THE BUY AND HOLD
REAL ESTATE STRATEGY

How to Secure Profits
in Any Real Estate Market

David T. Schumacher, PhD
with Erik Page Bucy, MA

John Wiley & Sons, Inc.

New York • Chichester • Brisbane • Toronto • Singapore

This text is printed on acid-free paper.

Disclaimer

The authors have endeavored to provide good, sound advice for a lifelong real estate invest-ment strategy and have made every effort to provide completeness and accuracy to the work. However, the field of real estate, especially the tax laws, changes too rapidly to guarantee ab-solute validity throughout. For simplicity, the term *mortgage* is used interchangeably with *trust deed*. Further, although the charts, tables, and examples presented are useful for illustrating concepts, they do not necessarily reflect the dollar amounts of actual transactions. Every real estate transaction is different; thus no general book on such an expansive topic could address every situation. By no means are we rendering legal or other professional advice.

Library of Congress Cataloging-in-Publication Data
Schumacher, David T.
    The buy and hold real estate strategy : how to secure profits in
  any real estate market / by David T. Schumacher with Erik Page Bucy.
        p.   cm.
    Includes index.
    ISBN 0-471-55602-5 (cloth)   ISBN 0-471-00962-8 (paper)
      1. Real estate investment.   I. Bucy, Erik Page, 1963–
    II. Title.
    HD1382.5.S38   1992
    332.63'24—dc20   91-41033

Printed in the United States of America

10 9 8 7 6 5 4 3 2 1

*This book is dedicated to the memory
of my identical twin brother and best friend,
Paul William Schumacher*

Investor to Will Rogers:
"What should I invest in?"
"Land, because they ain't making any more of it."

Acknowledgments

The author is especially grateful to John Wiley & Sons, Inc., for their interest in publishing this book. Special recognition goes to my editor, Michael J. Hamilton, for his help and inspiration throughout the project.

Words cannot express the gratitude I have for my dear wife, Margaret, for the herculean effort she put into this project. From the moment the idea of the book was conceived to the writing of the final manuscript, she offered encouragement and inspiration to see the project through to completion.

Special appreciation goes to my late twin brother, Paul William Schumacher, to whom this book is dedicated, for his vast knowledge of real estate and marvelous ability to comprehend complicated problems and explain them to others in understandable terms.

I am eternally grateful to my parents, the very best anyone could have had. Max Schumacher, my father, had outstanding business ability and always was willing to share his knowledge and experiences with others. Not only was he a fabulous father, he was a fabulous friend as well.

My mother, Minnie Louise Schumacher, was fantastic in her ability to get along with people. She knew when to say things and when to refrain from talking. My mother also had the unique ability to detect good real estate buys and keep properties occupied. During the Great Depression, she managed to hold the family together under very difficult and trying times.

Thanks to Susan Vilican, who has managed my properties in the South Bay area of Los Angeles County with remarkable skill and wisdom for over 18 years, and to Carmel Preciado, who assists us with our rental units in Orange County, California.

Many thanks also to Frank Swift, publisher of Marshall & Swift Construction Cost Services. His generosity in providing me with accurate, up-to-date construction cost information for the past 25 years has been a tremendous help in the preparation of this book.

I also wish to thank the National Association of Realtors, the California Association of Realtors, and the South Bay Board of Realtors for their contributions in gathering data for this project. In addition, I am grateful for the support of the following societies, from which I have obtained professional designations: Certified Commercial Investment Member (CCIM); Society of Real Estate Appraisers (SRA); American Society of Appraisers (ASA); National Association of Independent Fee Appraisers (IFAS); Certified Business Counselors (CBC); and Certified Review Appraisers (CRA).

Finally, I am very grateful to my dear friends, William Adams, Jack Bliss, Donald Haggerty, William Gorman, Patric Barry, and Thomas and Grace Collins for their generosity in sharing their ideas and concepts as well as for their faith in my endeavors.

David T. Schumacher, PhD
Hermosa Beach, California
March 1992

Contents

Introduction   1

1   Weighing Investment Decisions: Savings Plans and the Stock Market versus Real Estate   9

2   Determine the Best Type of Real Estate Investment to Fit Your Needs   26

3   Set a Realistic Objective That Investing in Real Estate Could Accomplish   43

4   Analyze National Trends Affecting Environmental Factors and Economic Growth   56

5   Assess How These Trends Will Affect Your Region, Metropolitan Area, and Community   72

6   Assess How National Trends Will Affect Your Immediate Neighborhood   96

7   Select the Right Property and Make an Analysis of Its Growth Potential   120

8   Forecast Your Property's Market Value in 20 Years Based on Available Data   136

9   Time Your Investment to Get a Boost from the Economy   151

10   Negotiate the Purchase Considering It to Be a Long-Term Investment   160

11   Advantages of Using a Real Estate Broker   175

12   Pyramid Your Initial Investment without Overextending Yourself   185

13   Manage Your Investment for Maximum Yield and Satisfaction   198

14   How to Make the System Work to Your Benefit: Refinancing and the Tax-Deferred Exchange   223

15   Protecting Your Investment and Accomplishing
      Your Objective   232

Appendix

A   Schumacher's Real Estate Axioms   242

B   The Appraisal Process   246

C   Outline of Factors Influencing the Value of
     Residential Property   274

D   Code of Ethics and Standards of Practice of the National
     Association of Realtors   279

Index   293

Introduction

Although a great many authors have written otherwise, there is really only one assured way of making money in real estate: buy property in growth areas and hold on to it for long-term appreciation. The *Buy and Hold Real Estate Strategy*, centered on this concept, is based on my 45 years' experience as a real estate appraiser and investor. Consequently, this book is not another untested get-rich-quick scheme or spin-off on the "no money down" idea, but a practical, step-by-step guide to a profitable lifelong investment program.

Ideally, you should begin to map out a long-term investment strategy in your twenties so that by the end of 30 years, when you're going to retire, you can retire on $10 million rather than a small monthly pension. No matter what phase of an investment program you are in, *The Buy and Hold Real Estate Strategy* will assist you in the process of wealth accumulation. The investment strategies and pyramiding techniques discussed apply to all types of real estate purchases—everything from single family residences and apartment buildings to shopping centers and industrial properties. The concepts and advice dispensed are just as relevant to the first-time buyer as they are to the seasoned investor.

In 15 easy-to-understand chapters, the book takes you through the multifaceted process of choosing the best type of real estate investment; analyzing the overall market and assessing a specific area's growth potential; deciding on the right property to buy; forecasting its market value in 20 years; timing the purchase to get a boost from the economy; negotiating the best deal possible; deciding whether to use a real estate broker; managing the property for maximum yield and satisfaction; and pyramiding the investment into other ventures.

The book begins with an analysis of the benefits and drawbacks of different types of investment options, comparing savings plans and the stock market to the advantages manifest in real estate. Since the best guided are those who have the clearest vision before them, the book advises potential investors on the importance of setting a realistic objective that investing in real estate could accomplish, in order to avoid going off in several different directions.

When I decided on real estate, my first investment was a four-unit apartment building in Hollywood, which I purchased in the mid-1950s while working as an appraiser. From that initial investment, I have pyramided my holdings into a $15 million estate that includes five ocean front apartment buildings on the Southern California beach, seven single family residences in the neighboring area, and some 30 condominiums in Orange County, California.

Some properties that I purchased with less than $3,000 down are worth more than $1 million today. Price isn't important; it's what you put down and what you take out of your pocket each month—as long as there's not a balloon payment off in the distance. If you can live with the terms, inflation will take care of the rest. The right piece of property is like gold; it can't do anything but increase in value. Buy real estate today for the long haul and you're going to get rich. Not only that, you will have wonderful financial security.

This book is written to give you, the investor, a choice—to stimulate your thinking, whet your appetite, and get your creative juices flowing in the hopes of achieving some tangible benefit. Realistically, I don't think 1 out of 50 people will follow the advice in this book. But I do hope that everyone who reads it will get some good out of it and that this knowledge will benefit someone in their life. If I am able to achieve this, then I will have accomplished what I set out to do.

When I taught real estate courses, I used to open one of my many lectures with a thought-provoking commentary: "Money, money, money, money, money—all we do is think about money!" People would perk up, and I would ask, "Have you ever thought about how much your house is worth? Think about how much your house, the one next door, and the one two doors down are worth. Now think about the wealth on your city block, There could be millions of dollars' worth of property. When you consider the community, you're talking about billions. When you consider the city and add up real estate values, you're into the billions and billions just in that city.

"By the time you get into the county, the figure becomes astronomical. By the time you get to a state the size of California, then consider the real estate wealth in our nation; it's into the trillions, if not quadrillions, of dollars. Now, the only thing we're trying to figure out is how to get a small piece of that action."

For most people, making money in real estate requires a fortune teller's ability combined with a thick wad of cash ready to plunk down at a moment's notice when that perfect investment opportunity suddenly presents itself. One point I like to emphasize, however, is that great real estate deals are not found. They are created. Finding a good real estate investment is not a matter of luck; it's being able to act when you should.

Almost everyone I talk to both in and out of real estate has a story about how they could have made millions if they only knew 10 or 20 years ago that property values were destined to skyrocket. This familiar tale is told countless times from coast-to-coast whenever real estate experiences a boom similar to the heady price gains of the mid- to late-1980s. But rather than acting on their impulses, the vast majority of investors and real estate onlookers are envious while others get rich and achieve financial security. This book explains how to identify properties with great growth potential and why you should act on the knowledge that good real estate markets will continue to rise.

Real estate is the best way of preserving and enhancing wealth. The right purchase in an area of appreciating land values can bring lasting prosperity. If you find a good piece of real estate, you will be able to do everything you want to do—build an estate, send your kids through school, travel around the world, invest in a new business, and so on. But the reward in real estate is commensurate with the risk you're willing to take. You have to take a chance, but you have to take one that's in your favor. Although the right location is key, you also need foresight to recognize the added potential. The thing you should never do is overextend yourself.

Successfully investing in real estate requires a long-term outlook that isn't subject to the ups and downs of short-lived adjustment periods. By evaluating what's happened to a given market in the past and making a realistic projection based on available data, it is possible to predict future market value.

Armed with this knowledge, buyers can then make informed investment decisions that are in their long-term interest. The best real estate investment is the one that relies the least on chance and emotion and realizes that patience above all else makes for profits; what you owe today you'll be worth tomorrow. If you're willing to buy property and sit on it for an extended period, the odds of losing are microscopic. Most people can't do that. They see a $500 profit and they grab it. Or they think the whole thing is collapsing, and they run for it.

Those who buy real estate on speculation usually sell too soon anyway, opting for limited, short-term profit at the expense of untold, forsaken value. It's usually the fourth or fifth owner of a piece of property who makes a killing. My philosophy is simple: Buy smartly and never sell. I believe in buying and holding. That's all I believe in doing. Land is becoming scarce. A good piece of property can't do anything but go up. But you have to commit yourself. When I buy, I'm not interested in what the property is like today, I'm interested in what it will be worth 15 or 20 years from now.

The tried-and-true techniques of long-range forecasting and limited risk taking outlined in the book, which I have employed for the past 35 years to assess the growth potential and to pyramid the scores of properties I now own, are based on courses I used to teach at Los Angeles City College and UCLA Extension.

Long-range forecasting basically entails making an analysis of a property's anticipated value by carefully considering the factors that influence its long-term worth. Long-range forecasting can, with a surprising amount of accuracy, predict the future value of a given piece of property. In my opinion it's much easier to predict the market value of a piece of real estate 20 years from now than it is next year or the year after, because we know what the overall trend of our country is. We know, for instance, that inflation is inevitable in a capitalistic country.

Given the climate of investor uncertainty surrounding the current recession and crisis in the financial industry, the message of how to build a real estate fortune with limited risk by maintaining a long-term outlook is more valuable than ever. The concepts presented in the book represent a realistic, bankable way for the average person to achieve financial security and make money in real estate.

This book is dedicated to the memory of my twin brother, Paul William Schumacher. One of the things I always admired about Paul was that he could study a real estate problem, dismiss the irrelevant details, identify the factors that really mattered, and work from there. That was a gift. My brother never made anything complicated. He always made it simple.

When my brother and I would go into appraisal meetings, he could describe how three or four corporations would all be affected by each other and how, for instance, certain patent infringements affected the products of other companies. He advised executives on what they should do and how they should value their assets to avoid any problems. My brother's professional advice always seemed to work, and yet he began his career, like me, without any formal training.

It's not a complicated process to become knowledgeable about real estate; you don't need a college degree, but you do need to develop a feeling for it. You also have to like it. When I was little, I used to sit down and read the want ads in the real estate section of the newspaper just for something to do. That was more interesting to me than reading the comic strips. Real estate investment doesn't have to be difficult. If you make real estate your hobby, pretty soon all the intricacies will become second nature.

My life has been a series of fortuitous opportunities and calculated successes. Having grown up near the Miracle Mile district of Los Angeles—

a stretch of Wilshire Boulevard between Fairfax and La Brea avenues that during the Depression was virtually immune to the nationwide economic crisis—I have an inherently optimistic outlook on life, one that has enabled me to bounce back in the face of financial adversity.

Before I became an appraiser, I worked for a few years during my early twenties as a real estate broker, although I never sold much property. One day, I was sitting in the office when a man came in and said he had a house for sale. It sounded like a really good buy to me. But another broker there said, "You don't know anything about whether this is a good buy or not." I asked him how he would know. He replied, "I would go get it appraised." That was the first time I ever heard the term *appraisal*. This was in 1945.

I went home that night and thought, Why should I sell real estate? If I can appraise it, I wouldn't have to ask somebody else how much a property is worth. I would know. Appraising sounded more interesting to me than sales, so I put an ad in the *Los Angeles Times* "situation wanted" column stating my interest in an appraising position. I wasn't interested in getting paid at first; I just wanted to learn. I figured that if I learned the business somebody would pay me what I was worth. If you have the knowledge, you are going to be rewarded. It is inevitable.

As it happens, a partner in the international appraisal firm Marshall and Stevens, Earl Marshall, called me up and asked if I wanted to come down and talk to him. At the end of my interview Mr. Marshall said he would start me at $100 a month working in the library. I had been there only two months, supplying information and keeping everything in order for the appraisers, when he said that he was doubling my salary. I told him that it was a mistake, but he said, "No, you're doing okay."

A few months later, around Thanksgiving, one of the senior appraisers was assigned to do an appraisal of a plant in Vernon, an industrial city just south of downtown. The job was supposed to be completed by that Friday, and the company had promised to deliver it, but the appraiser had gone out on a binge and couldn't be found. So the supervisor, who didn't know what to do and was becoming more and more desperate, asked me if I would help him. I said that I would.

So I spent my Thanksgiving weekend working on the project. I looked through the files of similar appraisals we had done to see how other appraisers had set them up, what kinds of information were included, and what types of results they were supposed to yield. I did my research and then sat down and wrote it. When I finished and delivered my report, the client was pleased. My boss was thrilled. I had come through at a critical moment, so he gave me another job. Pretty soon, I was appraising department stores, auditoriums, and all manner of commercial and residential property.

During the course of my 45-year career, I have personally appraised over 3,000 properties, including Bob Hope's home; the Jonathan Club in downtown Los Angeles; the Valley Hunt Club in Pasadena, where the Rose Parade is planned each year; Santa Catalina Island; the McDonnell-Douglas plant in Long Beach; the Las Vegas Racetrack; and numerous hospitals, restaurants, college campuses, and businesses.

Soon after my supervisor realized I had an aptitude for appraisal work, he asked my brother if he would like to come to work for the company. Although Paul, who was working as a shipfitter in the shipyards at the time, knew little about the appraisal business, I told my supervisor that we were identical twins, cast from the same mold, and so he couldn't go wrong. Sure enough, Paul took to the appraisal company as quickly and deftly as I had.

At Marshall and Stevens, where I worked until 1965, I held the positions of appraiser, district manager, and vice president in charge of training and research. My brother eventually became executive vice president of the company. When my brother and I left the appraisal company, we did quite well on our own because we could sit down and talk about the problem at hand and understand exactly what the other person was thinking.

While I was district manager of Marshall and Stevens's Los Angeles office, an administrator from Los Angeles City College called up and said he had a really serious situation. The instructor for an advanced real estate appraisal class decided not to present it. The class started that night. The administrator asked me if I had any ideas. I said, "What do you want?" He said he wanted someone to come out and teach the class that night. I said I'd be right out. After visiting his office and telling him what appraisers do, he asked if I wanted to take the class for the rest of the year. I said I'd let him know next week.

Over the next few days I wrote an outline for the college's board of trustees showing how I thought the class should be taught. They accepted my proposal. I taught advanced appraisal courses for five years at Los Angeles City College. During this time I wrote another course, "Real Estate Appraising for Investment Purposes," which I submitted to UCLA Extension. The administrator at Extension liked the idea, but said he wouldn't be able to offer it for a semester or two.

In the meantime, the University of California Extension division decided to present real estate investment seminars at its various facilities around the state. Because I had submitted a course outline, I was hired as one of the instructors, along with an experienced real estate broker named Ted Kessler. Together, we conducted about 10 of these two-day seminars, reaching a fairly substantial audience. This was about 1965.

One day, UCLA Extension was holding a conference in another division and had a speaker flying in from Salt Lake City to talk to real estate instructors on how to effectively present their courses. As it turned out, the speaker's plane was grounded at the Salt Lake City airport. So they called me and, reminiscent of my introduction to Los Angeles City College, I said I would come over and see what I could do. That afternoon, I had my office prepare a 20-page book on teaching techniques as they related to real estate and appraising. I delivered my presentation of the course as if I had been working on it for months and, much to their credit, they bought it. That's how I began my 16 years of teaching for UCLA Extension.

Having the opportunity to teach college courses and present professional seminars was one of the best things that ever happened to me. Students at night school who really want to learn have no mercy on the teacher. That inspired me to always have something valuable to say that would benefit the class above and beyond the course content. I think I learned more by teaching than I ever did as a student because I had to constantly research the latest developments to keep up with all the questions I was asked. Whenever a question was posed, I would never pass it off. Being an instructor enabled me to soar to new heights.

During my career as an appraiser, I also studied the commodities market. Unlike teaching, commodities never treated me that kindly. In 1956, I lost all of my savings—$12,000—investing in corn, wheat, rice, soybeans, and rye futures. That was a lot of money back then—enough to buy a house. So after nearly going broke in commodities, I resolved never to place myself at undue risk and make another bad investment again. I figured that there was no way of making a substantial amount of money other than through real estate. Many times during the early days, I just managed to squeak by. But no matter how close to the bone I was, I persevered with dedication and commitment with the goal of becoming independently wealthy. This perseverance eventually paid off handsomely.

A prominent businessman and friend of my father who lived in Philadelphia gave a lot of thought to matters that concerned him. In 1915, he said he couldn't figure out how the world's problems could be solved. He had no idea. Of course, this was in the middle of the First World War. Even so, I wonder how many times from 1915 to 1992 that great thinkers have believed the world's problems were so serious that they could not be remedied? And yet here we are in 1992, and the world, because of increased international cooperation, is probably safer from global warfare than at any other time in the twentieth century.

With this climate in mind, now is an opportune time to think about investing in real estate for the long term, because there probably won't be any serious international upheavals in the foreseeable future. When we have stable economic growth, it is easier to predict what might happen than before, during, and after a war. The end of the Cold War has created a completely different outlook. America is still at the forefront. And next to U.S. Government bonds, the safest investment you can possibly make is in real estate.

1

Weighing Investment Decisions: Savings Plans and the Stock Market versus Real Estate

Investors with venture capital have several options to choose from—namely, money-oriented investments, such as long- and short-term savings plans, stocks, bonds, and mutual funds—and real estate. Fortunes have been made by speculating in real estate and playing the housing market like the stock market. But in my opinion the wisest investment strategy incorporates a view that neither relies on frenzied Wall Street buying-and-selling practices nor leaves the fate of your investment to the vagaries of chance: Real estate investments located in desirable areas are bound to dramatically improve over time.

Nevertheless, it is useful to compare the advantages of a long-term real estate investment program in contrast to the volatility and uncertainty of financial investments. There are three basic ways to invest capital: (1) a safe return, (2) a speculation, or (3) a gamble. A safe return is something you can count on, while speculation depends on the whims of the market, and a gamble is left to chance. What determines a safe return, a speculation, and a gamble is the amount of risk you are willing to take. In monetary terms, a risk rate is equivalent to an interest rate. Do you want to take a gamble and go to Las Vegas and place all your chips on the black? Do you want to speculate in the commodities market? Or would you rather buy real estate in a desirable location as a long-term investment and get a safe return?

Much attention has been paid in the business press lately about how little Americans save their money on a per capita basis compared to other industrialized nations. But did you know that saving may actually be hazardous to your wealth? Savings plans don't begin to take advantage of the inflationary trend of our capitalistic economy. Say you were able to save $3,000 annually, earning 6 percent compound interest. After 20 years, your account would accumulate to $110,000. But since inflation averages about 6 percent annually, in 20 years that $110,000 will only be worth about $37,000 in today's dollars. Hardly enough to retire on.

9

TABLE 1.1
Types of Investment

	Safe Return	Speculation	Gamble
Interest/Risk	5 to 12%	12 to 20%	100% plus
Duration	1 to 20 years or more	Months to years	Seconds to months
Types	CDs, IRAs, mutual funds, pension plans, government securities, stocks, bonds, real estate, secure mortgage loans, fine art	Commodity futures, junk bonds, problem real estate, junior real estate loans	Money on the black, hunting for buried treasure, playing the lottery

Consider the different types of investments and their rates of return (Table 1.1). An investment is anything you put money in that will return capital appreciation.

INVESTMENT OPTIONS

The cash-rich investor has a variety of good investment options to choose from, including U.S. Treasury securities (bills, notes, and bonds), certificates of deposit, blue chip stocks and bonds, and high-rated mutual funds, which are among the safest investments available. However, most of these investments do not have the added advantage of capital appreciation, which well-located real estate does have.

F or a time in the early 1940s, I worked in the family store selling bakery goods. A regular customer of ours would delight in telling me how great he thought his insurance annuity was. This guy, who had a wife and three kids, said that he was paying $33 a month to an insurance company for 20 years. After that time, he was going to receive something like $300 a month for the rest of his life. I thought to myself, By golly, he's got it all wrong. Here's a father who can't even buy donuts and ice cream for his kids and he's putting money into something he has no control over. He had no idea what executives running that company would do, what decisions they would make with his and everyone else's hard-earned money.

━━━━━━━━

Look at the havoc being wrought by poor investment decisions within the savings and loan and insurance industries. In Rhode Island, 45 of that tiny state's banks and credit unions were closed on January 1, 1991, after the failure of their private insurer, the Rhode Island Security and Deposit Indemnity Corp. Although most of the institutions have since obtained federal deposit insurance and reopened, 14 were rejected when they applied for insurance and remained closed, leaving 300,000 accounts with total deposits of $1.3 billion completely frozen. Those depositors must not have had a very happy New Year.

━━━━━━━━

E xecutive Life Insurance Company in California is another example. Before it was seized by state regulators, who shopped around for a new buyer, some 350,000 policyholders stood to lose half their money and receive only 81 cents on the dollar at best. The ultimate fate of those policies is still uncertain and probably will be for a long time to come.

Assume that when you were 21 years old you started paying $50 a month to Executive Life and that today you're 65 years old and scheduled to receive an annuity from the now highly leveraged insurer. All your money is out the window if it goes broke. Moreover, the IRS has a $650 million lien against Executive Life, and the government will be the first party to be paid. I have never felt that acquiring an annuity was in anyone's best interest financially.

━━━━━━━━

Now, suppose that instead of putting your money into a company that spends millions of dollars in salaries for overpaid executives, accountants, and attorneys (who spend a portion of their time figuring out the most effective ways to beat their policyholders out of a few dollars), you had taken that $50 a month and put it into an investment that you had control over, such as real estate. To my way of thinking, it's better to have your own asset and let it appreciate than to allow other people and institutions to determine your financial future.

When most Americans get to be 65 years old, they have little or no security. They usually have to depend on Social Security, a retirement account, or some kind of pension fund they receive for having worked all of their adult life. But, increasingly, pension funds are being milked and are really in bad shape because of leveraging, junk bonds, and other types of creative financing. The holders of these accounts, the pensioners themselves, may end up with practically nothing. In this situation, you can find yourself in extreme hardship through no fault of your own by being the indirect victim of mismanagement. If you are not able to control your finances, you are not able to control your destiny.

But if you have your finger on the money that you are planning to retire on, you have the opportunity to build an estate and gain control over your financial future. I would much rather own an apartment building worth $1.5 million than a life insurance policy that I've paid on for 30 years that will only yield $800 a month when I retire and pay $50,000 if I die.

As an appraiser, I first got the idea of buying and holding real estate when I looked at a chart and realized that it will cost more to construct a new building tomorrow than it does today. Currently, an apartment building can be built at around $100 per square foot of livable floor area. Ten years from now, it might cost $150 per square foot to build the same apartment building. Even if costs don't rise that fast, you certainly know that it isn't going to be any cheaper to build in the future. Moreover, as the cost of construction rises, it tends to make older buildings more valuable. Figure 1.1 is a historical chart of construction costs for various types of buildings.

Let me pose a question. Suppose that someone were to offer to sell you for cash, today, the opportunity to receive $1,000 a month forever. How much would you be willing to pay in cash, today, for this opportunity? (Hint: The answer lies in the amount of risk you are willing to take.) In my many years I have heard answers ranging from "hundreds of thousands" to "millions" of dollars to "it just can't be calculated."

A thousand dollars a month is $12,000 a year. An investment of $240,000 with a 5 percent interest/risk (return) would yield $12,000 a year, or $1,000 a month. As long as the $240,000 is placed in a safe investment such as U.S. Treasury bonds and the bonds are not disturbed, and as long as the bonds pay 5 percent interest,

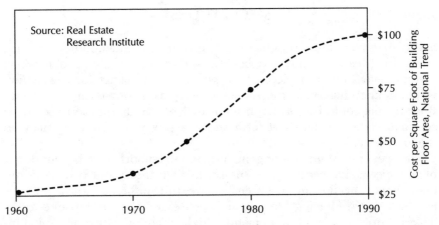

EXAMPLE: In 1960, if a building cost $25 per square foot to construct, in
1990, the same building cost $100 per square foot to build.

FIGURE 1.1
Construction Costs, 1960–1990

$240,000 invested this way will yield $12,000 per year, or $1,000 per
month forever (or as long as the government lasts). In this example,
the higher the risk and expected return (interest), the lower the capital
investment that is necessary to achieve the same result.

When you acquire any investment, you should be willing to accept
at least a modest amount of risk. Without a doubt, U.S. Treasury bonds
are the safest investment available. Another safe investment is a long-
term leased fee interest in a land parcel with a leasehold improvement
(building) worth considerably more than the land. I also believe that
the right piece of real estate is every bit as good as a U.S. Government
bond.

Good property located in growth areas should be regarded as an investment, as opposed to a speculation or gamble. The long-range forecasting techniques discussed later in this book will enable investors to
determine areas with the greatest growth potential. Providing you do
your research, the right real estate investment will take care of you for
life.

SPECULATIONS

Speculative purchases are sometimes a matter of mental attitude as much as anything because value, like beauty, is in the eye of the beholder. One investor may look at a piece of property as a purchase for speculation while another may view the same property as a long-term investment. Both people could be correct in their analyses, as the property could be speculative during the short term and a highly profitable investment in the long term.

In general, slum housing in difficult neighborhoods is considered highly speculative because it is subject to civil unrest and is hard to operate. Rent collection and maintenance are difficult because the conditions in which you are buying are rough. Expenses are likely to be quite costly. These properties therefore demand a higher rate of return on capital investment to justify the necessary expenditures. Consequently, they tend to be regarded as speculative.

It is important to analyze the community in which you are interested in buying to see that you don't make a poor investment. For instance, you don't want to purchase property directly adjacent to a community redevelopment project that will take eons to rebuild and force you to take a long-term negative cash flow. Granted, the property will eventually appreciate in value. But the question is, How long can you hold out?

Sometimes, it is impractical to acquire property on a street where the city has planned a widening project. Nor do you want to get into a situation where the highway authority plans to shave 30 feet from your front yard in order to create a major thoroughfare that prevents you from getting in and out of your driveway.

A real estate speculation doesn't necessarily entail a quick turnaround; it could be long term, too. A gamble in real estate could also be long term. For instance, today you can go out to the California desert or Colorado Springs or to some other places where desert subdivisions have collapsed because of their own costliness and buy up an old subdivision. Then you could sit on it for decades until growth catches up and somebody comes along who is willing to market it.

───────────

I have a friend who started buying vacant land in Kern County, California. He would go to these tax sales and, not having even inspected the property, put up a few thousand dollars to buy land and oil leases. Eventually, he ended up with about 65 parcels spread throughout four counties. Over time, land became valuable and a water district was formed that irrigated the land, and the land dramatically increased in value. It worked out really well for him. He could speculate without having to worry about tenants, maintenance, or other concerns.

———

A lot of people are in the business of buying older houses, fixing them up, and then selling them for a profit. Many of my friends and associates have bought fixer-uppers and have done a beautiful job rehabilitating them. When the newly refurbished property goes up in value, they turn around and sell it and move into a better house. That's not what I would do, but a lot of people are successful at it.

Say a person buys a house for $300,000 and puts $50,000 into fixing it up. Then the market falls off and the property can't even be sold for $300,000, let alone the additional $50,000 cash the owner has invested. Possibly, his only recourse is to hold on to his investment over a longer period of time by renting the property to offset his loan payments and remodeling expenses. Obviously, timing the purchase and acquiring property in a foreseeable up market is critical when speculating like this. Buying houses, fixing them up, and reselling them can be very lucrative if you are careful in your timing and selection of the right properties.

Speculating in real estate, in my opinion, is riddled with drawbacks. Even though it may result in a net profit, selling property exposes you to a tax on capital gains. Most people sell their real estate when they see a relatively small profit. Selling property in a neighborhood with appreciating land values prevents many income property owners from ever achieving a positive cash flow. It also limits the amount of equity they could have accumulated and borrowed against to make other investments. Buying and holding real estate for a brief period then selling is clearly a short-sighted approach to what is better regarded as a decades-long process of wealth accumulation by making a purchase that considers and allows long-term appreciation in value.

There are several inherent advantages to never selling the desirable real estate you acquire. Aside from qualitative attributes, there are four basic measurable benefits derived from ownership of income property, abbreviated by the acronym SEAT:

Spendable Income: With income property, you can realize a positive cash flow.

Equity Buildup: Building equity allows you to borrow against your property to make other investments.

Appreciation: Never selling enables property owners to realize substantial appreciation in value.

Tax Benefits: Property owners reap tax benefits by taking depreciation on improvements and personal property.

People who finance second mortgages receive monthly payments from the borrower. Second mortgages can be a fabulous source of income. But in down market, if the second mortgage comes due and the borrower doesn't pay, the property may have to be foreclosed on. Conversely, if the first mortgage holder forecloses on his note, the holder of the second has the option of taking over the property by making the payments. If you know what you are doing, the market for second mortgages and trust deeds can be fabulous because you should be able to make 15 to 20 percent on your money. But it's not for the investor who is just starting out.

The purchase or acquisition of second mortgages or second trust deeds is also speculative because they are junior liens to the first mortgage. They are in a secondary position in the mortgage line. If the holder of the first mortgage defaults on his payments, the holder of the second mortgage isn't paid until the holder of the first mortgage receives the full amount of unpaid principal plus legal expenses. It is very difficult to plan a long-term real estate investment strategy around speculation. Look what happened to Donald Trump.

MEANS OF FORCED SAVINGS

One of the primary benefits of investing in real estate is that making payments on property is a means of forced savings. Each month the owner of a piece of property must make a mortgage payment that, in essence, represents a deposit. Every time you make a payment you reduce the principal sum due on the mortgage, thereby increasing the equity. In essence, you're forcing yourself to save. It's a structured activity.

―――――――

When I was teaching real estate courses at UCLA Extension and Los Angeles City College, I used to invite a stock broker as a guest speaker to tell the class how fabulous it is to own stocks and bonds because they can be sold in two minutes. Then, after he would leave, I would emphasize to the students how it is even more fabulous to own real estate precisely because you *can't* sell it in two minutes. You can't sell real estate to solve your immediate financial problems because real estate is not easy to sell. You have to find another way to solve your problems. Some financial advisers think that it is a disadvantage.

But I think it is a terrific advantage because it compels you to think things over before you make the decision. Suppose you have a diversified investment portfolio and owned both stocks and real estate. Suddenly, a crisis occurs and you need $50,000. the first thing you would sell is the stock. If you didn't have any stock, you would figure out another way to solve your dilemma. You might borrow some money on your real estate or you might figure out another way to obtain a loan, but you aren't going to get rid of your real estate because it usually takes a period of time—weeks, months, or even years—to sell.

So you think of other ways to solve the problem. To me, that is a tremendous, built-in advantage of investing in real estate. It forces you to hold on to the property and, rather than receive a small profit, gives it time to appreciate. Maybe your dire financial situation or problem will pass. Once you get over that hurdle, you'll still be left with the property. If you hold it and keep it for the long pull, you'll be much better off.

═══════════════

You can count on your left hand the number of movie stars who made great sums of money in the 1950s and 1960s who did not maintain their wealth through the ownership of real estate. Many people who come into a lot of money don't have the ability to hold on to their riches. It is a foreign situation to them. Take Huntington Hartford, the heir to the Great Atlantic & Pacific Tea Company fortune. His spending habits were notorious. They made Donald Trump look like a lightweight.

In 1957 Hartford received a $90 million inheritance—over $325 million in today's dollars if you adjust for inflation. In the early 1960s, Hartford started spending money like it was going out of style. He invested in an art gallery, a magazine, and an artists' colony—one ill-advised scheme after another. He never failed to lose money. In a single-handed attempt to revive the West Coast theater scene, he bought a performance hall in Hollywood and renamed it the Huntington Hartford Theater.

Hartford, I last heard, lives in a little, cold-water flat on New York's East Side and receives a relatively small stipend from a trust fund. If he had considered a good real estate strategy, he could have had 10 times as much to squander!

TAX BENEFITS

Besides being a forced means of savings that yields a high rate of return, a real estate investment such as income property serves as an excellent tax shelter because the owner can take an annual tax deduction allowance or write off for wear and tear and obsolescence of the property's "improvements"—the physical building as opposed to the land.

Depreciation, the legitimate tax shelter the government grants to income property owners, is arrived at by dividing the value of the improvements (the building) by the number of years the Internal Revenue Code allows for depreciation—27.5 for residential property and 31.5 for commercial property. For tax accounting purposes, the purchase price is divided between the land and the improvements. The allocated value of the improvements may then be depreciated for tax purposes. The land is not depreciable for tax purposes.

Say you bought an apartment building for $500,000, with the improvements valued at $300,000 and the land valued at $200,000. The amount of your annual depreciation for the improvements would be $10,909, or $300,000 divided by 27.5 years. This is known as the straight-line method of depreciation, which reduces value over an extended period of time by equal increments.

Since the IRS allows depreciation to be deducted from net income, this can result in a paper loss. Suppose in the above example you received $8,909 in net rental income. With depreciation, you would show a "loss" of $2,000.

This is where the term *tax shelter* comes into play, because the amount of deductible depreciation partly or completely shelters the income derived from the property from tax liability. What's more, a tax loss can often offset other forms of income. So even as a building's depreciable book value drops, the real property value (in an area with solid growth potential) rises, resulting in an increase in equity wealth. Your accountant or tax preparer should be consulted on all matters concerning taxable income, as tax rulings change rapidly.

The tax laws also allow property owners, through a tax-deferred exchange, to sell a property and trade up for one or more properties of equal or greater value without paying income tax, unless there is "boot" (cash or other valuable assets) involved. Through an exchange, you retain the profit by acquiring the new property. Chapter 14 covers this topic in more detail.

Individual Retirement Accounts (IRAs), financial investments, are tax-deferred in the sense that you pay no taxes on the amount of money you put in until retirement. After that, you pay tax only on the amount you take out. However, there is a penalty for early withdrawal. Unlike real estate, your financial institution, following regulations set down by the government, tells you what you can do with your money and when you can take it out. With an IRA, you can take your money out only after a set time and not a day sooner (when you might need it) without paying a penalty.

Stocks, bonds, and commodities are very tax-exposed. With these investments, there is no way to exchange your holdings without forfeiting some of your profit to the government in the form of capital gains tax. Every profitable sale of shares or futures is taxed. The rancorous and unresolved debate in Congress over reducing the tax on capital gains speaks to this inherent disadvantage of the stock and commodities markets. With real estate, you can make and retain a profit by trading up without paying tax through the tax-deferred exchange.

Owning real estate also enables you to refinance the mortgage for up to 80 percent of the present market value of the real property and, if possible, to take out a second, third, or fourth mortgage loan against the property. The new loan money can be used to buy other real estate, improve your current property, or do what you want with.

A Comparison of Investment Returns:

Savings Accounts
$200,000 deposited in a savings account in a bank.

Real Estate
$200,000 invested in a commercial property. The premises are leased to a Triple A tenant.

Assume for this illustration:

10% interest per year is paid on the amount deposited.

10% interest (risk rate) is commensurate with the risk involved in ownership.

In both cases, this would yield $20,000 per year return on each investment.

Key Differences:

As long as the $200,000 deposit remains and as long as the institution pays 10% interest, the investor will receive $20,000 per annum. If these conditions are met, the $20,000 per year can be received forever.

The $20,000 per year represents a return on the investment in real estate comparable to the return on the savings account. The real estate investment also is entitled to a recapture of capital attributed to the building so that at the expiration of the life of the building, the investor will have sufficient money to replace the building.

In other words, if you have a $200,000 investment with a 10 percent return, you're entitled to a 10 percent return forever, according to this example. But since properly selected real estate has the added advantage of appreciation, you may be able to get well in excess of a 10 percent return. As Will Rogers once replied to a potential investor who asked what he should invest in, "Land, because they ain't making any more of it." On the other hand, there's no limited supply of savings accounts.

OUTSTRIPPING INFLATION

Besides being a reliable investment, real estate is in my opinion the only investment that, if properly selected, will outpace inflation. As previously mentioned, land values can rise much faster than inflationary trends because of local factors of supply and demand. Rather than yielding only a small interest payment or dividend, real estate in prime locations can appreciate at 20 percent a year or more. What savings plan can offer that rate of return? The principle sum in a bank account is not affected by inflation. It's a fixed amount of money accorded a moderate amount of interest. Real estate, on the other hand, is sensitive to the economy and can skyrocket accordingly, thereby acting as a hedge against inflation—providing you are in the right location.

HETEROGENEOUS NATURE

The wonderful thing about investing in the real estate market is that values are a matter of opinion, judgment, need, and desire. The same piece of real estate may be worth more to the person who desperately needs it than it is to the lukewarm buyer. Every property is a unique item. What may be good for one person may not be good for someone else. Even if you divided the Sahara Desert into lots and took two parcels that were side-by-side, one would be slightly closer to the Mediterranean Sea, the other slightly closer to the sand dunes. Values therefore vary with location and individual circumstance.

With real estate, an individual's need and desire are what's important, not necessarily what's happening in the marketplace. Sometimes you can buy real estate with little or no money down if the seller is distressed. The seller might need to move out of state on account of a job transfer or be in arrears on his payments and about go into foreclosure.

I've acquired much of my real estate with little or nothing down. I once bought an apartment building with three mortgages against it and put 15 percent down. At the same time, I was buying a house, and the broker agreed to use his cash commission from the apartment building as the total down payment on the house. He took a third mortgage on the apartment building so I could buy the house with nothing down. Essentially, I bought it with *his* cash and the broker was happy to make the deal!

There are so many ways you can go in real estate. Consider financing. A standard down payment with a conventional loan is generally considered to be 20 percent of the purchase price. However, with a VA loan guaranteed by the Veterans Administration to eligible veterans and spouses, no down payment is required. With a Federal Housing Administration, or FHA, loan, only 3 percent down is required on the first $25,000 borrowed and 5 percent on the remainder up to a specified limit when the residence is owner-occupied.

I worked on a deal just recently where I put 15 percent down on a condominium in Orange County, California. The market had fallen out, and the prices had dropped precipitously. The seller couldn't find a buyer, so I assumed the first mortgage and paid him 15 percent. As mentioned, banks usually want 20 percent down to make a loan. With non-owner-occupied property, however, if you can get the seller to carry a 10 percent second mortgage and you have 10 percent cash, oftentimes you will be able to comply with the bank's requirements with less than 20 percent out of pocket.

With real estate, you have the advantage of finding a buyer who has a particular set of circumstances that will fit your need. You may be able to sell a property to one person for more, or buy from someone else for less.

For example, I would expect to get more out of owning the place next door to where I live than somebody else would because it gives me control over the tenant mix and the noise. In addition, it enables me to easily collect the rent. It's ideal for me, so maybe I would be willing to pay more if the property came up for sale, especially if the current tenants were constantly disturbing the peace.

A few years ago, I bought a condominium from a savings bank that had REO (real estate owned) properties. This was a studio apartment within walking distance of an elaborate shopping center with every type of store and service imaginable. The condominium unit, which looked out onto the swimming pool, was located next door to a guy who loved to blare his stereo. One day I asked him if he would kindly turn the stereo down and he said, "No." So I went to my real estate broker and bought the unit.

Then, the tenant on the corner had a big dog who barked a lot, so I bought that unit, too. A few months later, the unit right above us came up for sale. Even though the sellers were asking 10 percent more than I thought it was worth, I decided to buy that one too because I didn't want somebody above me stomping around making a lot of noise. That's the American way to do it, isn't it?

━━━━━━━━━━
━━━━━━━━━━

I used to tell my students, bread sells for about a dollar a loaf. If you went to the bakery and said, "I'll give you 90 cents for this loaf," the cashier would tell you that you were crazy. The reason is that there are a zillion comparable sales that determine bread's price at a dollar a loaf. The same thing is true of General Motors or IBM stock. You pay the designated price depending on the market. If you own 10,000 shares of preferred stock, you know exactly what they are worth on any given day.

Not so with real estate, which has no absolute measure of dollar value. This places real estate into the same price category as an antique or object of art. Every piece of real property and object of art is heterogeneous. No two are exactly alike. The only difference is that real estate doesn't move. With an oil painting you can change the location of that asset to your advantage, say, to Paris, where you might be able to find a wealthier bidder. Real estate, on the other hand, is affected 100 percent by its surroundings. That's why location is so important—it's unchangeable.

A Comparison of Real Estate to Other Investments

Comparable Features	Improved Real Estate	Fine Art	Blue Chip Stocks
Value Based on	Highest and best use	Highest and best use	Present sales
No. of Identical Units Available for Purchase	None	None	Millions
Location	Fixed; neighborhood has strong influence on value	Portable. Can be moved to desirable markets	Portable, unimportant
Present Benefits from Ownership	Use, income, appreciation, pride of ownership	Pride of ownership, appreciation	Income and appreciation

Comparable Features	Improved Real Estate	Fine Art	Blue Chip Stocks
Terms of Sale	Can be very liberal	Usually cash	Governed by regulations
Return on Capital	Through use and/or income; eventual sale	Aesthetic value; eventual sale	Dividends
Liquidity of Investment	Sometimes difficult	Sometimes difficult	Good
Management	Can be troublesome	Proper care	Trouble free (generally)

DEGREE OF CONTROL

Being heterogeneous, real estate allows you to be creative. If you own a piece of real estate, you have control over how you're going to fix it up, how it is going to look, and, within certain regulatory guidelines, who you are going to rent it to. One of the things I used to tell my students was that if you want to make money in real estate, buy a piece of property and figure out a higher and better use for it. When you arrive at a solution and apply it, you're bound to do better. Through creative rehabilitation of real estate, you can create opportunities.

F or example, say you have a four-unit apartment building in which all the units have two bedrooms and two baths. If your city would permit you to convert the four units into eight single apartments, you might be able to generate as much as 30 percent more rent. That would be a higher and better use for the property.

Or, if you owned a single family residence in an area that was zoned for commercial uses, perhaps you could convert it into a restaurant. It might be fabulous. During the energy crisis of the 1970s, a lot of gas stations that were put out of business were converted into flower shops, nurseries, and convenience stores—essentially, higher and better uses.

Regardless of the real estate investment, there is no exact formula to tell you what the ultimate outcome will be. But with a good property located in a growth area, you can foresee its potential future value. Moreover, you can improve or alter the use to generate additional income.

═══════

I once owned a five-unit building on Camerford Avenue in Hollywood. It was located just around the corner from Paramount Studios and a few blocks up from the Wilshire Country Club. Despite these auspicious landmarks, the place was a real dog and needed fixing up. The property was flanked by an alley in the rear, and trees and shrubs were overgrown on the lot. But between the back of the building and the alleyway, there was a back yard about 30 feet deep. Soon after I bought the property, I discovered that whenever I would go to collect the rent, I was not able to find a parking place. People who worked at the studio would take up all the street spaces, and there was no on-site parking for the tenants.

The old street parking arrangement simply could not accommodate the current population density. Realizing this, I immediately hired some workers to tear out the growth in the rear portion of the lot, thereby clearing room for five parking spaces—one for each tenant. By creating this new parking, I was able to raise the rents dramatically. The people who owned the building before me could have made the effort to provide parking for the tenants, but they probably didn't think about it. I paid $3,000 to have the shrubs removed and the area paved with asphalt. But I got my money back in 12 months.

═══════

With real estate, you have this added opportunity to be inventive, to express some of your own thinking to improve your position. You don't have this option with stocks, bonds, savings plans, or any other types of investments I know of because you don't have control over them. But with real estate, an innovative idea can be a real boon. Let your ingenuity unfurl and creativity soar, and the sky's the limit! This points to another great advantage to investing in real estate—it's not structured. Being successful in real estate requires experience, knowledge, education, and the guts to get out and do it. But there's no pattern. Every piece of property is unique and requires a slightly different approach.

Stocks and bonds, which don't have this flexibility, cost the same regardless of who buys them. Moreover, the stock market is hypersensitive to world events and the national mood and will fluctuate wildly based on rumor, whereas the value of real estate is determined by local economic conditions that in areas like Los Angeles and Seattle are stable and consistently outperform the national average.

In the stock market, everything's standardized. You can't get someone to pay more for a given stock than what it's selling for. Stocks are also highly volatile. Nobody knows or can really understand the stock market. You can read a company's annual report and the latest financial statement, but you have no control over how that corporation is being run.

Information on the judgment and ability of the people who run the company you buy stock in is not available. Consider former tycoons Charles Keating, the wily former CEO of Lincoln Savings and Loan, and fallen junk bond king Michael Milken. Here are two media darlings who appeared to be really successful, who were looked up to and admired. Yet they were both condemned for their lack of scruples. As of this writing, Milken is serving a prison sentence for racketeering, breaching responsibility to investors, and misappropriating corporate assets, while Keating has been convicted on 17 of 18 counts of securities fraud stemming from the sale of his company's bonds.

Until just recently, the financial and insurance industries appeared to be rock solid. But now they are teetering on the brink of insolvency. If you think about it, banks and insurance companies have tremendous overhead. CEOs are paid million-dollar-a-year salaries, and lawyers, accountants, and senior executives earn six-digit incomes. Yet the savings and loan crisis has proven that highly paid doesn't necessarily mean well managed. When you invest in real estate, you can keep a much closer watch and maintain tighter control over your investment.

PRIDE OF OWNERSHIP

Qualitatively, real estate offers what property owners call pride of ownership. Property, besides having the potential of being changed to a higher and better use, can also be modified to the owner's personal liking. With real estate, you can build a monument to your own ego, acquire a lavish estate, or simply settle for having the nicest house on the block! Real estate is therefore an asset that can meet a specific personal need.

Real property, whether a residence, apartment complex, or a commercial or industrial building, is an investment that you can touch, feel, walk around in—one that you can physically appreciate, in other words. Real estate, unlike stocks, bonds, and savings plans, can have sentimental value. Real estate is the only investment you can live and work in. As we will see in Chapter 8, real estate has myriad values, only one of which is use value.

2

Determine the Best Type of Real Estate Investment to Fit Your Needs

Once you have decided to invest in real estate, it is important to determine the type of property that best suits your personality, skills, temperament, time availability, and practical needs. You wouldn't expect a 65-year-old widow with a dependent sister to own and manage a fraternity house anymore than you would expect a 30-year-old first-time investor to own a retirement home.

In considering the different types of real estate investments available, it is essential to find the right match between the type of property you are interested in and the individual needs that you have as a person. Real estate is classified into two basic categories: income or investment property, and non-income-producing property. The return on capital invested in investment real estate stems from net income produced, whereas the return on non-income-producing property is measured primarily in private or public use value.

Types of Income Property

- Vacant land
- Single family residences
- Condominiums and Townhouses
- Duplexes, triplexes, and fourplexes
- Apartment buildings
- Office buildings
- Shopping centers ("strip" and "anchored")
- Commercial and industrial properties

Non-Income-Producing Property

- Personal residences
- Churches
- Schools
- Parks

- City halls
- Courthouses
- Other government buildings

As a potential investor, you should look for property you are genuinely interested in and enthused about. Give consideration to the long-term investment concept rather than a quick buy and sell for a meager profit. What you want to do is find a property that not only suits you, but also has growth potential. I would never buy anything I wasn't interested in. When you first start out, it is best to buy something that you are familiar with so that you can analyze the growth potential of the community and neighborhood.

When I first decided to buy real estate and grow rich, I geared myself toward apartment buildings in Hermosa Beach, California, an ideally located, quaint (though at that time dilapidated) residential community in the South Bay area of Los Angeles County. When I started, I was single and liked the idea of having a home on the oceanfront—a recreational facility and residence all in one. My first purchase was a six-unit apartment building right on the oceanfront on a strip of land called "The Strand," which looks out onto the beach and the blue Pacific. (*Hermosa*, appropriately enough, is Spanish for *beautiful*.)

The property was close enough to downtown that I could commute to work. This particular building was ideal for my needs because it has so many different floor plans—3 one-bedroom apartments, 1 three-bedroom apartment, 1 two-bedroom apartment, and 1 small single unit. During my first few years of ownership, I couldn't afford to occupy the nicest apartment, so I lived in the smallest unit and rented out the best apartments, which brought in much-needed rental income.

RESIDENTIAL VERSUS COMMERCIAL PROPERTY

You should never invest in something you don't know anything about. I am a great believer in becoming informed. However, I also feel that most first-time investors are far more naturally suited to invest in residential real estate than commercial property because they live in a house, they associate with their neighbors, and they are more inclined to know how to treat residential tenants than commercial tenants. If you work for Coldwell Banker's commercial division, you might be inclined to invest in commercial property. The majority of investors aren't, however. Consequently, if you happen to win the lottery tomorrow, I would advise investing in what you feel most comfortable with, which in most cases probably would be residential property.

Vacant Land

There are many different kinds of vacant land acquisitions that are good investments. There are also many vacant land purchases that are purely speculative, some of them bordering on gambles. Vacant land by itself produces no income until it is improved and put to a profitable use, the possible exception being vacant parcels that are used for parking, storage, or land fills. In general, any profit derived from vacant land usually comes from the increased value of the land over a period of time. The following work increases the value of raw, unimproved land, creating land that is *improved*:

- Landscaping and grading
- Installation of utilities
- Construction of roads, curbs, and gutters
- Construction of buildings

When you own a parcel of vacant land, it is very important to determine its highest and best use—meaning the most profitable use—so that the land can produce the greatest return over a period of time.

Many years ago, Ringling Brothers, Barnum & Bailey Circus used to come to downtown Los Angeles and erect their huge circus tent on a vacant lot close to Washington Boulevard and Hill Street. The circus usually occupied the land parcel for about two weeks out of the year. Obviously, the circus was the highest and best use of that lot during the two-week period it was in use. However, the land would sit vacant the other 50 weeks out of the year.

Duration of use is very important to consider when contemplating a vacant land purchase. Sometimes, the most profitable return from the vacant land parcel is not measurable in monetary terms, but rather in community services, such as schools, parks, playgrounds, or libraries. Vacant land parcels that lend themselves to monetary returns should be carefully analyzed to determine the best profitable use over the longest period of time.

Oftentimes, it is very difficult to determine what the highest and best use of a vacant land parcel should be until the surrounding area is developed or shows signs of positive development. If you have a land parcel in a populated area, especially if it is in the path of future growth, the property can increase in market value as the community improves.

An expensive parcel of vacant land requires substantial holding power on the owner's behalf until it can be developed and be put to a profitable use. *Caution* is the watchword for the first-time investor considering vacant land for a long-term investment. It is generally unwise to purchase vacant land for an investment unless you can see an immediate use for the property.

RESIDENTIAL PROPERTY

Single Family Residences

Single family residential property is great if you have the right tenant. If you don't have the right tenant, it can be brutal. Successfully finding the right tenant to live in a house is the best thing that can happen. I have some tenants in a house I own in Los Angeles who think and act as if they own the place. And they don't want me bothering them. I also have a house in Hollywood. The tenants there recently wrote me a note saying they spent about $400 fixing up the yard and wanted to know what I thought about it? I said, "Wonderful. Send me the bill." And that was that. They always pay their rent on time and never complain about anything. It works out just super.

A good strategy to employ when buying residential property is to look for an older house in an area of high density that is, or eventually might be, zoned for multiple residential use. Oftentimes, it is possible to purchase the entire property—land and improvements—for about what the land alone is worth. If the property is in a prime location and increases in value over time, you can pay down the mortgage and end up with a desirable development site for an apartment house.

A friend of mine once purchased two adjacent single family homes on a parcel of land that measured 100 feet × 200 feet. Zoned for multiple residential use, the land would permit the development of 30 apartment units. The property was purchased in 1960 for $60,000 with $7,000 down. After three years, the rent from the two houses was bringing in enough income to make the payments. With a land parcel already paying for itself, my friend had no trouble getting a construction loan and was able to build his 30-unit apartment building. The neighborhood has improved in 30 years' time and today that property is worth about $3 million. Not bad for $7,000 down!

Condominiums and Townhouses

When you own a condominium or townhouse, you must belong to a home-owner association and pay monthly dues. There is a set of guidelines you must abide by from the association known as CC&Rs (covenants, conditions, and restrictions). These rules govern the use of real property. The homeowner association of a condominium complex, for instance, could limit the number of visitors who can stay with a homeowner or tenant at any given time. Some property owners find CC&Rs restrictive. As a landlord, I tend to look on them favorably because they ensure that tenants respect the rights of others and adhere to a set of uniform standards.

As mentioned, homeowner associations charge a monthly fee. It goes toward maintaining the grounds, pool, common elements, the building exterior, security, and waste removal. For me, this works out just fine. I own 30 condominiums in three separate projects that are virtually hassle-free. Whenever there is a vacancy, the on-site manager is responsible for filling it, so I don't have to worry about renting the places. All I have to do is pay $200 each time I have a vacancy. Altogether, I pay about $8,800 in homeowner fees per month. But my condominiums are all more or less self-sufficient. It's a headache-free situation, really. And that's well worth the expenditure.

For my wife and me, these condominiums are like having a vacation resort. We have one unit that we keep vacant for ourselves. The complex is close to a major commercial retail center, so numerous restaurants, department stores, professional offices, and movie theaters are all within walking distance. In addition, we belong to the local performing-arts center.

Similar to my apartments on the beach, these units have recreational and investment value. One day, they're going to make me a million dollars. Not only that, these little condominiums, which each have 500 square feet of floor area, are the lowest rent in the neighborhood.

One drawback to owning a condominium is that if your complex becomes embroiled in a lawsuit and your fellow property owners in the association vote to raise homeowner dues on account of legal fees or additional maintenance expenses, there isn't much you can do except comply and pay the additional fees.

Duplexes, Triplexes, and Fourplexes

Duplexes are a good first-time investment because you have the option of inhabiting one unit and renting out the other(s), which helps make the payments and pay the taxes. A four-family flat, or fourplex, does even better and generally takes no more effort to take care of than a duplex.

If you live in one unit and take care of the other three, you're already on the property to deal with whatever problems and situations arise.

A duplex, triplex, or even fourplex is usually a mom-and-pop operation. The owners may need the rent to help make the payment on the loan and pay the taxes. Maybe they figure that someday as they get along in years their mother or father might live in one of the units so they can keep an eye on them.

For a number of reasons, many people don't like the idea of living in an apartment. But certainly to get started, if you can buy a two- or four-unit building and live in it for a while until you can raise the rents, then refinance it, taking the money and buying a single family residence, you would have a good start on the road toward building an estate.

Buying real estate is a long-term investment. When I first started investing in income property, I had to hold on to property for about seven years before the cash flow would go from negative to positive. I bought most of my properties with very little down, so my mortgage payments were comparatively high. If you find a good piece of real estate, you'll be able to do wonders with it. But the key to the whole thing is to find the right property that you know through your research and analysis will increase in value.

A doctor friend of mine once wanted to buy a dilapidated forty-unit building in downtown Los Angeles. It upset me because here was a respected physician who helped people get well, and yet he was thinking about acquiring this run-down property. It was available at a cheap price, but that purchase would have forced him ipso facto to become a slumlord. The property didn't fit his need. After thinking about it, he decided to buy a place on Burton Way in Beverly Hills, and he eventually made a killing without having to compromise his position.

Apartment Buildings

It is not easy for first-time buyers to start off with an apartment building, unless they have inherited the property or a lot of money from a rich uncle. This said, an apartment building is one of the best investments there is. A friend of mine who had accumulated a substantial amount of equity in four single family residences and two duplexes recently decided to trade his equity for a 38-unit apartment building in the San Gabriel Valley, which he bought for $2.5 million.

Since the mortgage on the apartment is high compared to the income, he has a negative cash flow of about $2,000 a month. But he has faith in the area and believes that in a few years he will experience a positive cash flow. In 30 years, he will own an asset worth at least $6 million and have no outstanding mortgage on the property. There aren't many investments that offer this certainty, and size, of return.

To own and manage a large apartment complex with a negative cash flow requires a certain amount of income and discipline. But the rewards can be fantastic. If you are thinking about buying an apartment building, it is important to decide what you like and what kind of people you can work with. Then, locate a property in a good location that fits that quirk in your personality.

Before making an offer to purchase an apartment building, be sure that the size and configuration of the rental units conform with the demand factor for similar apartments in the neighborhood. Study the building's occupancy in relation to community facilities. For instance, a three-bedroom apartment building that attracts families might work fantastically near a high school, whereas studio apartments for single professionals would probably be a poor investment choice if they were situated next to a grammar school.

Study vacancy rates, planned construction projects, and the developments in the surrounding area that act as a source of employment for potential tenants. Such developments may include hospitals, shopping malls, colleges, financial centers, business parks, and the like. With a specific property in mind, it is useful to look at the neighborhood and the subject building as a potential tenant would. The following is a checklist of items to consider when assessing the property:

- Is the outside appearance as attractive, or more attractive, than competitive buildings?
- What is the condition of the balconies, porches, sidewalks, common areas, and landscaping?
- Are there any roof leaks or signs of water damage? Are the gutters and downspouts adequate?
- Does the apartment complex have adequate parking?
- What advantages does the location offer, such as proximity to traffic arteries, public transportation, shopping centers, churches, and schools?
- Are there any detrimental influences, such as adjacent noisy streets, railroad tracks, or obnoxious odors or excessive noise from industrial plants?

- How do the size and configuration of individual apartment units compare with the competition?
- How do the rents compare?
- Does the subject building offer the same number of amenities as the competition, such as parking, swimming pool, recreation center, and workout facilities?
- Are there any structural defects or visible building flaws in the foundation, roofing, or framing?
- Are the walls and floors soundproof so that noise from one apartment will not disturb other tenants?
- Are the apartments clean and well maintained?

The importance of knowing the physical characteristics of the apartment property before making a firm commitment to purchase cannot be overemphasized. Be sure that all mechanical appliances in individual apartment units are in good working order, including refrigerators, ranges, dishwashers, garbage disposals, exhaust fans, individual air conditioners, heaters, and laundry facilities. Building-wide, inspect the electrical service, as well as plumbing and heating, in sufficient detail to determine if there are any major, foreseeable problems. In addition, it might be necessary to obtain a termite or other infestation report. Finally, to determine whether the building is settling, you might want to place a marble on the floor and see where it rolls. (For a detailed discussion of an apartment appraisal, see Appendix B.)

COMMERCIAL

Office Buildings

Office buildings are a difficult first investment. Adequate income is the key. If you decide to buy an office building, be sure to make a thorough tenant-demand analysis for the subject property. Briefly, a demand analysis would include a forecast or estimate of the need and desire for office space in the community over a long period of time and what the future competition from other similar existing and proposed projects might do to the office building market. If there is nothing in the immediate area renting for $1.20 per square foot of floor area per month, it would be virtually impossible to get any more for your space unless you have a better quality building.

It is not advisable to buy an office building unless you really know what you are doing or have an immediate need for it. The current glut of vacant office space in most major metropolitan areas makes investing in this type of real estate quite hazardous.

About 15 years ago, I made an appraisal of the Wilshire Medical Building at the corner of Wilshire Boulevard and Bonnie Brae Street in downtown Los Angeles. When I finished with my appraisal, I met with a group of doctors who owned the medical building as well as a large lot in the rear of the complex. I told them at the time that they ought to build a hospital on the lot because if they didn't, they would have a difficult time keeping the medical building leased. Other developers would come into the area and build office buildings adjacent to the medical buildings, driving the medical tenants out.

The best arrangement for a commercial property is an owner-user. For any commercial property, whether it's a restaurant, business, supermarket, hardware store, or clothing store, the ultimate tenant is an owner-user. If you own a medical office building, it is best to have doctor participation. To keep commercial tenants in the building over a period of time requires that they get a piece of the action. If you are interested in buying an office building, you might want to syndicate it through a partnership, corporation, or trust with a group of professionals who will occupy the space.

I represent a company that has seven office and industrial buildings. The company leases these buildings from the employees, who own the properties in a profit-sharing trust. This trust is set up through the Securities and Exchange Commission. The company leases these buildings on a short-term basis, and every three years they have to be appraised to figure out how much the employees have made to increase their pension fund benefits.

If you are planning to purchase an office building for an investment, be sure to obtain expert, unbiased advice before you commit yourself to anything.

Specialty Investments: Miniwarehouses

Similar to other types of commercial real estate investments, a specialty investment such as a miniwarehouse requires that you know how to operate it. The key to a thriving miniwarehouse business is a good location. If you owned a miniwarehouse in a high-density resort community or bustling metropolis, you'd be a millionaire because there is such a high concentration of people who have wealth and all sorts of junk they don't need or want. A storage facility would attract ample customers. Even so, it's more of a speculative investment, really.

Recently, a friend of mine who owned a miniwarehouse went broke. He's one of the smartest guys I've ever met. He's brilliant, absolutely brilliant. He understands the tax laws and the economic forces of finance. He's given many lectures on these subjects. But he had to file bankruptcy recently because the miniwarehouse he owned and operated was so poorly managed. He didn't know how to generate enough interest and enthusiasm to fill up the building. He basically didn't know how to market his product properly.

With expensive commercial investments, there is a lot of money going out each month, so you've got to be sure that it comes back in. That might not sound difficult, but sometimes it takes tremendous effort and expenditures to first find suitable tenants and then to get everything that is coming to you, even when you have signed leases.

Shopping Centers

There are two basic types of shopping centers: "strip" and "anchored." A strip shopping center, or mini-mall, consists of a collection of independently operated or franchised retail stores with a common parking area but no "anchor" or main tenant that dominates the complex. An "anchored" shopping center, on the other hand, is characterized by a substantial commercial tenant, such as a major drug or discount store, supermarket, or department store, that serves as a primary tenant to anchor the project.

Strip Shopping Centers: Mini-malls

Mini-malls can make secure investments if you have a good long-term lease with reliable tenants and you understand the retail business. With some understanding of the commercial real estate business, you can probably make it work. But all kinds of outside factors can change the value of that property. The traffic pattern can change because of a decision by the state transportation department; the local planning commission can recommend a zoning change; a key store in your complex can declare bankruptcy and go out of business. You're vulnerable to all of these factors, plus the rulings and decisions of local, state, and regional agencies.

Moreover, some cities are difficult to do business in. They'll impose taxes and assessments. They won't allow you to put up a sign, to set up a display in front of your store, or to erect any kind of awning that upsets the character of the street. They'll ticket anyone who is two seconds over the parking limit. Whether by design or happenstance, some cities do everything they can do to harass customers and keep them away.

I've seen this happen in many cities. On the one hand, the city council says it likes business, but on the other it does everything it can to undermine economic activity. The city won't provide adequate parking; the meter maids will ticket too much; a laborious permit process makes new construction virtually impossible. By doing such things, the city destroys the business incentive and, along with it, the value of commercial property. Instead of leasing their commercial space at market value, property owners are generally obliged to accept reduced rents on account of severe restrictions imposed by the city government.

If you are going to invest in commercial real estate, you have to know how to get around these kinds of problems. A person who is not oriented to fight city hall has no business owning property affected in this manner.

Anchored Shopping Centers

A good anchored shopping center will do tremendously with a strong anchor tenant because it will yield a percentage of the gross income from the retail activity. We once owned a building occupied by a furniture store in the San Fernando Valley. Our monthly income was about $1,200. From the lease, we received 6 percent of the gross income with a minimum of $1,000 a month. Beyond this, if the store did $100,000 a month or more, we were entitled to 6 percent, or at least $6,000.

If you have a calculating mind, an anchored shopping center can become a source of great revenue. But, as with a mini-mall, there are many things you have to look out for. When you own a shopping center, your main concern is competition—the type of stores next door, down the street, in the neighborhood and surrounding area. In addition, new innovations, new commercial developments, and new ownership of existing centers can all take a bite out of your business, especially when money in the form of construction loans is available for development. It takes a person with great foresight to accurately assess the risk involved, find the right complex to invest in, and succeed.

It's far riskier and takes more ingenuity and more knowledge to own a shopping center than to own, say, an apartment building. Even in an economic downturn, people need a place to live, so the residential market remains relatively stable despite periodic dips.

First-time investors are not likely to buy commercial properties unless they have uses for them. Commercial real estate involves a completely different set of factors to consider than residential property. Quality of tenants, amount of income derived, and possibility of increased income are important factors to analyze, along with the duration of income. Long-term commercial leases are good to have in a recessionary market because they ensure a steady income stream. However, under inflationary conditions, short-term leases may be more desirable because of rapid increases in leasing rates during the upward cycle.

Industrial Buildings

Generally, industrial property doesn't fluctuate in value like residential real estate does. Most industrial buildings are single-purpose buildings built for one specific use. If the economy changes, that can create problems.

Smokestack industries are being hit from all sides. Oil refineries, chemical plants, and other hazardous industrial plants are restricted in many areas because of smog and other environmental conditions. In addition, the whole manufacturing process is constantly changing in response to the introduction of new technology.

The best time to invest in industrial property is when long-term demand is the greatest. Our world is changing dramatically from a technological standpoint. And sometimes, industrial real estate doesn't keep pace with these changes. A building can become functionally and economically obsolete before it begins to physically deteriorate on account of factors ranging from new processing techniques to lack of demand for the product.

For every 400 people who could buy an apartment building, there are probably 10 who should buy an office building. And for every 10 people who should buy an office building, there is probably one who could buy an industrial building and understand what to do with it. Whether you are experienced or just starting out, an industrial building is not an easy investment.

THE TIME FACTOR

When deciding the type of property that is right for you, the amount of time you have to maintain it becomes an important consideration. An older building, for instance, typically requires more upkeep and maintenance work than a newer building. A triplex or fourplex may require direct oversight and many owners often live on-site. But with a large apartment building or commercial complex, a property management company can be hired to take full charge of finding good tenants, collecting rents, and providing proper maintenance and repairs.

LOCATION

Residential

With both residential and commercial real estate, location is critical. But with a commercial property, you can have a good location today, and it could become a lousy location two years from now because of adverse influences created by governmental actions.

Municipal and county governments can change the traffic pattern or widen the street in front of your business, taking part or all the land in front of your property for public use as a right-of-way. They can also impose restrictions to the property that make ingress and egress difficult. When one-way streets are created, they sometimes cause tremendous problems for commercial property owners. Most cities also have the authority to limit the size and style of business signage. I could think of a whole host of actions they could take that would have a negative impact on commercial property.

A different set of rules seems to apply to residential real estate because people live in these properties; and when residents band together as a unified group, they can strongly influence elected officials. Many public servants in city hall have a different perspective. They are representing the people who put them in office. And so if the sentiment in the community is antigrowth or antibusiness, the city council is likely to vote in favor of restricting commercial activity.

Oftentimes, the local electorate will be up in arms if you change a concept that has to do with housing. The council chamber will be filled. But if you have a change of concept that has to do with commercial property, usually very few people show up for the public hearing.

If you own a single family residence and you have a low mortgage so that it is almost paid for, you'll never lose it. Our representatives in Congress wouldn't do anything to dramatically affect American homeowners because they would all lose their jobs if they did. (Interestingly, the National Association of Realtors has the largest lobby in Washington, D.C.) The same is true of local elected officials.

As mentioned, the location of residential income property is vital. In certain locales, beachfront and resort property are considered to be solid investments. However, many beach and resort communities have had very difficult times. The specific location you choose to invest in cannot be considered too carefully. Recreational properties located in areas that have year-round tenancies attract a certain type of renter, one who is prone to a carefree life-style, frequent parties, and loud noise. Many investors may find that type of tenant undesirable.

I do better with people on the beach than most other landlords I know, because I've been on the beach for so long. I know what to look for. I know how beach people are. I know what some of their traits are, their likes and dislikes. A lot of people aren't willing to become property owners in a beach community because of all the characters and problems you have to deal with. Admittedly, I've had to put up with quite a bit. For me, it's well worth it. But a great many landlords can't put up with loud noise, swearing, beer drinking, and the like.

In 1957, a few years before I bought the beachfront apartment I live in, there was a riot in front of the property that caused a lot of damage to the building. When I moved in, I vowed never to get mad at the people on the beach because if something were to happen, they are going to be the ones to protect your property.

A few years ago on the Fourth of July, I was at another beachfront property of mine where a second riot started. These guys created a big rumpus and started throwing rocks and everything else. Because I got along so well with my tenants, they stood guard to protect my building when the mayhem started. I bend over backward for the guys and gals who play volleyball in front of my places and in return they've paid me back in ways I never would have imagined.

I'll do anything I can for someone who rents from me, as long as they're paying their rent on time and not disturbing anyone else. But a lot of property owners won't do that. They get easily disturbed.

A friend of mine owns a six-unit building down from me on The Strand. For the life of me, I can't figure out why he owns the place. He can't keep it occupied. He doesn't know what to do. He doesn't know how to treat people who live by the beach. He goes over there every other day and pesters the tenants and won't leave them alone or give them any privacy.

On the other hand, if they make a little bit of noise, he gets mad. If people talk back to him, he doesn't know how to handle it and gets all upset. If his tenants pound a nail in the wall or accidentally break a window, he threatens them and raises a ruckus. It's not in him to accept these things. But why worry about a three-dollar window? He gets $1,500 a month from that one apartment. What should he care? It's all relative.

I've been renting out property for 30 years, and I've never had any serious trouble with a tenant. You just have to know how to treat people. A lot of it depends on your attitude and your approach. If one of my tenants busts a window, I'll make him replace it. But it doesn't bother me.

Very seldom do you find a tenant who will take care of the property like the owner will. One of the questions you have to ask yourself when you purchase an investment property is, Can I emotionally handle it if someone doesn't take care of the place the way I would? It is important to treat your investment as a business and not take it personally if someone trashes the place. It may not make you happy, but don't become ill over it because it probably will happen more than once.

Different localities engender different mentalities. As well as I understand and get along with people at the beach, I once bought a single family residence in Hesperia—a rural town about 80 miles from Los Angeles—and I never had so many problems in all my life. We couldn't communicate with the people there at all. We finally had to get rid of it.

Besides solving communication problems, living near your income property can also serve a valuable utilitarian purpose. When I started teaching real estate appraisal courses at Los Angeles City College in 1956, I acquired a four-unit building in Hollywood. I bought the property for two specific reasons. First, I needed a place to stay that was close to work and the campus. It was ideally located. Secondly, I used it as the subject of a hands-on exercise for my students, an assignment to physically go through the steps and prepare an appraisal of the property at its current market value. So this purchase satisfied two specific, practical needs I had at the time.

Commercial

In addition to location, the positioning of commercial property is extremely important. A bakery next door to a church is not as good for the bakery as a location next to a post office, because a church is typically used only one day a week, whereas a post office is open six days a week. In the downtown business district of a community, where building codes may not be as rigid as suburban areas, whoever owns the property decides what they think would be a good development. Oftentimes, this results in a hodgepodge. Because of this situation, many opportunities are created.

By contrast, a shopping center under the same management and ownership that is governed by a master plan may strive to put stores and activities that benefit each other side-by-side. You might find a flower shop next to a jewelry store because it helps the jewelry store. Or they might put all the shoe stores together so customers won't have to walk from one end of the complex to the other to find another shoe store when their mind is on shoes, or all the clothing stores, candy stores, or restaurants together. Everything is strategically placed, giving individual business owners less control over what they can do. That would be a point for analysis and study when investing in commercial property.

FINANCING

If you have only a business to use as collateral, you aren't as likely to have the security that banks require for a loan than if you own a piece of real property free and clear. If you have a business and a residence as your basic assets, the institutional lender is very likely to give you a substantial loan with good terms.

Today, you could get a loan on the residence for 8 to 9 percent interest and loan on the business for 15 percent or higher. But, whereas you can get a 30-year loan on a house, you can probably only get a one- or two-year loan on the business.

As far as financing of residential property is concerned, if you own from one to four units, it's relatively easy to get a loan. Generally, residential buildings with more than four units are considered apartments, so they fall into a different category. An institutional lender would require a substantial down payment. Lenders are more critical and more concerned about the net income derived from an apartment building. They would investigate the transaction more from an income standpoint.

LANDLORD RESPONSIBILITIES

Another important consideration in determining the best type of investment to fit your needs is whether you are comfortable with the role of landlord and all the attendant responsibilities of dealing with other people. Technically, a landlord is someone who *surrenders* the right to use their property for a duration of time in exchange for an agreed sum. People who are bashful about imposing on others will have a difficult time imposing on their tenants or asking for the rent.

Before investing in a property, you should ask yourself several questions. Can you get along with other people? Do you know how to go out and collect the rent? When do you get mad? When do you not get mad? How are you going to find somebody to clean and rent your apartments if you work all day? Are you competent enough in accounting to keep your own books? Can you do your own handiwork? There's a host of things to consider before you leap.

Residential versus Commercial Property

If you own a commercial property and you're leasing to a guy who runs a store, you're dealing with him on a business basis, and you can be hard-nosed. But when you rent a residential property or apartment unit, your tenants live there. It's their home. If you're dealing with a guy who has a wife and two kids, there can be a lot of emotion involved. It's harder to throw them out, or even make decisions that will affect them adversely.

Before buying, the most important thing is to become as informed as possible in the type of real estate you're going to be investing in, whether it's a single family residence, condominium, duplex or triplex, apartment buildings, or a commercial or industrial property. How do you acquire and then manage the investment? And how do other people who are successful operate their investments?

Learn everything you can. Read books on the subject. Go to night school. And realize that when you own a piece of real estate, you have the opportunity to become independent. It's not like going to a job where the boss can tell you one day, "Well, we don't need you anymore. Goodbye." With real estate, you have something that can make you self-sufficient. You therefore owe it to yourself to learn as much about the type of property you are interested in as possible.

Most of all, learn from other people's mistakes because countless others have tried before you. There are those who have failed miserably, and there are those who have succeeded beyond their wildest dreams. It's up to you to determine which category eventually best describes the type of investor you turn out to be.

3

Set a Realistic Objective That Investing in Real Estate Could Accomplish

In *Alice's Adventures in Wonderland*, the Cheshire Cat says to Alice that, if it doesn't matter where you are going, then "it doesn't matter which way you go." Investing in real estate can be like a trip through the looking glass if you are not sure what you hope to accomplish. When it comes to buying, it is important to have an objective, even one that may eventually change over time. Everyone changes their mind at some point. That's not the important thing. The important thing is to have focus. The worst thing in the world is to go off on a hundred different tangents.

People who have concrete goals, even ones that are difficult to achieve, find they can keep their mind better focused on what they set out to accomplish. These are the people who, more often than not, turn out to be the great achievers.

If a college graduate decides at the age of 21 that he wants to be a lawyer and he stays in it for the duration of his career, the odds are pretty good that he will be successful. But if that same person goes in with the idea of being a lawyer and after a few years maybe switching to something else because of uncertainty, he might wind up in a soup kitchen, degree in hand.

Before I became vice president and director of training and research for an international appraisal firm, I ran the Los Angeles office and held the position of district manager in charge of hiring. Now and again, somebody would come in and want a job as an appraiser. I would interview them and ask what type of appraisal work they could do. If an applicant would say, "I can do anything," I'd show them the door. Those are the kind of people you don't want. You want someone who has expertise in a particular field and who is decided about what to do.

Those who have a direction or goal and know what they want to accomplish are very fortunate, particularly if they know it early on. Lots of people in their forties and fifties have no more idea what they want to do in life than the man in the moon. Ask them what they can do, and, like the would-be appraisers I used to turn away, they'll say, "anything." Those are the kind of people who have difficulty being successful.

When you go to college, I think it's important to know what you intend to learn and what you hope to get out of it. Likewise, when you buy a piece of real estate, it's important to look at it as a vehicle to accomplish some objective. Do you want to make a million dollars? Do you want to buy property for the long-term to ensure your security when you get old? Do you want to buy five properties in 10 years? Whatever your objective is, you should look forward to it.

Many buyers don't have a long-term objective when they acquire a residence, other than to live there and raise a family, which is an objective, of course. But if you broaden your definition of what real estate can do for you and buy with a definite goal in mind, you're going to be far better off than just buying on a whim because you will have a plan of action. If you can buy an income property in which you could house your business or otherwise use to enhance your position, that would be a superb position to be in. The property will be twice as valuable in a sense.

Another reason for an objective is that it places your investment choices and decisions in long-range view. Investing isn't an end in itself. With a solid goal before you, it is easier to hang on to a piece of real estate over the long pull and actually realize the property's contemplated future potential than if you had no objective in mind and were enticed to sell the first time it rose in value. In addition to making a profit, an objective could include:

- Using real estate as a tax shelter
- Building an estate to leave for your children or heirs
- Generating additional income through rental properties
- Accruing a source of retirement income
- Sending your kids through school
- Accumulating equity to start a business
- Acquiring property for philanthropic purposes with the goal of eventually donating your estate to a church, college, or charity
- Having something to keep yourself occupied in retirement

Regardless of your age and station in life, when first starting a real estate investment program, it is important to assess your needs and desires and to lay out a blueprint of how you want to accomplish your ultimate goal. A 65-year-old retiree with a substantial life savings and a lot of free time will have an entirely different objective than someone who is 25, single, and making $30,000 a year. If you develop a framework to act out of and adhere to it, the odds are in your favor that you will succeed.

If you acquire a good piece of real estate and build up substantial equity, you will be able to do many things. But, as explained in Chapter 1, the reward in real estate is commensurate with the risk you're willing to take. You have to take a chance, but you have to take one that's in your favor. The thing you should never do is overextend yourself.

It shouldn't be a question of, "Well, let me think about it, and maybe I'll do it and maybe I won't." Once you begin your investment program, you can't be noncommittal or depend on someone to make your decisions for you. You'll miss the boat that way. If you can chart out a journey and set sail with your compass headings in the right direction, your destination will become clear at an early stage of the voyage. If you can do this, you will be in great shape, and it is obvious what will happen.

Consider the example of a former student of mine, a moderately successful real estate broker who started with more dedication than money. With a small savings, he was able to purchase a house and, by buying in the right location, was able to trade up after a few years for a duplex. One by one, he acquired six properties. Recently, he consolidated all of his holdings into a brand-new 59-unit apartment building. He was able to pay the down payment, decided to buy it, and focused on getting it rented. His objective is as clear as crystal. All he has to do is keep that building rented for the next 20 years and he'll be a multimillionaire, because he will be close to paying the mortgage off and the building will have appreciated to about $15 million by that time.

TAX SHELTER

A tax shelter is created by a transaction that reduces tax liability by providing tax deductions or credits. Income property is one of the best ways to shelter your wealth. Many real estate investments can be set up to provide all of the income derived from a building tax-free and allow you to reduce other taxable income by showing a paper loss. This paper loss can be the result of allowable depreciation from the building.

If you sell investment real estate for cash or term financing, you are required to pay capital gains tax on your profit. Profit is defined as your property's tax basis at the time of sale subtracted from the adjusted sale price. The adjusted sale price is the total sale price of the property less certain allowable costs of sale. If you had been taking accelerated tax depreciation, a portion of your gain could be taxed as ordinary income. Another method of transferring your profit into another property and deferring capital gains tax is through a tax-deferred exchange (see also Chapter 14).

If you have saved your money over the years and built up a nest egg, you can make a real estate investment and expand the investment into a like-kind income property of equal or greater value by doing a 1031 Tax-Deferred Exchange. The exchange becomes an extension of the original investment and, as long as you are trading up and don't take any cash out of the transaction, you can defer any tax on capital gains. If you have inherited a large amount of money and don't know what to do with it, real estate can provide a good tax shelter if you are real estate-oriented.

If you bought a commercial building that has a substantial long-term lease, you would have a tax shelter in the form of allowable depreciation on the improvements. If the property was in a growth area where the value would continue to rise, the purchase of an industrial building might be a good investment, provided you had or could find substantial tenants. The quality of tenants is extremely important. Triple A tenants, those with unquestioned financial strength, are the best.

BUILD AN ESTATE

When I started investing in real estate, I resolved that I wanted to make a million dollars by the time I was 50. It might have taken me a year or two longer, but I've since reached my mark and then some. And once you make your first million, it's easier to make your next million. My net worth now is about $15 million, which represents about $500,000 for each of the 30 years I've been serious about investing in real estate.

I remember as a boy thinking about whether I'd ever be "rich." My mother used to tell me you have to think high to rise. She used to talk about a distant relative of ours who vowed not to get married until his net worth was $250,000. When he reached the $250,000 mark, he decided he wasn't going to get married until he made $500,000. Some people never think they're successful no matter how much they make.

T he sooner you realize that there is no easy way to get rich, the better off you're going to be. If you are going to make money as a writer, you have to work tirelessly. If you are going to make money in your own business, you have to be committed. If you want to make it as an appraiser, you have to work at it. Similarly, if you want to make money buying and holding real estate, you have to realize that it takes knowledge, dedication, and hard work.

There is no easy way to make money, and real estate is no exception. But the difference between real estate and other endeavors is that you can identify a long-range objective and know where you are headed. You can't live beyond your means and do this, however.

Nothing is greased on all sides. The advantage to investing in real estate is that you can continue to work full-time and invest in property on the side. Once you have your money in the right place, it grows for you. It's going in the right direction. I don't know of any get-rich-quick schemes that work, unless you figure out a way to win the lottery.

Trying to get rich quick in the commodities market brought me to this realization. I tried three different times over a period of four years before I realized that commodities were not for me. I even took night school courses studying the commodities market with brokers who were really well versed in it. I hired them as consultants to advise me on what to do. But I lost all my money in spite of that.

During this time, I had a job working as an appraiser. One day I decided that maybe I'd be better off putting my efforts investing in real estate, a field I knew something about, rather than going for broke in the commodities market, which mystifies me to this day. So instead of going to night school to learn about commodities, I decided to redirect my efforts toward investing in real estate. My first deal worked out so well, I decided to continue buying.

Building an estate to leave for your children or heirs can be very advantageous for your family and a good way to get your kids started in life. Investing in real estate enables you to put property in a trust so that the children will have benefits when they reach a certain age.

JOINT TENANCY, COMMUNITY PROPERTY, AND TENANCY IN COMMON

When a piece of real property is purchased by two or more people, it is necessary to have a proper ownership deed to meet the needs and requirements of those participating in the transaction. Depending on the laws of the state you live in, there are three different ways to take title (legal possession) to a property—in joint tenancy, as community property, or as tenancy in common.

Joint tenancy is ownership by two or more people with the right of survivorship, or the right to acquire the interest of a deceased joint owner. Upon the death of a joint tenant, the interest in a property does not go to the heirs but to the remaining joint tenant. When real estate in this situation passes into new ownership, it is assigned a stepped-up basis to reflect present market value. Depreciation on the improvements for tax purposes can then start over, providing the property is income producing.

For example, say a hot property in a booming area was purchased for $100,000. The owners, in this instance a retired husband and wife, hold on to it for 10 years, during which time the value swells to $500,000. Since they own the property as joint tenants with the right of survivorship, the husband has a $250,000 interest and the wife has a $250,000 interest. When either spouse dies, the entire property will pass to the other without probate, as survivorship prevents heirs of the deceased from making claims against the property.

Assume the husband passes away. Under joint tenancy, the wife automatically inherits the husband's interest in the property. Although the property's former basis for tax purposes was $100,000 (with $50,000 allocated for each spouse), the wife's new basis now increases to $300,000—her $250,000 interest in the current market value of the property plus half of the old basis. For tax purposes, the wife can start taking depreciation on that stepped-up market value, the new $300,000 basis.

A different set of circumstances occurs when real estate is held as community property, which is defined as real and personal property accumulated through the joint efforts of a husband and wife after marriage and owned by them in equal shares. This method of ownership exists in a handful of western and southern states, including Arizona, California, Idaho, Louisiana, Nevada, New Mexico, Texas, and Washington.

Say a California couple decides to get a divorce. Half of all the property acquired by joint effort during the marriage goes to the wife and half to the husband, regardless of which spouse earned a greater income or invested more money in acquisitions during the marriage. One of the advantages of living in a community property state is that when one spouse passes away, the surviving spouse receives a stepped-up basis on income property, which allows a greater tax write-off through depreciation.

In community property, the stepped-up basis is equal to the increased value of the whole property. If, for example, a house was acquired for $100,000 and the property is now worth $500,000, the stepped-up basis would be $500,000.

When a person who owns real estate as community property or in a tenancy-in-common arrangement passes away, the estate has to go through a probate process to establish the validity of the will. An estate consists of the total assets of the decedent. Probate is handled by a court administrator to ensure that all those involved in the will are treated fairly. When the residue of an estate is passed on to an heir or heirs, the estate must first pay inheritance tax. The court can then distribute the assets or sell the real estate. Probate takes one year, two years, sometimes longer.

Placing your real estate into a living trust, family trust, or similar instrument alleviates the need for probate because the property is named specifically for the people in the trust. If you place your assets into a trust, you, as the trustee, hold the property for the benefit of another, the beneficiary named in the trust.

Tenancy in common is ownership of real property by two or more people who hold an undivided interest *without* the right of survivorship. After the death of one of the owners, the deceased's share in the property is passed on to the party or parties designated in the will. Under this arrangement, all of the investors have to sign the deed in order for the entire property to be conveyed, but each tenant may convey his or her share independently. Real estate syndication groups, a method of selling property whereby a sponsor sells interests to investors, may take the form of a tenancy in common.

SOURCE OF INCOME

Another goal that investing in real estate could accomplish is generating additional income through rental properties. Many people put their money in the bank and draw on Treasury bills or certificates of deposit. Whenever I received any excess income, I put it back into real estate. Every investor has different ideas and different needs. One person might buy a vintage automobile; another may start a new business. After losing all my money investing in the commodities market, I always thought the safest way to make money was in real estate.

It is difficult to predict the amount of net income that can be generated from a multiple-unit income property. Generally speaking, the larger the building, the more cash flow it will produce if properly financed and managed. But, all factors being equal, the larger the complex, the more business-oriented you must be to turn it into a paying entity. Duplexes and small unit properties can be more casually managed by people who have other occupations and lack property management experience than larger unit buildings.

Obviously, financing is a key factor in determining cash flow—the money left over after subtracting all property-related expenditures from rental income. In addition to monthly mortgage payments, property-related expenses might include renovation costs, vacancy and credit losses, maintenance costs, taxes and insurance, and utility bills. If the property is free and clear of debt, it should produce an immediate positive cash flow.

If you own a heavily mortgaged income property in a good growth area, it could take 7 to 10 years, or more, to realize your first positive cash flow where the rental income is enough to carry the mortgage payments and pay all property-related expenses.

Many people have the idea of making a million dollars in their lifetime. A young guy I once knew wanted to make a million dollars by the time he reached the ripe age of 40. Since California did not have a state lottery at the time, the only way he could see making his fortune was by investing in real estate. So he figured out a way to acquire a fourplex with a low down payment and obtained a 20-year mortgage on it. He knew that if he paid off the mortgage, at the end of 20 years he would have a million dollars in real estate, which is every bit as good as cash.

Sure enough, by the time he was 40, he had the thing paid off and owned an asset worth a million dollars. Had he not been structured in his activities, his success story might have had a much different ending. But because he had a definite goal and knew to stay true to his course, he became very disciplined and figured out a way to do it. The best decision he made was to select a property in a growth area where a 20-year appreciation factor could be forecasted with a degree of certainty.

Let me tell you about one of my college students. She used to attend the Church of Religious Science in Los Angeles and believed in the power of positive thinking. She once told me she was interested in making a lot of money, so she took this series of evening classes in positive thinking where the instructor taught her how to keep her mind active and focused on her objective at all times. To help visualize her goal, she bought a coin book that had a picture of a $10,000 bill printed on the cover. She then made photocopies of the simulated bill and pasted them all around her apartment. She had them in her living room, her bathroom mirror, all over the place. She also had her car painted gold and gold-colored carpet laid in the living room.

She did all this to condition herself to think only in terms of making money. Now, at the time I knew her, she had very little savings. But with this money, she went out to the desert and bought a large parcel of land with a partner, a very shrewd fellow. Simultaneously, they started selling off smaller parcels of land. They did this until they had enough money to put a down payment on a dilapidated apartment building back in Los Angeles.

After sitting on their first apartment building and getting it to produce a positive cash flow, they started buying run-down 30- to 40-unit buildings in problem areas, old brick structures that the city was about to condemn. Because these brick buildings did not meet stringent earthquake requirements, they were able to purchase some of them for nothing down because the owners were concerned about their personal liability should a severe tremor occur.

Although these two started investing in real estate without much capital, they were conditioned to visualize a golden objective, and they took a chance. Today, they must own about 10 apartment buildings on the fringe area of downtown Los Angeles and they've since made all their buildings earthquake resistant. Together, they're probably worth about $25 million. Focusing on an objective and being persistent can pay off in incalculable ways.

═══════════

What is your definition of a genius? Most people think a genius is a special person who can come up with ideas nobody else can. My definition of a genius is quite different. A genius to me is a person who has the ability to clearly visualize the overall objective, someone who doesn't allow himself to be distracted by all the trivia of daily life. In other words, a genius can see and understand what the future result will be and avoid being bogged down by the unimportant details. If your objective is clear to you and you don't let the little things in life interfere with the ultimate goal you're trying to accomplish, you could be a genius, too.

A friend of mine recently asked if there was anything I did when I first started investing in real estate that enabled me to survive during lean times. I told him that the most important thing to me that kept me going was the drive to be financially independent and not have to rely on someone else to be successful and pay my bills.

One day my brother Paul and I got to thinking and discovered that there are only about 200 beach-facing lots in the entire city of Hermosa Beach. We reasoned that if we enjoyed the view from The Strand, the row of houses facing the beach, there must be other people who think it is worth something, too. With only a limited number of properties and very few for sale, the demand was bound to push prices up over time.

After concluding that the area was unique, I decided that if I could buy a property on the oceanfront, regardless of what I had to pay, it would be an excellent buy—as long as I could live with the terms and my monthly mortgage payments. Once the area became saturated, those who wanted to live here would have to pay more because of the scarcity and uniqueness of the housing. I never lost sight of that even when property values started to rise. I was able to keep my focus because I liked the beach and was aware of the potential appreciation. I starting buying more property on the beach when, a few years later, it became obvious how good the market was going to be. If you can find a property you derive enjoyment from in an area with growth potential, you can't lose. In addition to having a good investment, I now have a place to live and for visitors to stay.

If I explained this concept to an auditorium of 500 people, I'll bet you there wouldn't be five people who would follow my advice. Most investors would probably agree that this is what they should do. But very few would act. Instead, a decade from now, they will be telling all their friends, "Well, 10 years ago I should have bought that piece of property over there because now look at what it's worth." With an objective, you won't regret missing opportunities like that. When they present themselves, you'll recognize how they can fit into your overall program and you'll act on them.

COLLEGE EDUCATION

In the mid-1950s I did an appraisal for a guy who bought a commercial property in Beverly Hills with the ultimate objective of providing money for his child's college education. When this man's son was born, the child's grandmother gave the boy $4,000 to be invested in an asset to further his college education. The father decided that, rather than putting this money into a meager trust fund, where the money would accumulate interest and the child probably would end up with about $50,000 at the age of 21, he would invest in a piece of commercial real estate.

The property was a single story retail store, which the father intended to use as a retail outlet for his printing business. The purchase price of the property was $40,000. He bought the property with a 10 percent down payment, or $4,000, and the seller carried back a first mortgage for $36,000. The interest rate on the loan was 6 percent, amortized over 20 years.

The father negotiated the transaction whereby he purchased the property in his son's name through a trust where the father possessed power of attorney. The deal was structured so that the son, having a 100-percent interest in the property, owned it as an individual. The father then "leased" the property from the son. This rental income was sufficient to make the loan payments, as well as pay for the property taxes, insurance, and maintenance costs.

At the end of 20 years, the mortgage was paid off. During this time, the property experienced a tenfold increase in value, to $400,000. Clearly, the son had an asset worth considerably more than if his father had invested in an annuity. Not only was this property, which is owned free and clear, able to finance a top-flight college education, it also provided him with an excellent start in life. The $4,000 his grandmother gave him turned into a prized asset. This illustrates one of the many ways an ingenious investor can accomplish a worthwhile objective by using real estate as a means to achieve a desired end.

Another use of real estate to help underwrite a college education was demonstrated to me by a client of mine who had four daughters ranging in age from 4 to 13. The father realized how costly it was going to be to send all of his daughters to college. So when the oldest daughter was 15 years old, he visited the local university where he felt the children might be happy studying for their degrees and purchased a two-bedroom condominium within walking distance of the campus.

Over the next three years, he rented the condominium until his first daughter was old enough to enroll in college. In the decade that followed, the condo became a second home for his daughters during their college years. They could walk to classes without needing a car. Instead of charging rent, the father insisted that each daughter work part-time while attending classes to help make the mortgage payment. Their portion was still considerably lower than what renting their own apartment would have been. This program worked out extremely well for the entire family and, after the last daughter graduated with her degree, the father put the property on the market and sold it for about seven times the original purchase price.

PHILANTHROPY

I've known people who, because they are dedicated to their church, buy property with the goal of donating it; others accumulate large sums and give it to charity, to a children's hospital, or to cancer research. I had a friend who owned a large estate in Laguna Beach, California. When he was getting along in years, he decided to donate his property to the city for artistic and cultural activities.

He purchased the property because he liked the area and realized how valuable the property would be as a public service and donation to the city. That was his objective. It worked out well for him because he got to use the house for the duration of his lifetime, while the city owned the property. Because of this, he didn't have to pay any property taxes. I did an appraisal for him segregating the value of the estate into five separate portions, allowing my friend to donate one segment of the estate to the city each year for five years. By doing this, he stayed within IRS limits for gift tax donations. It turned out well for everyone, and the city received the property after he passed away.

———

Another goal might be to set up a foundation, charity, or scholarship program to give something back to the community. I figured out a way to convert one of the properties I have into a very worthwhile use. The property consists of three small apartment units attached to a spacious four-bedroom house with a large living room, dining room, and patio area in the front. I want to convert this property if I can into a seven-bedroom single family residence with five bathrooms and one small apartment for a caretaker.

———

My plan is to transform this property into a charitable retreat for underprivileged Indian children. Eventually, I want to have it endowed in such a way that the property will accommodate a full-time live-in housekeeper. I estimate that about 10 kids and three parents can spend the weekend there. A different group could go each weekend for nothing. But right now I don't think the city will approve the use change. A few vocal homeowners in the neighborhood don't like the idea because they think it might lower their property values. I don't think it will adversely affect property values or the neighborhood. Eventually, this is what I am hoping to do. So that is a very practical objective that can benefit people through real estate. You see, you don't have to be Andrew Carnegie to set up a charitable foundation.

———

OWNING AND MANAGING PROPERTY
AS A RETIREMENT ACTIVITY

One of the main advantages to owning real estate, in my opinion, is that it gives you something to do in your old age. I think that is very important. When my father sold his business and wanted to retire, he bought a three-unit complex on Fountain Avenue in Hollywood. He bought this particular property because he liked the people who lived there and it kept him occupied. He would sit down and talk to the tenants for hours.

When he came home, I'd say, "So Dad, you went over there to collect the rent?" And he'd say, "Yeah" and then start telling me about all the problems everybody had. I'd ask, "Did you collect the rent?" And he would say, "Oh, I knew I forgot something." That property was a terrific thing for him. It kept him busy. On the other hand, he would have had nothing to do if all his money were in stocks, except call his broker and watch a little blip on a computer screen.

The three units my father purchased were very unique. Each was a two-bedroom structure. The unit in the middle had a bright, canary yellow kitchen. It was a beautiful paint job, but when you walked into the room, the color resembled that of a kindergarten playroom. We looked at it and decided we could never rent the place with a kitchen like that. But we put a sign up anyway and a lady came by who said, "You know, I've always wanted a kitchen that was bright yellow. I'm so happy. You don't know." That was funnier than a ham sandwich without the ham.

4

Analyze National Trends Affecting Environmental Factors and Economic Growth

This chapter begins our discussion of long-range forecasting methods. The first step in analyzing a given area's growth potential is to place it in the greater context of what is happening to the economy. The national economy and the actions of the federal government can have a profound effect on every usable piece of real estate in the nation. Therefore, it is useful to assess:

- Whether the gross domestic product (GDP) is in a growth mode or in a period of contraction
- Whether the overall number of jobs is increasing or falling off, and what the rate of unemployment is
- Whether construction and home building on a nationwide basis is up or down

By looking at these and other economic indicators, such as interest rates, you can begin to get a feel for the direction of various national trends important to the real estate market. And by studying past trends and cycles, it is possible to predict what will happen in the future. For instance, the U.S. economy has endured 10 recessions since the end of World War II, but overall GDP (formerly GNP) has more than tripled despite these temporary setbacks. Real estate appraisers often look for this type of historical data to formulate their opinions of a property's current— and future—market value.

INFLATIONARY/RECESSIONARY TREND

If you have a good piece of real estate, such an investment will act as a hedge against inflation because it will increase in value with the inflationary trend of the overall economy. In fact, real estate values frequently increase much faster than inflation because of supply and demand.

The best time to buy a piece of property is when the country has hit the depths of a recession and is about to start up again. If you can get in and hold out for two or three dips over a 10-year period, you'll probably be out of the woods, even if you bought for very little down and have relatively large payments. Recessions are hard on the economy, but land values in good areas can still appreciate because of inflation. Real estate prices probably will double again over the next decade. After a recession, we're almost always at a higher level. (In a depression, however, real estate prices tend to fall more rapidly than overall price levels.) As long as you can live with the terms of your financing, inflation should take care of the rest.

In a capitalistic economy, you can rest assured that inflation will always exist because it makes it easier for the government to function. The government, which borrows money at the present rate through the sale of savings bonds, pays back its obligations 10 years from now with soft, or inflated, dollars. Within this system, it always takes fewer of today's dollars to pay back yesterday's loans.

Real estate goes in cycles. Substantial downturns in the real estate market have happened at least a dozen times in my lifetime. But I'm not interested in the dips. What you want to do is consider the long-term trend of the country. Will it continue for the next 20 to 30 years? Read the newspaper with your long-term objective in mind and don't get tripped up in all the minutiae. Remember, a genius is a person who has the ability to clearly visualize the overall objective, who isn't distracted by the trivia of daily life.

National economic trends are most pronounced when our country experiences some kind of major crisis, such as a war, recession, or depression. These developments are accompanied by dynamic forces that affect the market value of real estate. They create a change in the government's demands for resources and supplies, and they change the population's demands for goods and services. If the economy has a normal annual growth rate of 2 to 3 percent, that indicates an inflationary trend and a healthy growth pattern in my opinion.

If you study history, you can predict the future. You don't have to be an expert to be in the know, but you do have to do a little research, and you've got to stay informed. There is no substitute for knowledge. Read as much as you can, study trends from state and regional agencies as well as public utilities, talk to state and local chambers of commerce, and make inquiries to local, state, and national real estate associations.

Inflation versus Depression

A depression is hard on a lot of people, but overinflation or hyperinflation is a total disaster for everybody. Even during the Great Depression, when there was 25 percent unemployment, some areas of the country still managed to do pretty well. I grew up in the 1930s, when things were at their worst, about a block-and-a-half from an area in Los Angeles known as the Miracle Mile district—a stretch of Wilshire Boulevard between Fairfax and La Brea avenues that was virtually immune to the nationwide economic crisis—and witnessed this firsthand.

But, when you have inflation, it effects every single person in the country because everyone's cost of living goes up while their buying power drops. Whether the economy is on an inflationary or recessionary trend, you have to be cautious and not overextend yourself. To ensure against any unforeseen adverse developments, you should have at least six months' cash reserve on hand to be able to make your mortgage payments and pay your bills. You can withstand a tremendous recession if you do that.

Interest Rates

Interest rates are extremely important. The lower the rate, the more money there is available for construction and housing, and for economic activity in general, such as consumer spending. When the housing market is good, home building and buying surges, which in turn creates jobs. And when houses are sold, it stimulates demand for hard goods, such as refrigerators, stoves, other appliances, furniture, carpets, drapes, and other long-term investment items. This type of spending helps boost the economy tremendously. (Soft goods, as opposed to hard goods, are items that wear out or are used up in a short period of time, such as clothing and apparel, food stuffs, and other nondurable or perishable items.)

I f you look at money as a commodity and interest rates as its barometer, when money is in short supply and harder to get, interest rates go up. Conversely, when there is a lot of money around and the demand or pressure is reduced, interest rates are lowered. It's a question of supply and demand. If you look at money as a nondurable good, as an essential item like bread, it becomes something you have to have. Everybody has to eat bread; otherwise, you're not going to have a balanced diet.

Now, if all of a sudden only half of the bread baked in America were to be available tomorrow, some people would invariably go hungry and their diet would suffer. In this circumstance, bread is going to become extremely valuable. Whether you like it or not, it will go up in price. In fact, the price of bread under these conditions is probably going to go out of sight. Again, it's a question of supply and demand. If, on the other hand, somebody bakes more bread than is needed and there is so much of it that you can find it lying on the street and can buy it for almost nothing. The same situation is true with money. So it is useful to think of money as bread.

―――――――

When there is a slow real estate market and interest rates are low, it can be an optimum time to buy. When interest rates are high, like they were during the 1982 recession when they reached upward of 20 percent, buying becomes more treacherous because of the unfavorable financing that is available. For people who are in a position to buy property, high interest rates are not necessarily a hindrance because they force sellers to be realistic. Of course, there is more activity when interest rates are low— much more. I think it's good to assess the condition of the economy, but not to be too concerned about interest rates.

Real estate sales activity can't always be good. But a lull may depend on what segment of the market you are looking at. If one part of the market is bad, such as high-priced single family homes in expensive suburban areas, another area, perhaps condominium sales in lower-priced urban locations, might be good. There is always a good segment, regardless of what interest rates are doing and regardless of the state of the economy.

Even if interest rates are high, the investor who is sharp, who is educated, who is knowledgeable, who is shrewd can go out and still make a lot of money because he or she understands the problem and knows that certain sellers will always be motivated irrespective of the economic climate. If you have capital and are familiar with your subject, there never really is a situation where you wouldn't want to buy real estate, except if you could foresee a serious depression.

Another factor to consider is that at some time in a person's life, real estate might become a burden. Say somebody passes away and the property goes into probate. No matter what the economy is like, the court must distribute the assets of the estate. If real estate is involved, it might be necessary to sell the property to pay inheritance taxes or satisfy other outstanding obligations.

POPULATION GROWTH

In one of my first real estate lectures in 1956, I predicted that "the trend is toward the Far East, with Los Angeles fast coming into its heyday." Just as the East Coast flourished when Europe was rich and powerful, so the

West Coast would thrive when the economies, and populations, of Pacific Rim countries began to intermingle with the western states. I don't claim to have a crystal ball, but my prognostication has come true. Of course, and I said this back then, the handwriting was on the wall.

Over the past decade, the migration of people from Asia, the South Pacific, and Mexico to the United States has never been more pronounced. A lot of Americans object to this. But I think this influx of population gives the United States a tremendous advantage. During the late 1800s and early 1900s, great numbers of European immigrants, including people from Germany, France, Italy, Great Britain, and Ireland, came to America. They were willing to come here and take a chance. They had the guts, the ideas, the stamina, and the foresight to do it. They helped make this country what it is.

The same is true today. I still think people who migrate to the United States are those who are willing to take a chance, who have vision and foresight, and who are willing to work toward a new and better life than they had in their old country. And in putting their skills and ideas to work in new ways, they benefit our country. The difference now is that instead of Europe, the new immigrants are largely from Asia—namely Korea, Japan, Vietnam, Singapore, Indonesia, and the Philippines—the Middle East, India, and Mexico. Roughly half of the nation's population growth of 23 million during the last decade resulted from increases in the Asian and Latino populations, according to the 1990 Census.

Many Americans are frightened by foreigners. People here think they are coming to take our jobs; I don't. It was reported that the Japanese firm Mitsubishi Estate Co. bought Rockefeller Center in New York City; they didn't. For $846 million, they acquired a 51 percent stake in the Rockefeller Group, amounting to a 14.5 percent controlling interest in the center. They don't own the center; they don't operate it; they only own part of it. But the news media never say that. Instead, such developments lead to sensationalistic trend stories where the sellers are charged, in effect, with economic treason. The headlines might as well read: "Oh my goodness, look what's happening." In my opinion, foreign investment, as well as immigration, provides a tremendous infusion of new labor and capital to the economy and gives it a tremendous boost.

And as more and more people move to the United States, the population density will increase. The fact is that we live in a vast country. We have miles and miles of desert land that can be converted to productive, habitable uses as long as there is an adequate water supply. The United States still has a relative abundance of raw land and natural resources that can accomodate a tremendous amount of people.

But population density doesn't necessarily create wealth. Think of India. With roughly 600 people per square mile, India is one of the most densely populated countries in the world. In the United States, population density averages about 60 people per square mile. When you have people come into a community who are industrious, who have the ability to do things, and who may have a little bit of money, then you are creating wealth. Population alone can be a detriment, but population combined with industry creates wealth.

Japan has been successful because of its industry. But that country has a very rigid economy. A handful of people at the top of the government oversee all of the industries, and they decide what is best for the country. One of the reasons Japan is so successful is that industries are integrated, and that a small group of people has the authority to tell the rest of the citizenry what to do.

That explains why they have such severe trading and immigration laws. But as a consequence of this, Japan doesn't have the infusion of new energy and ideas that we get from people who emigrate to the United States. In Japan, people are told what to do more than anything else. In America, people are allowed to think. That's the great thing about America. They are allowed to participate. They are given the opportunity to invest in property and build an estate.

Despite all the hoopla about the Japanese people's ability to save, they still are nowhere near as well off as we are. The average person living in Japan has a much, much lower standard of living than we do because they do not have the distribution of wealth or the natural resources that we do. Most of the land in Japan is not arable. Their sanitary conditions, their housing, their variety of food are all compromised.

We read in the newspaper how we have slums and a growing number of poor, but America primarily is made and dependent on the middle-class and middle America. That is what really makes America the great power that it is. The guy who goes to work and puts in an eight-hour day and makes $35,000 a year, which is about the average salary; and his wife who has a job earning $20,000; and their two kids, two new cars, and a house—they are the backbone of the economy. And they are living in superb luxury compared to the rest of the world.

Our inflationary economy makes it easier for them to buy big-ticket items with just credit. If you had a job working in a bank and you were making $35,000 a year, you could buy a new car without making a large downpayment. You can buy a new house, and you only have to put about $5,000 down on it. If you wanted to furnish the house, you can go to the furniture company and say, "Look, I've got a brand new car. I've got a brand new house. I'm a success. Why don't you loan me some money to buy the furniture?" And, if you have a good credit history, they will.

I've traveled all around the world, from Africa to Eastern Europe, from South America to remote destinations in the South Pacific. Citizens of other countries can't get credit like we can here in the United States. In fact, it is easier to obtain credit in the United States than it is in any other major industrialized country I know, easier than in Canada, Australia, Germany, France, Japan, or Great Britain.

Eastern Europe shows what happens when you have a rigidly structured economy and a controlling governmental bureaucracy that rules every aspect of citizens' lives, telling everybody what to do and for how long. When, all of a sudden, the rulers are gone, nobody knows what to do. Their ingenuity, resourcefulness, and standard of living drops. Look at the wretched conditions in Romania, the former Soviet Union, and what used to be East Germany. Decades of totalitarianism made people dependent. It's like feeding wild animals in a national park—pretty soon, they forget how to fend for themselves. Similarly, all the grain and the corn stalks rot in the fields while the people in the cities go hungry.

In California, the most populous, productive, and diverse state in the union, there are more Nobel Prize winners than in all of Japan. California has more Nobel Prize holders than any other state or country, except the United States. That creates wealth. America is on the cutting edge of everything because of our industriousness and ingenuity. In America, it takes a major crisis to get people moving. But when Americans are put to the test, we get the job done. Competition here is more intense than any place else in the world. Now, what if this knowledge and competitive spirit was spread out to other parts of the world? It would be fantastic.

If the United States nullified some of its antitrust laws so companies could work together and do research and development to their mutual benefit, they could take on competition anywhere. Companies together can do some pretty remarkable things. But when they are hampered by fair-trade or antitrust laws and industries in other countries aren't, that can tip the scales.

Many people think our antitrust laws are obsolete. I tend to agree. We're dealing in the world arena, not just on a domestic front. Leading corporations such as GM, AT&T, and IBM are tailoring their products and services to meet the needs not only of U.S. customers, but international clients as well. But with so many restrictions on it, corporate America has a hard time keeping pace with the rapid changes in the world economy.

I have great faith in America. It's a wonderful place to live. Of course, we have our problems, but if you travel to other continents, you'll find that most countries have it a lot worse than we do. Why do you think all these people from foreign lands want to live here?

FISCAL POLICIES

Federal Spending

Many people are frightened by the national debt, the sum of all the debts that the government has amassed, which is about $3 trillion. Yet the gross domestic product of the United States is about $6 trillion. If you were to calculate the present market value of all the assets the federal government owns, you would arrive at a figure probably in the hundreds of trillions of dollars. By comparison, our $3 trillion debt is negligible.

The federal government doesn't do its bookkeeping like a business or individual would. How do you measure the market value of Yosemite National Park? Or Yellowstone? Or Glacier? You can't measure the value of these national treasures. Even the assets that can be measured—public housing, military bases, millions of acres of land not a part of the national park system—all of this is valued and on the books according to the cost at the time of acquisition or construction.

In the depths of the Depression when Roosevelt came to power and implemented his New Deal, he took the government off the monetary standard and switched it to gold. Roosevelt maintained that we have to spend money in order to be successful, so he created national work forces.

He created conservation corps around the country so that when people couldn't find a job, the government would give them something to do. They built a lot of construction projects for public uses, including state capitols, schools, library buildings, and cultural institutions. Instead of putting people on welfare, the idea was that they would work on these various projects, be paid by the government, and eventually these projects would be publicly beneficial, which is exactly what happened. Public works projects on that scale aren't being undertaken very much anymore. Yet this type of federal spending is extremely important. It is the kind of thing that makes America strong.

———

The construction of the Grand Coulee Dam on the Columbia River, the largest concrete structure in the world, was extremely costly and time-consuming (construction lasted from 1933 to 1942) because it is situated on difficult terrain. But once the Grand Coulee was up and operating, the arid land of the Columbia River basin in Washington state became a blooming oasis. In addition to being an enormous source of hydroelectric power, the dam now provides a water supply for the irrigation of over 1 million acres of land previously used only for dry farming and grazing.

The Hoover Dam is another example. Located on the lower Colorado River on the Arizona-Nevada border, the Hoover Dam is one of the most efficient electricity-generating plants in the country, providing water for domestic, industrial, and municipal use as well as low-cost electric power for Arizona, Nevada, and California. It also created the largest artificial lake in America, Lake Mead, which is now used for recreational purposes. It is very difficult to put a dollar value on these types of assets, yet they create astronomical wealth.

The Grand Coulee and Hoover dams have turned desert lands into fertile areas, creating thousands of jobs and enhancing the economies of entire states and regions. The dams have also created wealth in the form of produce and other crops that can be sold around the world. Many people regard public works projects such as the Grand Coulee and Hoover dams as the unsung heroes of World War II. The electricity generated from these power plants provided energy for building warships, cargo vessels, ice-breaking ships, aircraft, rubber and metal products, and a host of other materials necessary for the war effort.

Other public works projects, such as boat harbors, rural electrification systems, and superhighways, also create value. Any well-planned public transportation project is bound to enhance value. The ability to move goods, services, and people is very important to the economy. From an investment standpoint, the important thing about public works projects is to analyze whether they are prompting change in a positive direction. Buy real estate when you can be assured of change in a positive direction and when you know that the subject property will be in the path of growth.

I believe the nation's railroad systems will be improved over the next 10 to 20 years. Similarly, during the Eisenhower administration, the freeway systems were improved with the passage of the Federal Aid Highway Bill. If rail systems are upgraded throughout the country, it will create more mass transit, and that in turn will create value. In Los Angeles County, the County Assessor has started to assess the properties where the new Metrorail subway stations are going to be at a higher rate than normal. The Assessor's Office recognizes how the Metrorail project will increase the value of the surrounding properties.

The construction of highways, freeways, and railways affects housing prices because it provides easier access to more areas. When you have a shift in transportation activity, it creates tremendous value. But property can also lose value if there is a negative impact from that shift. Look at all the little towns along old Route 66, which stretched from Lakeshore Drive in Chicago to Ocean Park Boulevard in Santa Monica, that were doing superbly before they put the Interstate in. All of sudden many of them went bust.

Aerospace spending is extremely important because space is unlimited, and we can explore from here to eternity. That explains why the planned space station is so important. To distinguish between space and defense, space exploration is not like the defense industry where we are building nuclear weapons for mass destruction. You don't get your money back from building war machines. But you do get your money back from space exploration, maybe not in dollars, but in other ways because the scientific and medical experiments the astronauts conduct in space improve our living conditions and ability to do things on the ground.

I remember when the astronauts' main mission was to take pictures of Earth using infrared photography from various points in space. By analyzing the photographs, oceanographers discovered a barrier shelf just beyond the Gulf of Mexico that prevented fish from getting into a huge area of about 500 square miles. So a project was initiated to remove part of that barrier so fish could get into this giant feeding area. This one action, by the added fishing it allowed, created hundreds, if not thousands, of jobs and fed maybe hundreds of thousands of people.

Table 4.1 illustrates, for selected years since 1930, the annual gross domestic product (then called gross national product) of the United States, the annual expenditures and average dollar amount spent per day by the federal government, and the size of the U.S. population.

Free Trade Agreements

The free trade agreement that the administration is currently trying to negotiate with Mexico (one already exists between the United States and Canada), which would phase out tariffs and restrictions on most goods and services traded between our countries, will have a tremendous effect on real estate. In my estimation, it will be a monumental boon to the border states of Texas, New Mexico, Arizona, and California. The easier it is for businesses to move back and forth across the border, the more economic activity will be generated within those states. And with more business activity comes more employment opportunities, increased population, and overall prosperity. Once average income levels start to rise, real estate values will increase because people will demand a higher standard of living.

The removal of trade barriers between our three countries will also result in a greater level of productivity because each country has what the other needs. Canada still has abundant natural resources. America has the financing, free market economy, creativity, industrial infrastructure, and entrepreneurial orientation. And Mexico has a good, available supply

TABLE 4.1
Federal Revenue and Expenditures

Year	President	Gross National Product	Annual Federal Expenditures	Avg. Amount Spent Per Day	U.S. Population[a]
1990	George Bush	$ 5.7 tril.	$ 1.3 tril.	$ 3.6 bil.	249.6
1985	Ronald Reagan	$ 4.0 tril.	$946.3 bil.	$ 2.6 bil.	239.2
1980	Jimmy Carter	$ 2.7 tril.	$590.9 bil.	$ 1.6 bil.	227.7
1975	Gerald R. Ford	$ 1.6 tril.	$332.3 bil.	$910 mil.	215.9
1970	Richard M. Nixon	$ 1.0 tril.	$195.6 bil.	$536 mil.	205.0
1965	Lyndon B. Johnson	$705.1 bil.	$118.2 bil.	$324 mil.	194.3
1960	John F. Kennedy	$515.3 bil.	$ 92.0 bil.	$252 mil.	180.6
1955	Dwight D. Eisenhower	$405.9 bil.	$ 68.0 bil.	$186 mil.	165.9
1950	Harry S. Truman	$288.3 bil.	$ 43.0 bil.	$117 mil.	152.9
1945	Franklin D. Roosevelt	$213.4 bil.	$ 93.0 bil.	$254 mil.	133.4
1940	Franklin D. Roosevelt	$100.4 bil.	$ 9.4 bil.	$ 26 mil.	132.2
1935	Franklin D. Roosevelt	$ 72.8 bil.	$ 6.4 bil.	$ 18 mil.	127.2
1930	Herbert Hoover	$103.9 bil.	$ 3.1 bil.	$ 8 mil.	123.0

[a] Population in millions.
Source: U.S. Dept. of Commerce, Bureau of the Census.

of labor and some natural resources to boot. With this trade agreement, the economies will enhance each other in a way they're not doing now. A Bank of America study of the proposed North American Free Trade Agreement concluded that the amount of trade between the United States and Mexico would triple if the agreement were ratified.

If this ever happens, many of the manufacturers currently having their products made in Korea, Thailand, Singapore, China, and the Philippines will opt to invest in Mexico, which offers affordable labor plus the opportunity to closely monitor and exercise control over the manufacturing process. Since the primary market for goods is in the United States, the demand will remain right where it is.

I f a free trade agreement existed between the United States and Mexico, I believe a fantastic real estate arrangement could be negotiated to the mutual benefit of both countries. With the cooperation of Mexico, the U.S. government could lease some of the undeveloped land on the Baja California peninsula in exchange for debt relief of outstanding loans. Camp Pendleton, the U.S. Marine

Corps training facility just north of San Diego, California, could then be moved from its present location to a new leased site in Baja.

The advantages to the Marines would be enormous. The new location would provide the training camp with greater insulation than it has now, with the Pacific Ocean bordering the land on one side and the Sea of Cortez on the other. In addition, the Baja Peninsula is sparsely populated, allowing room for possible expansion. Camp Pendleton's present location north of the border could be parceled out and sold to private interests for development. The income from this land would represent a large, albeit indirect, contribution toward the settlement of Mexico's foreign debt burden to the United States. And, by selling the Camp Pendleton land to private interests, the U.S. government would be able to recover a large portion of monies loaned as indirect compensation for the nonpayment of Mexico's debt to the United States.

Attitude toward Taxation

To my way of thinking, the move toward higher taxes destroys incentive. I think that what must be done on a macro level is to curtail government spending. I think that no matter how much money there is, for Congress it will never be enough. And I think the more you give the Congress, the more it will spend. And the more it spends, the deeper we get in debt. It's really disturbing when Congress raises taxes but doesn't cut spending. If it did both, then that would be fine. But that isn't what happens. Like they say, a penny saved is a congressional oversight.

Higher real property taxes remove incentive for people to buy property in an area. That is one of the reasons why I recommend acquiring existing housing in an established area; there is no guarantee people and jobs will move into a newly established area, especially when taxes are higher because of the financing of all new roads, facilities, and public buildings.

One of the best things about our tax system is that it keeps the money supply circulating. A person can make all the money desired while living, but after death, the government claims most of it through inheritance tax. If you make a tremendous amount of money and are put into a higher bracket where the taxes are severe, you might not like it, but that also puts money back into circulation for others to make. The tax system also encourages the creation of charitable trusts, endowments, scholarship funds, nonprofit foundations, and other innovative financial vehicles.

As money recirculates through the economy, a growth pattern occurs as new money becomes available. The big problem in many third world countries, such as Brazil and Argentina, is that maybe one-half of 1 percent of the population owns 99 percent of the wealth. And there are only minor tax laws on the books, doing little or nothing to mitigate this fact. Few third world countries have a substantial income tax or inheritance tax.

And so the elite continue to inherit money from their families, and they are the only ones who can afford to attend college and become well educated. Because they know more, they continue to drain the country of all its wealth and the weak tax laws ensure that the wealth will never be evenly distributed among the people.

COST OF GOVERNMENT

The more you take out of the gross domestic product to invest in the business to stimulate growth—the government being the business—the more long-term prosperity you can expect in return. So if the government is spending a lot of money on public works projects and private/public partnerships, that activity is inevitably going to stimulate the private business sector and create more opportunity.

The effect of an increase or decrease in spending depends on what the government is spending the money for. It is important to look at what things the administration spends money on. If the government spends money on housing and employment programs that are beneficial to people, that people can use to elevate their position, then they are likely to benefit the economy. If, on the other hand, money allocated for social services is distributed in the form of handouts to people who then squander it, then I don't see how it benefits the economy or even really helps the people it is designed to assist.

If, by some miracle, the government were to spend less money for nonessential services, services that don't enhance the community, and more on projects that add to community growth, that could be very advantageous. It's easy for the government as well as individuals to spend money in the wrong places. If you, your father, or anyone else who invests capital, puts it in the wrong place, it isn't going to do anybody any good. And the government is not immune to that.

At the regional level, some states have strict rules governing what public funds can be allocated for. The tidelands (coastal regions) in Long Beach, California are a great example. The City of Long Beach was able to buy the Queen Mary, build a surrounding breakwall, and set up the great oceanliner as a tourist attraction largely through the use of tidelands money—profits that came from oil wells located in the tidelands.

The City Council was prevented by state law from taking those monies and depositing them into the general fund. They had to be spent whence they originated. Over time, the city accumulated a huge fund and was able to buy the Queen Mary and spend all the money necessary to convert it into an attraction. By spending the tidelands money wisely, the City Council enhanced the city's reputation and attracted new business to the community by acquiring an asset that is known worldwide. Strategically, it was a sound move. Such thoughtful public investments greatly enhance land values in the surrounding area.

FEDERAL PARTICIPATION IN HOUSING

Subsidized Housing Programs

Subsidized housing programs are intended to improve the living conditions of people with moderate, or minimal, means. The general problem with housing programs is their political nature. The billions spent on these projects address only one aspect of the total need—shelter. Other considerations should include the development of community services, education, and employment-assistance programs to improve the outlook and socioeconomic position of the recipients who occupy these buildings.

The sad part of subsidized housing programs is that these building projects oftentimes become slums. Typically, public housing developments are in the downtown district of a city or in low income areas. The theory behind most public housing projects is to provide adequate shelter for people of moderate means to help get them on their feet and find jobs, thereby contributing to the local economy and helping to improve the city. Frequently, however, it doesn't work that way.

In many major cities, housing projects have become havens for drug dealing and gang activity. It's terrible, but it doesn't have to be this way. In Philadelphia and other cities around the country, tenants are starting to organize with the goal of buying back the public housing buildings in which they live from the city with funds from the federal government.

In St. Louis, several families recently united to reclaim a public housing project that was virtually destroyed over the years by tenants who had no concern for the property. The building in question was originally built as part of an urban renewal project in the 1960s. These families asked the government for help in clearing out problem tenants and rehabilitating the building so that responsible tenants could once again enjoy living there. They then created a board of directors and picked new tenants who agreed to follow the rules. Those who didn't adhere to the new guidelines were kicked out. The building association enforced their conditions to the letter of the law and in a very short time turned a once woebegone project into a desirable place to live.

If the government invests in a lot of subsidized mass housing projects, it generally does not improve the growth potential of the surrounding real estate because of this pattern of neglect. However, smaller subsidized housing projects—for instance, housing for senior citizens—may enhance a community. If new housing is built in an old residential area, it can't do anything but improve the neighborhood.

The amount of federal funds allocated for community and regional development shrank by almost 50 percent over the past decade, from $11.3 billion in 1980 to an estimated $6.3 billion in 1989. At the same time, housing has become less affordable to first-time buyers because wages have not kept pace with inflation and escalating real estate prices. Perhaps this explains why federal housing assistance in the form of cash payments or checks issued almost tripled in the 1980s, from $5.6 billion in 1980 to an estimated $15.3 billion in 1989.

R egardless of income, how people live is a matter of mental attitude. The condition of the beach in front of properties I own is a matter of mental attitude. If the hoards of people who visit the beach every weekend during the summer leave garbage on the sidewalk and throw their trash in the sand, the beach pretty soon will look atrocious. This is exactly what happens every Memorial Day and Labor Day—the beginning and end of summer. Fortunately, county maintenance crews come by the next day and rake the sand clean with giant tractors. Concerned residents pick up the rest. Yet if peoples' attitudes were different, this effort and expense would not be necessary.

Once, while visiting Leningrad (now renamed St. Petersburg), Russia, I took a stroll on a Sunday afternoon through a park adjacent to the Neva River on my way to a sight-seeing trip. People were sprawled out everywhere in this park, sitting on the grass and having lunch. When I came back at night, you couldn't even tell that the place had been used. There wasn't one speck of trash anywhere. Now if this had been a weekend at the beach in front of my apartment complex, you could imagine how the place would have looked. It's all a matter of attitude.

Insured Mortgages

The federal government, through the Federal Housing Administration, or FHA, insures many types of home mortgages by providing mortgage insurance to private institutional lenders for construction and home loans. The FHA charges the borrower a 0.5 percent annual premium on the average outstanding loan balance to insure the lender against loss. If a mortgage is insured by the government, the lender is assured that its money is safe and will be repaid. This enables the bank or savings and loan association to borrow against this secured asset, thus allowing future growth.

To ensure liquidity, most institutional lenders package their mortgage loans along with other mortgage loans and sell them to the secondary market, namely, the Federal National Mortgage Association ("Fannie Mae"), the Government National Mortgage Association ("Ginnie Mae"), and the Federal Home Loan Mortgage Corporation ("Freddie Mac"). Portions of these loan commitments are then sold as securities to the public, backed by a guarantee from the U.S. Treasury. The lenders, in turn, get their money back and are able to offer it for other people to borrow. In this way, a steady supply of money remains available for future transactions.

Mortgages that do not meet government requirements are not insurable. Second mortgages usually aren't insured by the government because they are a junior lien to the first mortgage and typically involve very little collateral. As such, they are a far riskier investment. Because they aren't protected, uninsured mortgages and second mortgages command a higher interest rate than insured mortgages. Private party mortgages from so-called hard money lenders also fall into this category.

Money Supply

If the government is a machine and the economy its engine, money is the grease that makes its operation possible. The supply of money is vital to economic activity. Fluctuations in entrepreneurial activity because of the availability of financing affect the health of the economy nationwide. The money supply is largely determined by the actions of the Federal Reserve Bank through the buying and selling of U.S. Treasury securities. The Federal Reserve Board controls the fluctuation of prime interest rates, which in turn determine consumer lending rates. Interest rates in large part influence economic growth. High interest rates tend to restrict expansion while lower interest rates typically stimulate economic activity.

5

Assess How National Trends Will Affect Your Region, Metropolitan Area, and Community

THE REGION

Generally, a segment of the nation set apart from other areas by geographical boundaries, which typically comprises a cluster of states such as New England, the South, Southwest, Midwest, Atlantic Seaboard, Pacific Northwest, and so on.

One of the most salient indicators of regional growth is the current and anticipated population trend of the region. In my opinion, there will be continued migration to warmer climates in the West and Southwest because it's an easier life and there will be more opportunities than in the slow-growing Rust Belt regions and industrial north. Data from the 1990 Census confirms that the nation's population continues to move west and south, as it has since the 1940s.

California's population swelled by more than 6 million people over the last decade, from 23.7 million residents in 1980 to 29.8 million in 1990. Yet I believe that the southern part of the state hasn't even started to grow yet. Information from the state department of finance projects that 5.5 million *more* people will be moving to the five-county greater Los Angeles area over the next 20 years because of a huge supply of new jobs. This influx represents the greatest migration of people to an American city since New York at the turn of the last century.

As mentioned previously, population combined with industry is what creates wealth, and there is an abundant supply of both of these vital factors in the Golden State. If California were an independent country, it would rank as the fourth largest stand-alone economy in the world. I think

Southern California in particular is the garden spot of the garden spot of the world.

Economic Considerations

In times of economic downturns, or upswings for that matter, different regions of the country are affected differently. Take the current recession. Regions like the Pacific Northwest are holding their own, while New England is experiencing considerable hardship. In this chapter, our focus is on how important trends affect the region, metropolitan area, and community you are planning to invest in, so you can decide whether that area shows enough promise.

Southwestern states, including Texas, Arizona, and Colorado, are prime examples. The collapse of the real estate market in those states really has been brutal. In hard-hit cities such as Houston, home prices sank by 30 percent in the late 1980s. The Resolution Trust Corporation, the government agency responsible for the S&L bailout, has taken over scores of savings and loan associations and billions of dollars' worth of property in these states primarily because of poor real estate loans.

Real estate prices went out of sight for a few years in the mid-to late 1980s, then fell right back down. When the S&Ls had to take scores of foreclosed properties back at 50 cents—or less—on the dollar, they were not able to sell these properties. The ensuing failure of many S&Ls attributable to bad real estate loans has had a serious effect on the regional economy, mainly because of loss of jobs. Here you can see the causal relationship between the economy and real estate. When people lose their jobs, they can't afford to make the payments, so the number of foreclosures increases and the housing market falters.

But there's no doubt that someday the housing market in those areas is going to pick up again. Land values are already starting to improve because oil prices are stabilizing. The economy in Georgia is going to be good because of all the aerospace contractors who have relocated their operations. A recent report in the *Wall Street Journal* noted that Nevada and Arizona are projected to have the fastest growth rates in personal income, employment, and population between 1988 and 2000. The U.S. Department of Commerce predicts Arizona's population growth during that period will be 21.4 percent. Just a few years ago, these states were supposedly "dying on the vine."

More than any one factor, a positive attitude can bring about a boom. If people think in terms of wealth and the success of the economy, then we will have a robust economy. Only a handful of people ever got rich during the Gold Rush of 1849. But people flocked to Sutter's mill in California because they *thought* they could get in on the action. If everyone thought we were in a depression, it wouldn't matter what the actual economic conditions were, we would be in a severe crisis. People would adopt a siege mentality. They wouldn't spend their money. Instead of eating porterhouse steaks, they'd be eating franks. People would conserve electricity. Our country is very wasteful, but when we go into a depression mode, people double up. They live in apartments together. They don't turn on unnecessary lights. They start figuring out ways to conserve. It's a state of mind as much as anything else. On the other hand, if people think times are good, they go out and spend money; they buy new cars; they purchase new homes; they take trips around the world.

Over the past few years, there has been a tremendous housing boom in Las Vegas, spurred mainly by retirees from California and the East Coast seeking a more affordable and comfortable life-style. Las Vegas is unique. If the economy flattens out or goes bust, the housing market there could collapse. At the very least, it would be very dramatically affected. There's not much industry there to keep the economy going except tourism and gambling. If the California state legislature enacted a legalized gambling law, it could have a strikingly negative impact on the Nevada region.

In the next 10 years, when Castro finally gets kicked out of power and Cuba becomes a free country, there's no question that it will go back to what it was before Castro. It will be one of the hot spots of the Caribbean. The U.S. government won't have control over taxation, rules, and the like. In my estimation, hotels and casinos will be built that are very comparable to what you see in Las Vegas right now. Before Castro's revolution, you used to be able to go to Cuba by ferry from Key West. If that returned, imagine what would happen to the economies of Miami and the Florida keys. They would be bolstered by an influx of tourism. On the other hand, Atlantic City would probably suffer.

LEGISLATIVE ACTIONS

Environmental Regulations

Political trends and legislative decisions at the national and regional levels can have a tremendous effect on the value of real estate. Environmental legislation, such as the Clean Air Act of 1990, has dramatic impact on the smokestack industries—oil refining, automaking, steel manufacturing, and so on. If the EPA (Environmental Protection Agency) or Congress imposes restrictions on emissions for automobiles, then that affects the car industry.

Other types of environmental restraints include the imposition of restrictions on the fishing industry off the Pacific Coast, the timber industry in Oregon and Washington, mining operations in the Sierra Nevada, the California water supply, and the debate over nuclear power plants for electricity. All these actions either create jobs or destroy jobs. They either enhance the economy or undermine the economy. In Southern California, there are severe air-quality regulations, which is driving out business. Whether you have a change for the better or for the worse, it affects the market value of real property.

In addition to economics, the actions and attitudes of people create as well as destroy value. Sometimes it happens overnight, sometimes it happens over a long period of time. Slow-growth attitudes have dramatic impact on property values, usually causing existing properties to increase in value. Disputes between slow-growth advocates and developers can take years to resolve.

E nvironmentalists can have a monumental effect on the market value of land. About 15 years ago I did an appraisal at one of the largest privately owned parcels of land in Oahu, Hawaii. A Japanese group wanted to buy this property, which extended for thousands of acres, to develop it. This parcel included about $1\frac{1}{4}$ miles of beautiful frontage along the beach, with a big ranch and a little village. About 80 percent of the land was in an environmental preserve.

The investment group wanted to build a yacht harbor, two or three golf courses, condominiums, and a hotel development. The owners of the property wanted $32 million for the estate. This was about 20 to 25 years ago. The buyers asked me to do an appraisal of the property and tell them how much they should pay for it. So I flew to Hawaii, studied the problem, and figured out that if they were able to develop the land in the way that the sellers said they could, the property would be worth $32 million. The owners said they could develop this preserve, but the environmentalists were so strong there that they couldn't do a thing. This is a prime example of slow-growth attitudes curtailing activity in a community.

Environmental restraints are very important to watch. If restrictions are imposed on cutting down trees to protect certain endangered species, then the lumber industry is going to suffer. The lumber industry is going to affect the value of real estate because it will cost more to build houses. If no new houses are being built, the existing ones are going to increase in value.

On the other hand, for a city like Seattle, part of the attraction is that there is a lot of forest and mountains in the area. So if the logging companies cut everything down, that would hurt the value of the property. It works both ways. You have to have a balance.

Here is another controversy. In California, there is a very serious water problem, a five-year-long drought. If the water shortage gets really serious, regional authorities aren't going to issue any more water meters, and that will impede growth—huge tracts of subdivisions would not be built in the fast-growing Riverside and San Bernardino areas. If this occurs, the value of existing housing is going to increase sharply. A few years ago in San Clemente, California, a development group started a housing project and laid out all the subdivisions. They he had all the streets in. But the city decided that the water shortage was severe enough to curtail development and refused to issue permits for water meters. The developers had millions tied up in the project. It was really brutal. As a consequence, values of existing houses in the adjacent tracts have started to skyrocket.

With the diversity of the Southern California economy and its proximity to the Pacific Rim, many people have high-paying jobs, and that means that they can afford to pay a high price for prime real estate. At the same time, millions more people are projected to move to the area over the next 10 to 20 years. If the water shortage continues and it is not possible to build new housing to compensate for this influx, you will have a situation like you have in Tokyo, where houses are worth millions and millions because of the shortage. It changes the nature of financing. You get into hundred-year loans. It can have a tremendous effect.

Environmental restrictions by regional agencies, such as the South Coast Air Quality Management District in Southern California, that limit the amount of toxic pollutants in the air are driving a lot of business out of the area, resulting in corporate relocations to Georgia, Arizona, Texas, Oklahoma, Missouri, and other less-restrictive and cost-prohibitive states. In the short-term, this may have a detrimental effect on the regional economy, but other people will move in with other types of businesses, compensating for the outflow. It is important to be aware of environmental factors and what affect they are having on the housing market and the economy.

With environmental regulations, you have to be extremely careful about your liability as well. I once heard a story about a guy who owned a piece of desert land worth about $10,000. One day, somebody decided to dump some sealed barrels of toxic waste on his land. Somebody else then came along and shot the barrels for target practice, causing the chemicals to seep into the ground and taint the water supply. Two miles downstream, somebody noticed pollutants in a well and traced it back to this property. The owner was liable for cleaning up the hazard. The cleanup amounted to about $2.5 million and cost him everything he had—his house, his business, everything. He had to file bankruptcy. He had never even been to the property. He didn't even know where it was. He had inherited it. The moral of the story is to be as informed and careful about your liability as possible.

CLIMATIC CONDITIONS

Generally speaking, if you have a nice recreational community in an area where you have sun most of the year, property values are going to soar. Housing prices are generally higher in temperate climates. Look what's happened in Honolulu, Hawaii, where single family homes sell on average for $339,800, compared to Green Bay, Wisconsin, where the median price for a single family residence is $63,100. The competition to find a good investment in Honolulu is tremendous. On the other hand, not too many people want to invest in Green Bay. You need a polar bear instinct for at least part of the year to live there. In my opinion, Florida is a fabulous place to invest. However, I don't like the bugs. But many people don't mind. Palm Springs and the Las Vegas area are other examples of how warm weather can enhance the housing market.

One way of gauging how climatic conditions affect land values is by analyzing the median price of homes in different regions of the country. Also, look at the strategic decisions made by industry. Corporations such as Disney, which decided Anaheim, California was the ideal spot for Disneyland and Orlando, Florida, the best location for Disneyworld, don't invest in a given location blindly. Both Anaheim and Orlando are densely populated areas with highly desirable climates. Disney's recent announcement to go forward with a $1 billion expansion of Disneyland in Anaheim speaks volumes about the potential of the Los Angeles area.

Climatic conditions, therefore, can have a direct effect on the regional economy. In addition to hospitality and tourism, the sporting industry thrives in warmer regions. Southern California is able to host more sporting events than any place else in the world because of the temperate climate. The facilities can always be used, and because of that, more sports arenas and stadiums have been built to accommodate the year-round demand for indoor and outdoor sporting events. Although Florida is clement for most of the year, it does have a hurricane season, which makes coastal development difficult, and freezing temperatures in some areas during the winter months, which puts a damper on the economy.

Smog conditions also have much to do with the value of real estate. About the only area that is smog-free in Southern California is the beach, where some of the highest property values are found. Much of the appeal of states like Oregon and Washington has to do with their clean air and pristine environments.

The northern states have a tremendous disadvantage in my opinion: The climate is not as conducive to industrial development than that of the southern states. A manufacturer can build a plant in San Diego, California, and, provided that the pollution level isn't too high, operate it every day of the year. In some of the northern states, such as Maine, Vermont, upstate New York, and Minnesota, there are certain days when the weather is so severe that people can't even get to work. The high cost of construction to protect workers and equipment from extreme weather is an added burden to doing business in harsh climates, whereas in most of the western states you can practically build a Quonset hut and work there year round without adverse effects.

AGRICULTURAL PRODUCTION

Agriculture production can be absolutely essential to a state and region. In California, agriculture production is an important segment of the state economy. If a region has a lot of agricultural activity, that can create tremendous wealth.

A guy I know bought 100 acres of land in Indio, California, a few years ago for $100,000. Today, it's probably worth $200,000 to $250,000 because other landowners in the region have developed irrigation systems. The regional authorities formed a water district, and now this investor has the opportunity to make use of the water on his land. That makes his property considerably more valuable than it was before the water district was formed.

In a good stable farming community that grows truck crops—vegetables such as potatoes, tomatoes, celery, lettuce, and cucumbers that are hauled to market by truck at regular intervals—the economy is usually quite stable because everyone eats vegetables. Farming communities that grow oranges and lemons and other citrus crops are more exposed. If a serious drought or freeze occurs, it can affect the economy of the whole community. People will have a difficult time paying on their mortgages, and it could impact the economy.

The United States is the only country in the world that has two crops of wheat, winter wheat and summer wheat (hard wheat and soft wheat). America has enough farmland to feed the world, so we always have a surplus of certain crops. And with our modern technology, we're always improving our ability to grow crops and to grow more on smaller parcels of land. We have mechanized agriculture to the point where the system favors the large farmer because of cheaper labor costs and a higher volume of production.

Sometimes there's a tremendous profit in agriculture, but sometimes it's very risky because of insects, weather, harvest rates, demand—a whole slew of unpredictable and uncontrollable factors. Locusts can fly across the plains and eat up all the wheat fields in their path. Or the Mediterranean fruit fly may contaminate a vitally important crop. The result in either case can be disastrous.

On the other hand, when there's a surplus, farmers can't always make enough money to survive. Agriculture in a way is speculative, which explains why commodity markets and farm subsidies were established to help stabilize the markets. If farm subsidies are lifted, many of small- to medium-sized farmers are going to get caught in the fallout, and that's going to have an impact on the regional economy.

GOVERNMENT ACTIONS

Subsidized Industries

Although it doesn't contribute to the extent that other industrialized countries do, the U.S. government subsidizes many important industries, including agriculture, aerospace and defense, aircraft production, utilities, waterways, even automakers such as Chrysler. As long as government subsidies continue and there is proper growth and economic development from these subsidies, then they will enhance the value of property in the area.

When the government closes or curtails spending at military bases, it shifts the economy dramatically because the government pours millions and millions of dollars into these facilities. The bases provide a tremendous amount of direct and ancillary employment. Many of these bases are so valuable that, if they were handed over to the cities in which they are located, the real estate they occupy could be put to a higher and better use. It would result in loss of jobs, but it would create a lot of opportunity, too.

The greater the change, the more opportunity that is created. Just imagine what will happen when some of these bases targeted for closure go out of business. There are thousands and thousands of people in the surrounding towns who will be affected. Every one of them will suffer dramatically. But these bases will eventually be put to other uses. If municipalities were to gain control of the land, they might parcel it out and sell it to private individuals for new development. Or perhaps, as has been suggested, the bases could be converted into shelters for the homeless or into detention centers to get criminals off the streets and out of our crowded jails and into a place where they could do something constructive, which in turn would help the community. Of course, it will take an act of Congress to do any of this.

Drastic cuts in defense spending, which lead to cutbacks in the well-paying aerospace industry, lessen the demand for new homes and create more demand for apartments in communities that are dependent on defense. If homes are not selling and financing is hard to get, then the market for apartment housing gets better.

Taxation Policies

A growing number of states are experiencing serious deficit problems. Increased taxpayer demand on public services, combined with growing expectations for an ever higher standard of living, has seriously challenged state governments. At least 28 states faced shortfalls in their 1991 budgets attributable to the sluggish economy and growing demands for spending. At the same time, state governments are obliged to make infrastructure improvements, to highways, roadways, water systems, and utilities, to keep commerce competitive and prosperous.

In states that have a constant influx of people, particularly in the West, calls for new taxes can discourage new business activity. Moreover, if companies already in business decide they can no longer afford to operate in the state because of tax increases, they may relocate to other states, thereby weakening the economy and hurting the housing market. This partly explains why the legislatures in many states with budget deficits recently decided to raise or create taxes on consumer items rather than taxing industry.

THE METROPOLITAN AREA

A large center of population including one or more central cities and their adjacent satellite communities.

Population Trends

In the years following World War II, Americans participated in the greatest migration of people from one area to another in the history of the world up to that time. Millions of people relocated from the East Coast, Northeast, and Midwest to the southern and western states, most notably California, which is now the most populous state in the union. The desirable climate and great opportunities afforded by post-war commercial and industrial activity stimulated this mass influx.

People are always looking for a better life, both within and outside of the confines of their own country, and will relocate to areas where this is possible. Witness the recent migration of people from Mexico and Central America to the United States, as well as the exodus of Eastern Europeans to Western Europe.

Ever since the Bureau of the Census started tracking demographic shifts, it has been statistically proved that home building closely follows population trends. If population levels increase, residential-building and land values generally increase proportionately. Table 5.1 lists recent Census statistics showing areas with the largest population shifts.

The quickest way to solve a housing shortage in a crowded or growing area is by erecting new housing. Subsidized housing is another answer, but governments these days are hard pressed to find sufficient resources to fund that type of activity. When new housing is built, people in higher income brackets tend to move up, creating a supply of available, lower-priced, existing housing. A marked population increase in a metropolitan area therefore creates demand for both new and existing housing.

ECONOMIC ACTIVITY

Active versus Dormant Industries

Whether influenced by recession, global competition, or overproduction, industrial activity often goes in cycles. Heavy industries such as automaking,

TABLE 5.1
Metropoliltan Statistical Areas with Largest Net Migration, 1980 to 1988

Metropolitan Area[a]	Population 1980	1988	Net Migration
Los Angeles/ Anaheim/River- side, CA	11,498,000	13,770,000	2,272,000
Dallas-Fort Worth, TX	2,931,000	3,766,000	835,000
Atlanta, GA	2,138,000	2,737,000	599,000
Tampa/St. Peters- burg/Clearwater, FL	1,614,000	1,995,000	381,000
Phoenix, AZ	1,509,000	2,030,000	521,000
San Diego, CA	1,862,000	2,370,000	508,000
San Francisco/ Oakland/San Jose, CA	5,368,000	6,042,000	674,000
Miami/Fort Lauderdale, FL	2,644,000	3,001,000	357,000
West Palm Beach/Boca Raton/Delray Beach, FL	577,000	818,000	241,000
Washington DC/ Maryland/Virginia	3,251,000	3,734,000	483,000
Orlando, FL	700,000	971,000	271,000
Sacramento, CA	1,100,000	1,385,000	285,000
Seattle/ Tacoma, WA	2,093,000	2,421,000	328,000
Houston, TX	2,736,00	3,247,000	511,000
Austin, TX	537,000	748,000	211,000
San Antonio, TX	1,072,000	1,323,000	251,000
Las Vegas, NV	463,000	631,000	168,000
Jacksonville, FL	722,000	898,000	176,000
Norfolk/Virginia Beach/Newport News, VA	1,160,000	1,380,000	220,000
Monmouth/Ocean, NJ	849,000	969,000	120,000

[a]Metropolitan areas generally encompass the region economically attached to a large, central city.
Source: U.S. Bureau of the Census.

metals processing, building, and construction are prime examples. Whenever there is a glut of oil on the market, oil prices drop and petroleum production activity wanes. Right now there isn't much demand for copper, and most of the copper mills in Arizona are shut down. Steel is slow because Japan is manufacturing steel cheaper than we can do it. Heavy equipment manufacturers such as Caterpillar Tractor and John Deere, maker of harvest equipment, even motorcycle giant Harley Davidson, were in a lull for a long period of time largely because of competition from overseas. Ford, Chrysler, and General Motors have experienced recent profit losses caused by both foreign competition and decreased consumer spending.

If you are interested in buying in an area with dormant industries, make sure that there is some anticipated spark that will eventually stimulate the local economy. New technology may make many of these dormant industries all but obsolete. The large regional steel plants in Pittsburgh, for example, may never be able to compete with steel manufacturers that are more internationally oriented. The same is true of shipbuilding. On the other hand, industries that are globally competitive, for instance, high-technology, media, and entertainment, may have bright futures. It is important to do considerable research before making an investment decision.

Labor Market

A prolonged strike can have a detrimental effect on the local economy. The old *Los Angeles Herald Examiner* once had the largest circulation of any afternoon newspaper in the country. Then, in 1967, the paper's unions decided to go on strike, resulting in a prolonged labor action that lasted for 10 years. Advertisers fled, circulation plummeted, employees left or lost their jobs, and the local economy suffered. The strikers made their point, and they sounded the now-defunct paper's death knell. The recent strike at Eastern Airlines is another example of a prolonged labor action that can put a company out of business and result in the loss of jobs.

Job actions can have a dramatic effect on the area economy. When people are out of work, they can't afford new housing and the real estate market slows. It's important to invest in an area of diversified industry. Greater Los Angeles is ideal in this respect because of its size and diversity. In addition, the region has the resources, land, entrepreneurs, and utilities to do a lot of things. There are essentially nine basic industries in the area offering goods or services that people from outside the area want to buy. This, combined with the abundance of small- to medium-sized businesses, makes the local economy able to withstand periodic downturns.

Southern California is unique in the sense that there's such a diversification of industries. The important thing when deciding on a location is to select a community that has a good, solid economic base that will grow with the needs of the country over the next 20 years and more. Such a base could consist of the service and information industries, which are presently competitive and are likely to remain competitive over the long pull. Next to growth industries, look for stable industries, such as wholesale trade and distribution, transportation, agriculture, and health care, that aren't subject to wild fluctuations and that will provide a source of reliable employment.

Given the shift in the national economy from an industrial/ manufacturing to a high-tech/ service orientation, it's becoming increasingly important to look for areas with companies that employ thinkers. A thinker makes more than a guy who works in a steel mill. A service, consulting, high-tech, or think-tank-type of business is a clean business. It doesn't create smog, pollution, or much waste. But it does generate new ideas and solutions. Those kinds of businesses are ideal, in my opinion. They produce high-paying jobs, help to keep property values up, and enable homeowners to obtain loans, get better credit, and make their payments. And as the wages of the employees go up, you'll find that real estate values will go up in harmony, only more rapidly.

Southern California is probably one of the best places in the world to invest in because, for all its growth and activity, this area really hasn't taken off yet. There are so many advantages, and there are so many things that are planned and proposed that the future growth is going to be monumental.

Not too long ago I did an appraisal of an automobile junkyard in the Los Angeles Harbor area. The railroad was putting a turning radius in the location of the junkyard. From that analysis, I figured that the dynamic growth in the Long Beach/ Los Angeles Harbor area is going to be astounding. With increased activity in the Asian markets coming to the United States and the trade activity that has been improving around the harbor—the Los Angeles Customs District recently surpassed New York as the nation's busiest commercial gateway—not to mention the Greater Los Angeles area's inevitable expansion, it isn't a question of *whether* growth is going to happen, it's a question of *when*.

It might take 20 or 30 years, but indeed the factors are in place. Knowing that in itself is worth money. What do you think it will do to the properties in the surrounding areas? Long Beach and Los Angeles are the only major port cities in the world that aren't flanked by high-rise office buildings. Except for the recently constructed World Trade Center, there aren't any. It's just a matter of time before there are.

Some cities are dependent on one or two companies and industries. Take Seattle, whose biggest employers are Boeing and Microsoft. If Boeing's doing good, then Seattle's doing good. If the company has lucrative contracts (and it does, through the next century), then money's running out the front door. However, if Boeing loses its prized contracts, people will be standing in the street. That's a one-industry town if you ask me. Many towns are dependent on jobs provided by the city, county, or federal government. That's not the best situation to invest in either.

To find out about an area's economic activity and growth potential, basic industries, and the outlook for them, contact city planning departments, area chambers of commerce, state departments of finance or revenue, economics departments of major financial institutions, and area real estate boards and be sure to read newspapers, business publications, and real estate journals.

Recreational Facilities

When a coliseum or large sports arena is built, that changes the character of the area. Sometimes it serves as a physical barrier that limits or changes development, such as Hollywood Park in Inglewood, California or Wrigley Field in Chicago, Illinois. When they finally installed lights at Wrigley Field a few years ago, that further changed the character of the neighborhood. Not surprisingly, the people in the surrounding area fought tooth and nail against it because they didn't want the noise, traffic, congestion, and everything else that comes with night baseball games. Ideally, you learn about these developments before they happen, when they are still in the discussion phases, so you can plan your investment strategy accordingly. There's always a way to find out about up-and-coming projects and developments.

CONSTRUCTION COSTS

If shortages of materials or strikes cause construction costs to go way up, then existing housing and buildings are going to go up in value, provided there's a demand. A labor shortage usually means that it will cost more to build. If it does, then prices go up. In 1970, when the Airport Authority built the north runway at Los Angeles International Airport, there was a strike by concrete workers. Because of the shortage of concrete and demand from builders, the price of concrete went out of sight.

The time of year also affects labor efficiency. When I need a painting job done on my beachfront property in the summer, it takes twice as long than in the winter because there are more visual distractions and activities like volleyball tournaments going on. So it costs more to have work done in the summer. Conversely, in cities like Minneapolis or Buffalo, repair costs are much higher in the winter due to the harsh working conditions.

MAJOR IMPROVEMENT PROGRAMS

Redevelopment Projects

Many cities have redevelopment agencies. Oftentimes, members of the city council sit on the agency or have direct influence regarding the actions of the agency. Redevelopment agencies are entities established to improve the quality of life for the residents of a community or to improve the business or industrial climate of an area. Well-planned redevelopment projects can enhance the growth pattern. If the nature of the community is enhanced by a redevelopment project, then the project is justified. If not, the project shouldn't go forward.

Redevelopment plans that improve "blighted" or run-down areas generally raise a neighborhood's growth potential. In Baltimore, the city's historic waterfront area was recently improved through an impressive redevelopment project that gave the dilapidated docks a new lease on life. In Santa Monica, an area known as Pacific Ocean Park in front of the boardwalk was once the subject of a city redevelopment project that cleared about 10 blocks of run-down housing to make room for two high-rise apartment buildings that now sell for over $500,000 per unit.

The Bunker Hill redevelopment project in downtown Los Angeles, started in the early 1940s, made room for the many high-rise buildings that today constitute the city skyline. The development of the Bunker Hill project has had a positive effect on growth in the central business district because it put a once blighted area to a higher and better use.

My brother and I did a reuse appraisal determining the highest and best use of each designated land parcel surrounding the University of Southern California for a development known as the Hoover Street project. The study area was enormous, encompassing approximately 10 city blocks. At the time, there was a lot of privately owned land on the south side of Jefferson Boulevard that the university wanted for expansion of the campus.

In order to implement the project, the City of Los Angeles Redevelopment Agency had to condemn all the land and improvements in the vicinity of the university so the campus could be expanded and a buffer zone created for student housing and a community shopping center. The city had the legal authority to do this on the grounds of eminent domain, the right of a government or public utility to acquire private property for public use through the condemnation process, provided that just compensation is awarded for the taking of the property. In other words, the redevelopment agency is required to pay fair market value for property it acquires. Once acquired, the redevelopment parcels may then be sold to private developers who are entitled to low interest loans as incentive to develop the site.

A bout 1972 I did an appraisal of a redevelopment project in National City, California, a community located on the outskirts of San Diego. In the mid-1960s, San Diego was wholeheartedly dependent on the aircraft industry. When Convair, a defense contractor and maker of military aircraft, went out of business, the area had serious unemployment problems. So the city fathers went out into the suburbs and bought large tracts of vacant land for commercial and industrial use. They then sold it to businesses and based the price on potential employment.

If you were going to purchase the land and build a warehouse where you only had two people working, the cost of the land was extremely high. But if you were going to employ 100 people, you could get it for almost nothing. They practically gave them the land because they wanted employment. In this way, San Diego was able to attract new industry into the community and diversify its economic base. That's happening now with the flight of aerospace to such states as Arizona, Arkansas, and Georgia.

S ometimes growth can be measured in the time it takes to travel to certain places rather than the distance covered. My uncle was 91 years old when he passed away. First he walked to work, then he rode a horse, then he rode a bicycle, then he drove a car, and then he took the Red Car train. All the while, it took him about 30 minutes to get to work. Most people live about 30 to 40 minutes from where they work. If a freeway is built enabling people to live farther from work, it's going to change the whole transportation pattern. If you put a high-speed rail in, it would increase land values in outlying areas.

With an existing freeway, you know where the growth is. A proposed freeway is speculative because you don't know when or where they're going to build it. Most cities don't like the idea of having a freeway run through their town. Major improvement programs such as boat harbors and gateways, downtown office buildings, a world-class subway system, and redevelopment projects generally increase area property values but may have a short-term negative impact on the immediate community in which they are built.

When the city of Redondo Beach started building the breakwater in 1963, they condemned a large area adjacent to the harbor to start a redevelopment project. The surrounding property in the immediate vicinity was for sale for practically nothing, presumably because it was an undesirable area to buy.

Yet if you went down to the city Planning Department, you could see that the city was committed to going ahead with this project, that they had the rocks in the water and were starting to tear buildings down and condemn the land. That was the perfect time to go in and buy residential property because of the obvious potential that existed.

Once the commitment is made and the city starts building, you can project into the future and envision how the area will look after the 10 or 15 years that it's going to take to fully develop the project. Oftentimes, you can see that a certain development is going to be fabulous when they get through with it, and you're going to be sitting on top of a gold mine.

If there was a private development that had an impact great enough to change the character of the community, then I would have as much faith in it as a government project. Not many major projects are started that aren't completed.

———

After analyzing the Redondo Beach breakwater project, I decided to buy an empty lot for $12,000 with $500 down. It wasn't exactly a pretty sight. It was close to the harbor development and there was a lot of dirt and rubble and trucks going by. If you took most people to look at the lot, they would ask what's wrong with you. But I knew that the property would double in value after the marina was built. I wasn't looking at the mess sitting in front of me, I was looking at the long-range potential created by a harbor that would be there 30 years from now. Sure enough, today that property's worth over half a million dollars.

———

Although residential real estate is a good investment around a redevelopment project, commercial property in these instances may be a little speculative. In Pasadena, there was a massive redevelopment project called the Pepper Street Project, which encompassed about 10 city blocks. The city took an interminable amount of time—probably four or five years—setting up the project, obtaining all the necessary approvals, appropriating the money, appraising and condemning the properties, making the architectural drawings, and realigning the streets.

During this time, the properties adjacent to the project really suffered. The supermarkets adjacent to the development went broke, and all the dry cleaners and nearby small businesses lost their leases because of it. If you owned residential property, you may have taken a short-term loss. However, when the project was finally finished your losses would have seemed insignificant compared to the rents the market would bear.

———

For all of the big projects that are proposed, very few are ever completed. Yet once a project gets started, the odds are in your favor that it will be finished. So it was pretty obvious with the growth factor that was occurring around Hermosa Beach, even though the crumbs weren't spilling over from economic activity in surrounding communities, that we had a terrific advantage. When you see a substantial positive development of a community and there's no way that the community can turn back, then that is the time to buy. Visualize what a major development project will do for a community once the deal is committed, and take advantage of it today.

The investor must be concerned when purchasing property for a long period that there is no threat of imminent condemnation to the property and to the immediate vicinity of the property. I once represented the Airport Commission as an appraiser when the Los Angeles International Airport needed to condemn entire tracts of residential properties to build a new runway north of the existing airport grounds. In all, about 350 houses north of the airport were condemned for demolition. When the Federal Aviation Administration granted the local airport authority permission to expand the runway, it stipulated that no houses could be within 750 feet of the runway.

———

In 1968, some friends of mine wished to purchase a single family residence in Westchester, a suburb near Los Angeles International Airport. They were really enthused about the house, which had a beautiful backyard and was ideally located near a high school. But it was only a matter of time before the airport authority was going to expand and acquire homes in the area where my friends wanted to live.

I told them that 10 years from now they would not be living in the house they selected to buy. They refused to believe me until I obtained a map from the Airport Commission of the proposed acquisition showing where the new runway was planned. After locating their house on the map, I discovered that it was the second house from where the condemnation project stopped to acquire the land for the runway expansion.

We then pinpointed a location on the map that was about the same distance from a presently existing airport runway as their residence would be when the new runway was in full operation with airplanes taking off every few minutes. We then drove to the designated spot on the map and spent about an hour sitting in the car listening to the noise pattern.

I am sure you know the rest of the story. The noise was frighteningly loud. So they bought a beautiful residence in a suburban area about 12 miles south of the airport. Today, their house is worth well over 10 times what they originally paid for it. The place they once had their sights on still sits adjacent to the airport runway and isn't worth all that much more than they would have paid for it.

Although the acquisition of sites for building projects may enhance a community and make it more desirable, it is important to not get caught in the condemnation trap by failing to foresee any adverse factors that might affect your purchase. There have been other instances when condemnation has benefited investors.

A close friend and fellow instructor at UCLA Extension once owned a large parcel of vacant land in the San Gabriel Valley. Located on a main thoroughfare, this particular parcel was ideal for an automobile dealership. A few years after he purchased the land, the adjacent city annexed the community where his property was. After the annexation, the city decided it needed a new school site.

To everyone's amazement, the city decided my friend's property on a busy highway would be suitable for a grade school and, after initiating condemnation proceedings, offered $2 million for it. The price was conservative, so my friend said to the city negotiator, "I don't think this property is good for a school. If you want to buy it, I won't fight over the price. But I want to put a clause in the sale document to be recorded that the property is to be used for a public school only. And if the city does not use it for that specific purpose, I reserve the right to buy the property back for $2 million."

The city purchased this property but, for a variety of reasons, never built a school on the site. Fifteen years later, the city gave up and sold the property back to my friend for $2 million. On account of appreciation, he got a $20 million piece of real estate for a tenth of the price. And he didn't have to pay any real property taxes for the 15-year period while the property was appreciating in value because it was owned by the city. Condemnation was beneficial in this instance. And my friend's measured approach paid off handsomely.

────────

There is no substitute for knowing what you are doing. Think the problem through and consider the long-term effects.

Infrastructure Obsolescence

It is equally important to check with local and regional planning commissions, city councils, boards of supervisors, and the like, to find out what building restrictions may apply to a given area. Environmental considerations, like overloaded sewer and water systems or inadequate parking, could lead to building moratoriums and downzoning efforts in overcrowded areas, causing the value of land to skyrocket. From an investor's standpoint, these form an ideal set of conditions in which to become a property owner.

On the other hand, if you want to buy a "teardown" property for a low price and either remodel it or build a new structure, severe building restrictions can hinder the project's approval or result in exorbitant fees for building permits. You can never be too informed about the area you're buying into. With real estate there are so many intricate things that affect value. You have to take into consideration all of them to understand why something is happening.

THE COMMUNITY

That part of the metropolitan area composed of a number of neighborhoods that have a tendency toward common interests and problems.

Geographical Pattern

Natural terrain separates and defines community boundaries. Natural barriers, such as hills, valleys, rivers, forests, lakes, and ravines, tend to distinguish communities, providing a distinctive feel and enriching them with natural beauty. They create a unique condition beyond other geographic boundaries. Proximity to an ocean, lake, or river can increase value if it is desirable. Conversely, a swamp or cesspool will detract. With a river, you always want to live on the most desirable side, which is generally away from industrial plants, obnoxious odors, and other pollutants. The top of the hill is usually worth more money because it typically affords a sweeping view. When you buy property, be sure to get a sweeping view, not a view of the sweepings!

I f you lived on an unstable cliff in Malibu, your house could slide into the ocean after a big storm. Or a rock slide could shut down the highway. A big boulder once fell on Pacific Coast Highway, forcing people to drive 35 miles out of their way into the San Fernando Valley just to get to Santa Monica. The roads were so bad you couldn't drive on them for a week. That to me is geographically undesirable. I wouldn't buy in an area like Malibu. A friend of mine bought a house that sat out over the ocean. But he and his wife were raising three children. Now tell me where the kids are going to play when the tides come in—certainly not on the highway.

Natural barriers are often employed to partition industrial properties (business parks, factories, and the like) from residential real estate, although artificial barriers such as highways also serve this purpose. Barriers between different types of real estate are positive in that they limit the encroachment of one type of development on another. Typically, if a residential development encroaches on an industrial property, the industrial property gives way.

Unlike other natural barriers, undeveloped land areas are changeable. When undeveloped land is developed, it changes the whole complexity of the community. It probably will enhance the adjacent neighborhoods. Try to figure out what type of improvements will be made and how those improvements will impact the surrounding area. Find out who owns the property. The developer would never be able to do anything without approval from the city or county planning department. If plans or drawings have been filed, carefully examine them, then talk to the developer to learn more about the project.

I n the Marina del Rey area of Southern California, there is a massive, 887-acre planned development called the Playa Vista Project that is being built on what commercial realtors refer to as the premiere piece of undeveloped urban real estate in the country. The upscale project contains plans for 40 acres of new boating marinas, 5 million square feet of office space, 720,000 square feet of retail space, 11,750 planned residential units, and 2,400 planned hotel rooms. The effect it should have on adjacent property values will be stupendous. If you think property values around the marina are expensive now, wait until that thing goes in!

━━━━━━

Some developments may be detrimental. For instance, a furniture maker or auto body shop might create noxious odors. Positive developments would depend on the type of property you're looking at. If you're thinking of acquiring an apartment house and someone wanted to build a recreational facility or health spa across the street, that might add to the desirability of your property. A tasteful shopping center could have a similar effect.

In Chapter 6, we will consider the impact that artificial barriers can have on a community and the constituent neighborhoods.

Satellite Communities

In Los Angeles County, there are 88 separate cities including the City of Los Angeles. Regional shopping centers—major shopping centers that service a satellite community—and industrial complexes have a tremendous effect on values in suburban areas. If an industry or business is not smoke producing, toxic, or noise polluting but is instead clean and enhances the community, such as a semiconductor plant, it can be an asset to the community.

In my opinion, the best type of industries are the high-tech industries because they are relatively clean and have fairly high payrolls. Aerospace, computers, biotechnology firms, virtually all of the high-tech industries are fantastic as far as land values are concerned because they are usually kind to the environment and contribute to a higher average family income level. Think of the possibilities if a company such as TRW in Redondo Beach, which employs engineers, who are planning the future and designing communications satellites, more efficient credit systems, space transportation systems and the like, were to double its staff. Wow! It is self-evident what would happen to real estate values in a community should this occur.

━━━━━━

What do 100 new factory workers bring to a town? According to the U.S. Chamber of Commerce, 359 more people, 91 more school children, 100 more households, 229,000 more bank deposits, three more retail establishments, and 331,000 more retail sales per year. For every 100 aerospace workers, an estimated 67 jobs in ancillary industries are created. That's substantial. Now look at it in the other direction. What happens when a factory closes and 100 people lose their jobs? All this is taken away. Or most of it. So what you must do if you are going to invest in real estate is consider these kind of situations and assess the growth potential of the community.

CIVIC GOVERNMENT POLICIES

Assessments

If city or county governments impose taxes and assessments on your property, it doesn't help any. Hermosa Beach, the city where I live, is a bedroom community so the city has to provide services such as police, fire, health, schools, and utilities. If you have industry or a lot of good commercial activity, it can be very beneficial to the community. But cities that are dependent on residents for a tax base are bound to have problems because they can't provide enough services that people want and expect in proportion to what they pay. The tax rate in the nearby community of El Segundo is about half what it is in Hermosa Beach because El Segundo has so much industry.

Rent Control

Rent control has a tremendous effect on property values. Rent control limits the amount of rent that property owners can charge for the use of their rental units. It isn't based on economics or market conditions, but, rather, on legislative activity. When a community is totally developed and saturated, people claim that they can't afford the rent, and legislators sometimes respond by enacting a rent control ordinance. However, anytime legislative activity is separated from economic conditions, there is a tremendous spread and the property owner usually winds up taking it on the chin. Landlords need to raise the rents in order to keep pace with the spiraling costs of properly maintaining the building.

Affordable housing is a victim of controls. If you put rent controls on property, you're not going to have affordable housing because you won't have free enterprise. Depending on how hermetic the controls are, some people may have cheap rent, while others are excluded. When cities impose zoning restrictions or height and density limits, they make affordable housing more expensive because developers can't build housing of adequate quality or quantity.

A friend of mine has a six-unit apartment building in Santa Monica. It's a really nice place in one of the premiere locations in all of Southern California. But rent control allows him to get only around $300 a month for a one bedroom apartment. If it weren't for rent control, he'd probably get about $800 a month for the same unit. I remember once, when he had a vacancy, he put an ad in the paper, and it was an absolute circus. He literally had hundreds and hundreds of people lined up waiting to apply. How can you make a selection? In my opinion, it would be better for the city to build housing for the elderly rather than interfere with private enterprise.

Rents can only go as high as people can afford to pay. That's why rent control doesn't work and is artificial. When governments crimp or disrupt the free economy, it can have a tremendous impact on the natural flow of goods and services and can also impede growth.

For instance, the establishment of the California Coastal Commission in the 1970s, which has planning jurisdiction over any property within 2,000 feet of the coastline, has resulted in such severe building restrictions that many people have gone bankrupt. If the ocean damaged your house, the Coastal Commission wouldn't let you place rocks in front to protect it. They maintain it would impede the beach, even though the ocean was destroying your house. And if the tide did destroy your house, they might not let you build it back the way it was.

A great example of this happened in Malibu. After a certain point, you couldn't build any more apartments along the coastline. If an apartment already existed, it didn't have any competition, so the real estate values soared. It was a boon for the existing apartment owners, but it left everybody else high and dry. Some people had purchased lots figuring they would eventually build a couple of units, but they weren't allowed to do it.

The point of all this is to think about real estate in terms of the overall picture and for the long term. Economic, legislative, environmental, and manmade forces can have a tremendous impact on the value of real estate and should be carefully considered before an investment decision is made. In the next chapters, we assess the ways in which these factors can affect the immediate neighborhood of the subject property.

6

Assess How National Trends Will Affect Your Immediate Neighborhood

THE NEIGHBORHOOD

A neighborhood is a residential area with distinguishing characteristics comprised of people with similar interests. A neighborhood can consist of a city block, a street, or a handful of houses, so long as it is an area where there is a homogeneous group of people.

PHYSICAL CHARACTERISTICS

Overall Trend of the Area

Having narrowed down the likely location of your real estate investment to a specific community, it is important to determine the growth potential of the immediate neighborhood. The surrounding neighborhood has just as much influence on the value of a property as the property itself.

As with the outlying area, it is important to assess the neighborhood trend. There are really only three things that happen to real estate at the neighborhood level: Values remain stable, they increase, or they decrease. When a neighborhood reaches its peak growth stage, the cycle is upward. After that, values plateau. At the end of the plateau period, they begin to drop off. Every neighborhood goes through this cycle.

The best time to invest in a neighborhood is at the very lowest ebb of the cycle, when it has deteriorated but when you can see future growth potential because of the surrounding communities and activities.

If a neighborhood has already started to deteriorate, yet we can see that it has more or less bottomed out and is now at a point where growth is likely to occur and there are other factors that will enhance the value over the 20-year period, then that's actually a good time to buy. We're not interested in what will happen today; we're interested in what will happen 20 years later.

To understand the cycle of ownership, you have to look at the history of the area. Sometimes property becomes more valuable as multiple residential real estate is developed and land values go out of sight. Sometimes not. The only thing you can be assured of is change. And every time we have change it either creates or destroys value. Neighborhoods make up a community, so if the larger trend in the community is toward development, then you can reasonably expect development to continue.

When I decided to invest in Hermosa Beach, the two larger adjacent communities had tremendous growth potential. Redondo Beach, the next city over, was building King Harbor boating marina, while Manhattan Beach was removing hazardous railroad tracks. Hermosa Beach sits in the middle of this, so I concluded that even if Hermosa wanted to go back to a sleepy little town, it couldn't do it because the pressure from all sides wouldn't permit it. The adjacent areas simply wouldn't let it deteriorate any further. When I bought in 1960 I determined that the city's condition had hit rock bottom and couldn't get any worse because of this activity.

There are a lot of areas around the country where you can see this type of thing happening. But you have to do your homework, and you have to understand a little about the local economic conditions. Know what to look for. There are reams of information and material available if you want to find them, so you must be careful not to place too much weight on irrelevant details. There are only a few indicators that are truly important in your analysis. Don't get lost in the trivia; you might miss the forest among the trees.

Before anything can happen, you have to have the guts to do it. The easiest thing to say is that I won't take a chance because it will hurt me or I'm sticking my neck out too far. We all see great opportunities, but we're afraid to take a risk. That's the biggest problem many would-be investors face, their own reluctance.

William Zeckendorf was one of the greatest entrepreneurs of the century. After World War II, the United States government commissioned Zeckendorf to locate and arrange to acquire the property for the United Nations building in New York. So he went along the East River and found a site, which was a hog ranch, and advised the U.N. to build their new building on this site.

While he was negotiating a price, he bought a number of properties surrounding the subject site himself. Land that he paid $3 or $4 a square foot for before the U.N. building was built ballooned to $300 per square foot after it was constructed. And so Zeckendorf made a fortune on the deal.

═══════════════

Granted, he knew something that nobody else did. But it was possible to extrapolate the facts and come to the same realization just by reading the paper. Anybody could have found out, but not anybody was willing to follow up on it. A similar development recently transpired in Long Beach, California, with the building of the World Trade Center. Local economists were projecting that it would become the hub of downtown business activity as well as the focus of international trading activity for the ports of Long Beach and Los Angeles. But the point isn't to just be aware, it's to do something about it. In some locales, land is becoming scarce. There just isn't any more available for development. But some people have a hard time seeing an opportunity when it presents itself.

═══════════════

About six months before, I heard they were going to build a new World Trade Center building in Long Beach. So I drove down there and found a 34-unit apartment building that was up for sale within two blocks of the soon-to-be-built Trade Center. The developer had boxed off the construction site and had just dug the hole to lay the foundation. The apartment building was in terrible condition, a real dog. The people who owned it were letting it fall apart and didn't believe the area would ever turn around, even with the World Trade Center right at their front door.

I told my wife that we ought to make an offer on that apartment building and try to buy it because I knew we could make a few million off it. But she said, "Oh, no, no! I don't want to go near the place. I don't like the people. I'm afraid." I can guarantee you, whoever bought that thing would have been able to rehabilitate it, double or triple the rents, and change the tenancy dramatically.

It would be pretty hard to lose on a deal like that if you could get it at a realistic price. As soon as the World Trade Center building came out of the ground, people started scrambling. Once a new building like that is standing, the potential is obvious. What we want to do is get there before the potential is plain for all to see.

═══════════════

QUALITY, CONVENIENCE, AND
AVAILABILITY OF FACILITIES

A key indicator of the overall trend of a neighborhood is the quality, convenience, and availability of facilities that improve a community. If public schools, public transportation, shopping centers, cultural, recreational, and religious institutions are not top quality or don't work properly, then they're not going to do the neighborhood and, by extension, land values, any good. The reputation of a school district can have a direct impact on the desirability of a particular neighborhood. An effective local transportation system can have a positive effect on real estate values, so can a substantial performing arts center or civic amphitheater. The availability of utilities also has a direct bearing on a neighborhood's growth potential. Some rural areas don't have sewer systems. They still have septic tanks. Not all areas have natural gas. The availability of cable television might even be a consideration.

LAND AND IMPROVEMENT
CHARACTERISTICS

Street Patterns

When considering a neighborhood to invest in, look for a homogeneous street pattern. Irregular subdivisions that conflict with each other don't have through streets and because of that have frequent traffic jams and congestion. London, England, where streets run into funny alleyways and where you'll end up at someone's backyard or on a main highway, is as great an example as you'll ever see. That city had a number of topsy-turvy growth patterns. Subdivisions were laid down without regard to each other. The streets go one way, and you have to make a jog to get to another. Streets that are not predictable create all kinds of problems because the traffic flow is not normal.

Boston, Philadelphia, and Baltimore are also like that. They are all old cities that have had unique and unusual growth. The patterns are such that access is prevented from certain directions. How you get in and out of a neighborhood obviously is a matter of convenience. On the other hand, if you have poor street patterns, it might be an advantage to a family with children precisely *because* it prevents access and therefore reduces street traffic. It's always nice if a family can live on a cul-de-sac because there is no through traffic, and people are more careful when they drive.

A few years ago, my wife and I joined the Orange County Performing Arts Center in Costa Mesa, California. Because the center is too far for us to drive for an evening, we started looking around there to buy a condominium so we could attend the opera and ballet and have a place to stay overnight. So I went down there and looked around. Then I attended a local National Association of Real Estate Boards Certified Commercial Investment Members meeting where the marketing director for the South Coast Metro Association told us about the development that was planned for the community over time.

She had a bunch of statistics, so I sat there and listened. She talked about how they were going to build more high-rise office buildings and expand John Wayne Airport in nearby Irvine. After she was through, I asked what they were going to do about the traffic problem caused by all this planned development. She said, "We're thinking about widening the streets, or not allowing people to park on the streets, or changing the stop signs and signals." I told my wife that they were going to create one of the worst traffic jams in history. The apartments close to this huge, new employment/commercial center were going to be worth their weight in gold because the people living there would not have to commute to work. That was when I decided to buy my first condominium in Orange County. Now I own 30!

Similar Land Uses

A well-planned community generally has land uses that are segregated. For instance, a residential neighborhood might have main thoroughfares surrounding it so that it is completely separated and insulated from industrial property. What you want to do is find a homogeneous neighborhood where the land uses are more or less the same, where the homeowners are in the same basic income bracket, and where there is a similar family mix so that the attitudes are harmonious. This scenario lends itself to growth far more readily than areas with an incongruous mix of people and property.

As far as lot shape, you want a shape that's usable. A long, narrow, or irregularly shaped lot might present problems and prevent optimum use. A lot for commercial use that is only 25 feet wide is really difficult to use because it is important to have adequate frontage. In many cases a buyer won't even know what the actual dimensions are until a surveyor is hired to physically determine them. As mentioned in the previous chapter, I've been in many situations where people thought they were buying something they didn't get. Concerning lot orientation, it's generally considered desirable to have a house facing east with the bedrooms toward the west because it allows sunlight to filter into the bedroom in the afternoon while allowing you to sit in the coolness of the living room, where you are more likely to be that time of the day.

Percentage of Area Developed

A neighborhood usually reaches its peak value and will begin to plateau when about 85 percent of the area is developed. That's when the initial enthusiasm will start to subside and when the original families in the neighborhood will want to look for something better. When that happens, the secondary owners move in. The second wave of owners generally will keep land values at a constant level for a period of time.

After that, property values will either go up or down, depending on what happens to the community. If the neighborhood deteriorates from undesirable activity, they will go down. If people start acting in a negative manner—parking on lawns, installing cheap awnings that detract from appearances, letting yards go unattended, putting up with potholes, changing their cars' oil in gutters, tolerating excessive loitering—the neighborhood will cease to be a desirable place to live. Conversely, if everyone in the area has an attitude toward bettering the neighborhood, then the neighborhood will improve. Just as negative attitudes and actions will make property values go down, positive actions will make them go up.

A neighborhood that is about 85 percent developed may still continue to rise in value, but you know that the potential is there for it to start to level off. If the neighborhood is fully developed, then some of those people are going to think of moving somewhere else. Americans are always looking for the next best thing; they're always trying to design a better mousetrap or achieve a better life-style. In my opinion, the only way to solve the problem of affordable housing is to continue to build new houses, because the people who live in the upper level generally want to live in new housing. It's a chain reaction.

In performing a neighborhood analysis, you don't measure the real estate as such. Instead, it is more important to measure the actions, attitudes, and thinking of people. It may not be as easy to do, but if you think of psychology as part of the business of real estate, then you will be light years ahead of other investors.

For example, I own five apartment buildings with a total of 26 rental units on the oceanfront. When I have the opportunity, I ask people why they choose to move here because it gives me a better idea how I can advertise and attract the right type of tenant for the area. I want to know why they want to be here, why people buy houses 150 feet from the beach, why they will pay almost as much for a house on a walkstreet up from the beach as they will for a house right on the oceanfront. If you can commingle the attitudes of the people who live in a neighborhood, you'll have a much greater understanding of the forces that determine value.

Harmony of Development

Monotonous tract development, where there are hundreds or thousands of homes built all at once in uniform fashion, turns me off. It's like tenement housing. Every building is practically the same. I think it destroys the beauty of the landscape. I like to stay away from it unless you can get a real bargain, because mass-produced housing projects usually appreciate at a slower rate than custom homes. There's no feeling of uniqueness, and that limits your options. This also applies to condominium projects that take on the appearance of row houses. Developers are just creating future slums by building structures like that. A unique design is going to be worth more over time, not a prefabricated, mass-produced one.

I've always felt that buying a unique property in an established area was much better than buying something that made you feel as if you were part of a mule train. A neighborhood where the properties are roughly the same size, quality, and price but are different in design has a much more desirable aspect than a monotonous tract development, because it gives property owners a feeling of individual expression. When the neighborhood is established and has a certain reputation, people of the same income and socioeconomic status will generally go there.

The right location is the key to the whole thing. But you need the foresight to see the added potential. When you have a piece of real estate that is well located, it's probably better to own that property than build a new one if you're not sure what you're doing. The reason is that you have a past performance of what has happened to an existing building to study. With a new building, that type of information doesn't exist. You only have similar, newer buildings to refer to.

Generally speaking, if you have a tract of homes in a desirable area, such as Las Vegas, Nevada, or Riverside California, the value of those homes will reach their peak when the last property is sold. At this point, people who bought in first begin to want something more desirable and start looking for something else. If the neighborhood doesn't have true amenities to hold values—good schools, parks, recreational facilities, shopping centers, churches—it will generally deteriorate. The only thing that makes property in a monotonous housing tract valuable after that is a superb location. Otherwise, values become static and in some cases will fall.

MANMADE ATTRIBUTES

A s a consultant for a buyer, I once looked at a house that was located directly adjacent to a storm drain. I told my client that if he bought that house, the noise from the water in the winter time, combined with the animals that are attracted to that type of thing, could be a disaster. So my client didn't buy it, even though he had apparently already agreed to. The seller got furious when I told him and threatened to report me to the Department of Real Estate. Apparently, he didn't know about disclosure laws.

With a yacht harbor or marina, where there's leisure activity that attracts money, land values tend to soar. Take the Venice Canals in Los Angeles. When they were first built, they were fantastic—unique, original, a re-creation of Venice, Italy, complete with gondolas and a Bridge of Sighs. If they would have been kept up, the area would have a completely different character than it does today. My parents used to own a few houses in Venice, one right along a canal. Unfortunately, the canals became a filthy, terrible slum zone. That's when the city of Los Angeles annexed the property and incorporated it. Now there's a movement afoot to rehabilitate the canals, but for decades they have been a manmade eyesore detracting from real estate values.

Sometimes a school or university will act as a line of demarcation. Around UCLA, there are at least five different neighborhoods: Westwood, Brentwood, Bel Air, West Los Angeles, and Beverly Hills, each having a completely different character. In New York City, Columbia University separates the Upper West Side of Manhattan from Harlem.

Freeways and major highways also divide neighborhoods, usually resulting in values that are slightly higher on one side and slightly lower on the other. When the Hollywood Freeway was built over the Tejon Pass, there was a grade going up the hill. Obviously, trucks using this route would make a lot of noise, which was irritating to the people who lived in the apartment houses next to the freeway. A few years later, completion of the Golden State Freeway diverted traffic and reduced a lot of the noise from the Hollywood Freeway. Any time you remove a detriment such as traffic congestion or noise pollution from a piece of real estate, both the property value and rental value are enhanced.

I f a city added a stop signal to a corner, the house or apartment building next to that corner would be affected. The crossing might be safer, but the noise would increase because people would periodically be compelled to start their cars and motorcycles from a standstill. A friend of mine once told me that she had to move from a particular house facing a thoroughfare because the motorcycles would shift gears right at a point adjacent to her property.

When a city imposes traffic regulations, it directly affects residential real estate, many times in a negative fashion. But with commercial real estate, such as a restaurant or retail store, new traffic patterns can easily enhance values because motorists are obligated to stop, look around, and see what's in their immediate environment. What might be a disadvantage in one situation might be advantageous in another.

Other potentially negative developments may include a mini-mall or convenience store, which may add to the congestion problem and attract patrons who litter the neighborhood. But even these developments wouldn't deter me if I were able to buy a property at the right price. There's always a price at which a property is worth purchasing.

S ome of the condominiums we bought in Costa Mesa face the boulevard. Because of this, we were able to pick them up for only $45,000. Even so, all these units still rent for $600 a month, nearly the same amount I get for my other units inside the complex. Many people like to live on a busy street because they think there's something going on. It's the attitudes and thinking of people that determine value. You might find one person who thinks it's great and another who thinks it's terrible.

If you buy a house or apartment building in the center of a neighborhood, the surrounding houses will act as insulation and keep undesirable property uses away. Commercial and industrial property and multiple residential properties won't encroach. If a property is located on the edge of a neighborhood, it could have an encroachment, especially if the property is located next to a highway, used-car lot, or other type of commercial establishment. If a house is next to the corner, there could be a service station adjacent to the property that does bodywork on Saturday morning at 7:30 A.M. right under the bedroom window.

Zoning ordinances also act as artificial barriers. If a property is commercially zoned, developers are prevented from building any more houses in that direction. But buying a property next to another property with a different use might be better over the long term. A high-rise office building is an example of a positive development, particularly if people want to live near their work.

Another example is a proposed hotel development in a desirable beach community adjacent to an existing residential development. One of the houses directly across the street from the proposed hotel now rents for $2,500 a month. It was originally purchased in 1963 for $16,000 with no money down. If it takes two years to build the new hotel, then after three or four years the value of the residence, which is currently $450,000, might go as high as $600,000, depending on the economy and the state of the housing market. You only need one opportunity like this in a lifetime to get you going.

If a property is commercially zoned, that serves as a barrier. You can't build any more houses in that direction. Or if a property is zoned for low density, you may be prevented from building multiple units on that site.

Recently, we built a new house on a lot I've owned for 30 years. In 1961, I could have built two units on the land. Today, because it's been downzoned, I was only able to build one single family residence, and a scaled-back one at that. The city is trying to do everything it can to reduce the population density because if there are too many people, it's too hard on the utilities, it strains the maintenance budget, and it's hard for the police and fire departments to provide an adequate level of service. Most cities in areas of fairly heavy density are having these problems and yet I think they are some of the best areas to invest in because the restrictions eliminate competition.

Before you buy anything, you should have as many facts at your disposal as possible. Bernard Baruch, a businessman who from a humble beginning rose to become one of the wealthiest men in America and personal adviser to several presidents in the first half of this century, used to say that if you have a very important problem and gather all the facts and information about the problem at hand, the weight of the facts will answer the question for you or at least point to the direction of the solution. (Baruch was nicknamed "Dr. Facts" by President Woodrow Wilson.) In other words, the more careful the research, the more meaningful the final analysis.

It's important, however, not to go crazy over facts. Dwell on the *important* details and use the *un*important details for background. What's important and what isn't depends on the circumstances and the problem. The only way to know what's vital and what's extraneous is through education, knowledge, and experience. You just have to get out and do it; be proactive in your research and don't leave any important stone unturned. Yet remember too that the smart investor knows when to stop.

ECONOMIC CHARACTERISTICS

Degree of Home Ownership

In a newer single family residential neighborhood, or "bedroom community," the odds are pretty good that the homeowner will live in the neighborhood. But after the neighborhood has stabilized, homeowners start to move out and tenants start to move in. At this point, the neighborhood may start to deteriorate because renters don't have the same pride of ownership that owners do. They generally aren't of the mind to sweep the gutters or pick up stray trash. And why should they be? They don't have a long-term financial stake in the neighborhood.

Most lending institutions will bend over backward for homeowners because they represent stability, mom, apple pie, a white picket fence, and so on. They are substantial members of the community. On the other hand, banks aren't too enthused about speculators or absentee landlords because they tend to be less reliable.

If you're in a rental area and the properties are only half rented, the area will deteriorate. This has happened in numerous communities around the country, such as Kansas City, St. Louis, Detroit, Chicago's East Side, and New York City, just to name a few, where many housing projects are largely unoccupied, even though there is a housing shortage, because the area has become so dilapidated and run-down. Unattended property naturally detracts from the values of the surrounding real estate. To change things for the better, you have to give people an incentive to change their attitude, such as the option to buy their building. Ownership is a motivating factor because it gives people a stake in determining their own destiny.

If you are in an area with high rental rates and can see that the rents are increasing, then you know that the value of the real property is increasing along with them. Whenever I see a sign for a rental, I always ask how much the rent is. And then I note how long it takes to rent it. I used to write this information down and keep track of it pretty carefully. Rental rates are especially important when you have a lot of competition and you need to keep your own rents slightly lower than the place down the street because you're just getting by and need the rent to make your payments. In many situations, real estate values will increase more rapidly than the rents. It only takes one person to pay a high price for a property, but it takes a large group of people to pay higher rental rates, pushing the average up.

FAMILY INCOME CHARACTERISTICS

The income levels of people in a community directly influence real estate values. If people in a community are prosperous, then values are generally high. When the oil market bottomed out, the local economies of Galveston, Midland, and Houston in Texas, as well as Oklahoma City, all took a real shellacking. Moreover, many industries that were dependent on the oil industry went out of business, so all types of workers lost their jobs, lost their income, and had to foreclose on their real estate. When contemplating an investment, make sure that people in the area are gainfully employed and will continue to be employed. Ideally, find a location where the incomes are substantial and diversified and where the conditions exist for steady growth. If you consider the demographics of the community and the influx of people into the area, you'll find that as the wages go up, the price of real estate also goes up.

Percentage of Families on Public Assistance

Generally speaking, the more people who are on public assistance in a neighborhood, the less likely that properties will rise in value. When I did my appraisal of the redevelopment project in National City, California, I discovered that 50 percent of the people in the area were on public assistance or welfare of some kind or another. That kind of data, which is readily available from the county and state, if not the local newspaper, is a red flag for the potential investor. The local real estate prices in these areas may be cheap, but they're not likely to appreciate.

An important thing to consider when buying investment property is how much spendable income the people in the neighborhood have and what their attitude is toward living. Are the big money makers gangsters who bring in $200,000 a year by selling crack cocaine or are they mechanical engineers making $100,000 a year designing high-speed transit or the national aerospace plane?

SOCIAL CHARACTERISTICS

Density of the Population

W ith 20,000 people in 1.3 square miles, Hermosa Beach is one of the most densely populated cities in the state. The density is destroying the area in my opinion. Even before the current, nationwide trend of municipal budget crises, Hermosa always seemed to run a deficit budget. Hermosa is an old city with inadequate parking and dated infrastructure. And because the city has very little industry to provide a tax base, it lacks the necessary funds to run the city in a manner in which the community would like to have it run. High density can be a detriment in that respect, but when you own property, density increases land values because of the demand.

For the past few years, the City Council has been trying to down-zone everything in an effort to reduce the number of residents, so they make it extremely difficult to own a business, build a house, or re-model an apartment building. Plans for building a new house in Hermosa Beach may well sit in the city Building Department for a year. The drawings for a remodel I did to one of my buildings on The Strand took nine months to be approved. And then I had to seek approval from the state Coastal Commission, the city Planning Commission, and the City Council. Although this is an incredible inconvenience, it is also extremely beneficial because the city's downzoning efforts make the existing properties worth much more.

Composition of the Population

If you find people with approximately the same income and same mix of family arrangements, whether it is the traditional family, singles, single parents with children, or senior citizens, then you have a neighborhood because everyone is more or less thinking on the same terms. The outside appearance of property also helps shape and define the neighborhood, but mainly it's the homogeneity of the inhabitants.

I ncongruous economic and life-style patterns will create the po-tential for deterioration because of the lack of similar attitudes and values. Say you have a $300,000 house with a husband, wife, and three kids. In the house next door are five political activists who never fail to argue with each other into the early morning hours. Next door to that you have three bachelors. Next door to that you have a small, family-run day-care center. And the house next door to that doubles as an auto body shop. An incongruous mix like this tends to hinder the neighborhood from reaching its full potential. You want to consider the composition of the population *before* you buy.

If you want to find out about the characteristics of the neighborhood, you can go to grammar schools and see how the children are dressed. If they're neat, clean, and well-groomed, and have new shoes and everything else, then you know that you're in a somewhat affluent neighborhood. Some people even analyze the trash that people throw away. Although I've never done this, it's one way to measure the affluence of a neighborhood.

Harmonious Attitudes

A more subtle measure of a neighborhood are the attitudes of the people. In order for there to be harmony, everyone in a neighborhood has to think somewhat alike. Everyone has to like the idea of flowers in the garden, clean and maintained streets, and not having cars parked on the front lawn. Ideally, residents should have harmonious attitudes toward neighborhood things, which affect everybody. With harmonious attitudes, chances are that people will take pride in their neighborhood and see that it improves rather than deteriorates.

You can believe that when people allow their properties to deteriorate, they almost always have a deteriorating attitude toward themselves. As a property owner, if you allow people to leave their trash in the front yard and park their cars, boats, and RVs on the lawn, you are contributing to the demise of the neighborhood because that type of activity detracts from property values. If everyone around you has trashy attitudes, including property owners, then you're going to have a trashy neighborhood.

Don't be misled, however. The income level and outlook of the inhabitants are far more important than the outside appearance of the neighborhood. Remember, you want to invest in an area that has growth potential. If you see a neighborhood that has substantially declined but is in an area where the surrounding communities are good, you know that these growth factors will eventually increase the value of the depressed neighborhood. The investor has a slightly different outlook than someone who wants to buy a piece of property for shelter.

If you go into the worst neighborhood and buy the best house there is, you will lose money. But, if you go into the best neighborhood and buy the worst house, you can always make money. You can always improve a house, but you can't impose your will to change a neighborhood. A group of people may be able to, but you can't do it individually.

The investor should not be concerned with what a piece of property is like now, but what it will be like 20 years from now. Your objective should always be forward-looking. Buy something today and estimate what the property will be worth 20 or 30 years hence. If you can find a dilapidated district, that might be a real opportunity because neighborhoods change. They go through different phases as peoples' attitudes change.

PRIDE OF OWNERSHIP

Pride of ownership is defined not only by the way people maintain the interior and exterior of their property, but also by the attitudes they have toward ownership.

———

My brother used to own a 14-unit apartment building in Hermosa Beach. In 1965, the building, which he had purchased with pretty high leverage, had a negative cash flow of $2,000 per month, which was a lot of money at the time. It was costing him that much to own it. But for him it was worth it. He used to sit across the street and say, gosh, I own this thing. The satisfaction he derived from knowing that he was the owner of this big, impressive complex tickled him to no end. That's pride of ownership. Plus, the building's now worth about 10 times what he paid for it.

It makes me feel pretty good when I can walk on the beach and look up at my building, which sort of reminds me of a smaller version of a private beach club. That's pride of ownership, too. I felt it the first day I bought this place. I liked it from the very beginning. I was thrilled to pieces—even though it was vacant, in terrible shape, and there were big curtains right in front of the window that looked awful and faded red carpet on the living room floor. I knew I could always fix the building and the interior and that if I did, someday it was going to be worth something.

———

Civic pride is slightly different than pride of ownership. With civic pride, people may be proud of the fact they live in a certain area. It's more a pride of accomplishment, a feeling that you've arrived. These attitudes can also have a positive effect on property values.

For instance, if a group of people band together and start a neighborhood watch program to see that law and order are preserved, that will have a tremendous positive impact on law enforcement and help minimize crime. If something does happen, people will be up in arms and take action instead of shrugging their shoulders and saying, "Well, fortunately, it didn't happen to me, so I'll forget about it."

When people actively participate in neighborhood activities and show concern about their homes, they generally have a good attitude toward maintaining and improving the neighborhood. Similarly, if there are high enrollments, memberships, and participation in educational and cultural institutions, you can be assured that people want to improve themselves, better their condition, and strive for a higher standard of living.

Absence or Presence of Vice

If you get a bad feeling from an area, look at the crime rates. Crime rates can affect real estate values, drive people away from business districts, and take away revenue. Even so, it's important to weigh the amount of criminal activity against other salient factors, such as plans for new developments. If the city government is building a new hotel and convention center, expanding the harbor, or building a new sports arena, then I would be interested in buying a nearby property no matter how seedy the area is. Once the developer commits and gets these plans going, he can't go back. In this type of situation, I wouldn't give the crime factor much weight unless it's widespread.

———

E very area has crime. Just the mere fact that money is around will instigate it. Look for a neighborhood where you feel comfortable and can control the situation. I've never been afraid to walk on the beach at night. When I bought my home in Hermosa Beach, I figured that a burglar or attacker would only have one way to exit—inland (east). I thought about that very carefully when I was younger so that when I got older I wouldn't have to worry about it.

Sometimes, you can take the crime issue head-on yourself. I once knew a fellow who bought a 30-unit apartment building in one of the most notorious parts of South-Central Los Angeles. It was in really bad shape, so he fixed it up. Before he started renovating, he put a fence around the place and got a few guard dogs to patrol the property. The front entrance sat about four feet above the street level for some reason, so he had a ramp built across the sidewalk to the front entrance so that the dogs could run under the ramp and not disturb the tenants.

That simple solution solved a lot of problems. Even though that place was in a high crime area, it never got burglarized, and he was able to find good tenants. He transformed a run-down, dilapidated property into a desirable asset and turned it into a good-paying proposition. It took a lot of courage, but it paid off for him. Not only that, he wound up helping the people who lived there, and they appreciated his efforts.

Consider all the positive things that will make the property go up in value in 20 years. After you can see these things in your mind, then put down the negative. If you think of the positive qualities enough times, the negative attributes won't be as bad as they were at first. But if you start listing the negative aspects first and begin to dwell on them, you'll never finish making your list. Unfortunately, that's what many people do. They find something to criticize and drum up an excuse for why they don't want to do it. That's the wrong way to approach it. You should approach your investment program with a positive attitude like my friend did and watch as wonderful things start to happen.

REAL ESTATE SALES ACTIVITY

Number and Price of Homes for Sale

Before investing in a neighborhood, consider the number and price of the homes that are for sale to determine if you're in a buyer's or seller's market. This information should be available from your realtor or the local Board of Realty. But don't lose sight of the fact that you want to consider what the area will be like in 20 years. That's where you could make a critical mistake. If it's a buyer's market with a glut of properties listed for sale, you might be able to negotiate better terms. If you can get favorable terms, it could be well worth your while to buy even in the middle of a downturn.

If properties that are for sale in a neighborhood sit on the market for a long time, they are probably overpriced. If so, you can probably negotiate a good deal.

As we will see in more detail in Chapter 10, the down payment and the terms of sale are more important than the purchase price. Say a seller has an apartment for sale for $300,000. He or she has a $100,000 loan on the property and wants $200,000 cash out of the deal. You can come along and offer $300,000, offering to pay $100,000 in cash if the seller agrees to take back a second mortgage for $100,000. You go to lenders; you refinance the property. Say you get a $200,000 first and the seller agrees to carry the $100,000 second. At this point, you haven't got a dime invested.

Now, supposing he or she is very anxious to sell and is willing to take no interest or principal payments for 10 years on the second. How much will that note be worth if you tried to sell it on the open market? Probably only about $25,000 because of the terms, so you're really buying the property for $225,000, not $300,000. You never know what a motivated seller will do.

SALES CONDITIONS

Willingness of Lenders to Participate

The willingness of recognized institutional lenders to participate in the neighborhood says a great deal about the value of the property. If a lender, which is supposed to be conservative by nature in its lending practices, is willing to make a loan, then that is a major vote of confidence in the subject neighborhood. Also, if your real estate agent is on the ball and keeping track of what's going on in the community, he or she should be able to find out whether substantial down payments are being made on purchases. This suggests that the people moving into the area are solid citizens.

Number of Foreclosures

The number of foreclosures has an effect on the overall trend of the neighborhood. If people no longer have the ability to make their payments, they're going to let the property deteriorate. It's not the greatest thing for the quality of a neighborhood. If there are a lot of foreclosures, it indicates that the neighborhood is in a recessionary trend, although foreclosures don't necessarily cluster unless the people who live there are all employed by the same industry and that industry is in the midst of restructuring and mass layoffs. Similarly, if there are a lot of people in a neighborhood with delinquent taxes, they don't have the money to sustain themselves or they don't think much of the property. If you have a good broker, he should know these kinds of things.

GOVERNMENTAL CHARACTERISTICS

Taxation Policies

In most cities and counties, the assessed value for real property acts as the basis for determining the property tax rate. Real property taxes are the best revenue base there is for governments because property is always there. It is always possible to get a lien against a property because real estate is secure. It doesn't move. On the other hand, you can take a car across the state line and all your creditors can do is hire a skip-tracer.

If property taxes increase, there is far more expense in owning real estate. Given the dire circumstances that many local and regional governments are finding themselves in—40 percent of all counties nationwide with more than 100,000 residents reported budget shortfalls in 1991—the trend over the next five to 10 years will probably be toward higher property taxes. And when taxes go up, it takes money out of the income stream of property owners. However, higher property taxes probably won't result in lower housing prices. Usually, when property taxes go up, it is a sign that the neighborhood is improving. Taxes aren't usually raised in areas that are declining.

R ecently, I consulted some property owners whose real property assessments doubled over a two-year period. Incensed, these home and apartment owners formed an action committee to fight the dramatic increase. Amazingly, the County Assessor's reassessment proved to be correct. As a result, land values, as well as real property taxes, increased dramatically. Property owners were subsequently compelled to improve their rental units to bring in more income to pay the higher tax rate. There was an upside to these higher assessments, however. For in the process of making improvements to their units, the property owners stimulated the local real estate market and were able to ask for higher rents.

Municipal Fees and Assessments

Municipal fees and assessments are another burden on property owners and occur when a city decides to make general improvements to such things as roads and utilities. Even the smallest city governments have regulatory and taxing authority, which makes them powerful. In many cities, property owners now have to pay added trash-collection tax to fund recycling programs. The installation of new sewer lines can also result in a new assessment.

If a city has too much indebtedness caused by the passage of too many bond issues for public works projects, it could have a low municipal bond rating. Since the bonds are riskier, investors who buy them have to pay more interest. That means property owners would have to pay more money to accommodate that higher interest rate. If, in this situation, a city were to put new initiatives on the ballot to build new schools, resurface streets, and undertake a massive redevelopment project and all the measures were approved by voters, all city services would be placed in jeopardy on account of the precarious revenues.

Zoning Ordinances

When selecting property, obtain a zoning map and see how the area is zoned. If you're looking at an R-1 lot but the house next door is zoned C-2, you're going to want to know about it, because someday the owner could tear down that C-2 house and replace it with a video arcade or convenience store. You want the owner to know that you have this information so the price will be right. (Figure 6.1 shows a typical zoning map.)

If I were going to buy a property for which a zoning question was involved, I would make the deal contingent on zoning approval by the city council. That is a standard practice if you want to change a zoning designation. Unless, of course, you can buy the property for so little that it doesn't matter. The problem with zoning matters is that you need a seller who's willing to wait for up to six months to sell.

Typically, if a zoning change is approved, the property will become more valuable, in which case the seller could ask for more. Say a parcel is rezoned from residential to commercial. You probably would pay at least 25 percent more to build a restaurant or shopping center in place of a house or apartment building. But since these kinds of changes aren't guaranteed, you need to agree on a price assuming that the property will be rezoned. If it isn't, you might want to reconsider your purchase.

Wherever there are heavy population densities, there tend to be slow-growth movements that advocate downzoning. An elevator designed for 10 people can't hold 15 because it's dangerous. The same thing is true for a city. If a city's public services—streets, schools, utilities, and the like—are designed only for 10,000 or 20,000 people but 40,000 move in, you're going to have a colossal problem, and that is exactly what's happening in many popular areas. Cities in these instances have no choice but to downzone.

If a city decides to downzone an area, that generally means that existing properties become more valuable. Say you had a single family residence that is 5,000 square feet on a lot, and the city changed the setbacks

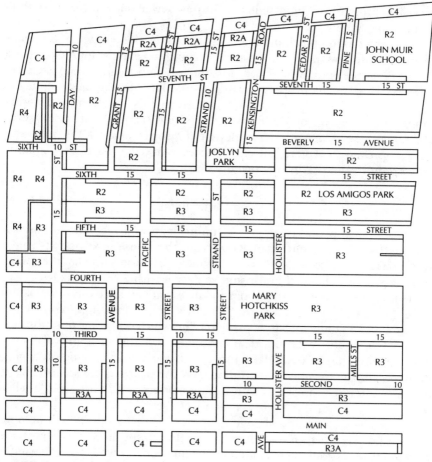

FIGURE 6.1
**Sample zoning map showing permitted land uses. (C = commercial; R =
residential; R-A = parking; R2, 3, 4 = allowable density, e.g., two units, three
units, four units.)**

so you have to be 17 feet from the alleyway before you can put in a garage.
And they've added setbacks on the side, so now you can build only 2,000
square feet on the same lot. The existing building, which now becomes
"legal nonconforming," could be worth much more than a new one.

Legal-noncomforming properties that aren't burdened with the factor
of functional obsolescence enable property owners to utilize the property
to the greatest extent. The six-unit apartment building I live in, which
became legal nonconforming in 1956 when the city changed its zoning

ordinance, is not functionally obsolete in the least. Even though it was built in 1938, it accommodates six groups of tenants as well now as it did then.

Everything that is manmade is a wasting asset. As soon as it's built, it starts to deteriorate and goes down in value. But my building, even though it is 54 years old, is worth more now than when it was built partly because of downzoning.

I have two lots in Redondo Beach zoned R-3. Individually, they're only big enough for a single family residence. But together, you could build three units. But you can't because of a new zoning ordinance that prevents accumulation of lots to gain plottage. Since it isn't possible to assemble adjoining lots for construction purposes, you aren't going to see any big apartment buildings erected in Redondo Beach any time soon. Single family residences, therefore, will rise in value. In these examples, external influences from governmental sources have had a marked effect on real estate values.

Creative Rehabilitation

Creative rehabilitation is the act of improving the present use of the building to a higher and better use by eliminating such negative factors as obsolescence and physical deterioration. Many older buildings are structurally sound but lack modern amenities, including modern electrical wiring, plumbing and heating systems, and insulation. When the basic structure is sound and modern facilities are installed, the value of the property is sometimes enhanced beyond what a new building would be worth on the same site.

Oftentimes, you can get more money out of an older building that can be rehabilitated than you can by constructing a new building, especially if the older building is legal nonconforming and has more units than the current zoning ordinance allows. There are examples of this in most areas. Typically, the city allows property owners to renovate a building that doesn't conform with current zoning laws without a special permit or variance as long as the renovation doesn't change the exterior of the building or add to the overall square footage. In high-density areas, a remodelling job often makes better sense than building from the ground up because you don't have to provide all the parking necessary for a new building.

Building Codes

Building codes are designed to provide the city building department with a uniform method of regulating the construction of buildings in keeping with health and safety requirements. These regulations are stipulated in the form of construction standards. In high-density areas, such as New

York City or Manhattan Beach, people attempt to modify and rent illegal apartment units, such as converted garages, basements, attics, and bedrooms. If building codes are vigorously enforced, this helps preserve the quality of the neighborhood. Still, many renters and owners do things without a permit. If you have any questions about a specific site, check with the city building department for building permits. They are a matter of public record.

Health and Fire Regulations

Health and fire regulations, such as laws that require smoke detectors, fire extinguishers, and sprinkler systems, can really become a costly issue in a high-density area. Just a few years ago, the City of Los Angeles passed an ordinance requiring all high-rise buildings to install sprinklers. To comply with a fire code like that is very expensive. Many older office buildings have asbestos in the ceiling, and in order to install sprinklers, the asbestos has to be removed. Sometimes conforming to new regulations can cost as much as rehabilitating the whole building. That's why investors who know the law and can work efficiently within it are going to be successful. The more you know, the more you can take into consideration when putting an offer in on a building.

A lot of people don't know what an asbestos ceiling is, let alone how to deal with the city when an inspector comes out. Asbestos is a hazardous material used for fireproofing before it was discovered to be dangerous, and its removal is governed by strict regulations. When an inspector walks through a building and notes that it has an asbestos ceiling in it and you can't put in sprinklers until you get rid of it, then some owners might get desperate, especially if the building isn't paying for itself at the moment.

When investing, strive to become educated and knowledgeable enough to realize what the important factors are that affect the value of the property you are interested in acquiring. Learn what contingencies and events might occur that advantageously affect the value of that property over a long period. Also become aware of the detrimental factors that can undermine the value of the property over that period. Those are the important things; the rest is secondary.

Dwell on these kinds of things, and look at them in the form of a trend. When you see that the trend is going in the right direction, act on it. When you see it going in the wrong direction, go on to something else. Understanding what factors are important is a matter of studying the problem. As we'll see in the next chapter, the surest sign that the value of land will rise is if average income levels are on an upward trend. Two other key indicators of long-term growth potential include population estimates and employment projections.

Knowledge is more important than money; once you're in an area with growth potential, you don't have to do nearly as much research and analysis. Once you've found a neighborhood where you know there is a growth factor going, you can hop on the bandwagon. You have only to go through one reasonable process of assessing a neighborhood's long-term prospects to be assured of a solid investment location.

7

Select the Right Property and Make an Analysis of Its Growth Potential

After identifying the right neighborhood, the next step is to select the right property to buy and analyze its growth potential. Besides physical appearance and other visible signs, a key consideration in determining the desirability of a piece of real estate is its zoning designation, whether high- or low-density industrial, commercial, or residential. Knowing the lot's size and precise boundaries can also influence the sales price.

The first thing you have to do is find a good real estate market where you know there is great potential. Most people find a place where they want to live and buy a piece of property there, and if they like the area, they might buy another one. When I came to Hermosa Beach, I studied the area very carefully before buying anything. It was run-down, terrible; you couldn't believe it. But I always looked at it with a long-term perspective. I wasn't so much interested in what the property was like when I bought it as what it would be worth 15 or 20 years later.

Ideally, you should spend a few months investigating as much as you can about a community. Before you buy, maybe rent for a little while, and give yourself some time to do a study and determine what you really want, what your objectives are, and how they fit into your overall program. Always, it's better for you to make an analysis of a community firsthand than to hire someone to do it, because you know what you're looking for.

Table 7.1 lists the many characteristics to be aware of when judging the value of income property.

A few years ago I spoke with a real estate broker who moved to Belmont Shores, an upscale residential community south of Long Beach, California. This broker told me that he spent two years studying the community, real estate market, and local economy before he decided to open his office there. He took it upon

TABLE 7.1
Factors that Affect the Value of Income Property

Land	Services	Facilities	Conditions
Location	Paving	Schools	Zoning
Topography	Sidewalks	Churches	Percent developed
Street width	Street lights	Proximity to mass transit	Type of development
Alleyways	Phone service		
Corner lots	Cable TV service	Neighborhood shopping	Appearance
Drainage	Utilities		Present use
Soil conditions	Transportation	Regional shopping	Highest and best use
Size and shape	Fire protection		
Filled ground	Police protection		Deed restrictions
			Assessed values
			Easements

himself to become thoroughly informed about all aspects of the community before he completed one transaction. During the next few years, he advertised the fact that he had become an authority on Belmont Shores and would invite property owners, prospective buyers, and other interested parties to attend seminars in which he shared his knowledge of the area. Needless to say, he developed a thriving business.

I n 1960, during the construction of King Harbor in Redondo Beach, I chartered a helicopter to survey the best land to invest in along the South Bay coastline. Since there wasn't any beach frontage in Redondo, I decided on Hermosa Beach, a dilapidated (at that time) seaside community whose proximity to the ocean, beachfront lots, and run-down condition suggested that things could only get better. I started at a time when Hermosa was so deteriorated, there was nowhere it could go but up.

Another advantage to Hermosa was the fact that the city—not the state or some other distant entity—owned the beach, so the chances of local authorities confiscating property to build a parking lot for public access to the beach, as had happened in neighboring Manhattan Beach, were minimal.

Most buyers are not aware of everything going on around a property. People don't think about real estate in that sense. They don't explore it in that depth. They say, "Well, I can get my broker to do something about it."

In Manhattan Beach you can talk to 90 percent of the brokers selling real estate and not find many who know that the beach is a state park and therefore owned by the State of California and not the City of Manhattan Beach. Most people are dumbfounded when I tell them that. What difference does it make? About 20 years ago, the state decided to put a car park in front of many people's houses in the north end of town and there was nothing they could do about it because they found out too late. If the state wanted to do that in Hermosa Beach, they would have to wrest control of beach access away from the city, and people would know about it and where to protest. But if you're dealing with the state, by the time you find out who ordered it, the parking lot would already be built. That's exactly what happened in Manhattan Beach. The few residents who rallied at the last minute against the parking lot did too little, too late.

Ironically, the City of Hermosa Beach, though crowded, is dormant. People here have little concern for whether it grows. They'd rather it didn't. They like this village atmosphere. But the surrounding cities of Redondo Beach, Manhattan Beach, Torrance, and El Segundo are entirely different. Redondo has built a marina and substantial hotel and the South Bay Galleria, which is a very successful shopping mall. Manhattan Beach has its own substantial Manhattan Village Shopping Center and is rebuilding the pier. Torrance is home to the largest shopping center in the world under one roof, and El Segundo has allowed the construction of several high-rise office buildings for aerospace contractors.

But Hermosa has done relatively little. What few projects the City Council does pass, it passes begrudgingly. Nevertheless, the economic impact of the developments in the surrounding areas has had a tremendous impact on the value of properties in Hermosa. That's why Hermosa was such a valuable area to invest in during the early days. Even if they didn't want it to grow, the residents couldn't do anything about it. They had no control over it. So even though the city was falling apart, everything else was falling in line.

On top of everything, several major aerospace contractors set up operations within a few miles of my house. The most dramatic thing to happen to this community, really, has been the influx of the aerospace and defense industries—high-tech companies that have created jobs of substance. In the early 1960s, the average income of people in this area was about $15,000 a year. Today, it's close to $45,000. The main reason is the number of well-paying professional jobs that have been created by companies such as TRW, Rockwell, Hughes Aircraft, General Dynamics, Aerospace Corp., Xerox, and Computer Sciences Corp., plus the fact that it's a desirable place to live. Similar situations exist all around the country.

Another reason that the land by me has gone up so much is that there's no land to build on. There's no room for expansion. And when that happens, you have two choices: either build up or tear down the old structures and build new ones. Either way, property values increase on account of construction costs and the tremendous demand. Owing to the influx of population with high incomes in an area of high density where there is little supply, the demand becomes astronomical.

My brother and I once did an appraisal of the California Rock Salt Company located in the Mojave Desert near Amboy, California. Amboy, a sleepy little town, had a population of about 500. The population of Amboy could probably double in a year or two, and it wouldn't affect the market value of land there. However, if you doubled the population in a confined area like Hermosa Beach, real estate values would go out of sight. They would be like Tokyo because there isn't room for expansion.

That is how people make a big mistake in going to outlying areas, where there are huge tracts of land, and buying houses for 10 percent down. When the house is built, the contractor moves on to the next tract. Pretty soon, there are thousands and thousands of houses in that district, and they're all competitive. If there is a slight recession, it's pretty difficult for people to handle. A portion of those living there are going to lose their jobs and won't be able to make their mortgage payments. And so some people will be able to come in and buy properties for less than what the original owners bought them for.

That scenario won't occur when there's no room for expansion because competition like that doesn't exist. When there's not a lot of room for expansion in a desirable area and people in that area have good jobs, you can be assured that land values in that area are going to skyrocket.

Another reason I decided to invest in Hermosa Beach is that I knew there was a scarcity of land. There are only about 200 properties on The Strand. Land values were destined to go up. And, sure enough, I haven't lost any money on the real estate I've invested in; it's all gone out of sight. Properties I purchased with $3,000 down or less in the early 1960s and made payments on are worth over $1 million today. It's easy to sit here now and say with hindsight that it was inevitable, but I am convinced that similar patterns will emerge in the future if you just pick the right area to invest in.

Today, you can't even buy a lot on or near The Strand for less than $800,000. Five years ago, it was about half that. The dollar keeps shrinking. There has to be three or four percent inflation a year just to keep the economy going (see Table 7.2).

TABLE 7.2
Inflation since 1960

Year	Annual Inflation Rate (percent)	Cumulative Inflation (percent: 1959 = 100%)	Value of the 1983 Dollar
1960	1.7	101.7	$3.73
1961	1.0	102.7	3.34
1962	1.0	103.7	3.30
1963	1.3	105.0	3.27
1964	1.3	106.3	3.22
1965	1.6	107.9	3.17
1966	2.9	110.8	3.08
1967	3.1	113.9	2.99
1968	4.2	118.1	2.87
1969	5.5	123.6	2.73
1970	5.7	129.3	2.57
1971	4.4	133.7	2.47
1972	3.2	136.9	2.39
1973	6.2	143.1	2.25
1974	11.0	154.1	2.03
1975	9.1	163.2	1.86
1976	5.8	169.0	1.76
1977	6.5	175.5	1.65
1978	7.6	183.1	1.53
1979	11.3	194.4	1.38
1980	13.5	207.9	1.22
1981	10.3	218.2	1.09
1982	6.2	224.4	1.04
1983	3.2	227.6	1.00
1984	4.3	231.9	.96
1985	3.6	235.5	.93
1986	1.9	237.4	.91
1987	3.6	241.0	.88
1988	4.1	245.1	.85

Source: U.S. Bureau of Labor Statistics.

In addition to the scarcity factor associated with land in high-demand areas, there's also foreign investment. Foreign investors can afford to pay more and afford to pay all cash. I've had a number of Asian buyers look at the properties I have. They're looking at the long haul. What you've got to remember about real estate is that you pay today for what you expect to get from that property years later, what I refer to as the contemplated future benefits.

Most investors are interested in what return they're going to get today, not what they're going to get tomorrow. Real estate is not that type of investment. In my opinion, you have to look at the long term. There are opportunities everywhere, areas all over the country that are going to be good. When I decided to invest at the beach in the early 1960s, I couldn't have gone to downtown Manhattan in New York City at 42nd Street and Broadway and bought a piece of property. This was all I could afford. But 50 years before, 42nd and Broadway might have been ideal and affordable for a guy like me.

When I was a consultant, I used to work with a broker at a real estate office. My associate invested five times more than I ever did. But he sold it all during the recession of the early 1980s because he thought the bottom was going to fall out of the market. I've talked to him since and he said, "I wish I would have done what you did—held on to my property." Uninformed investors make rash decisions to sell under two emotional circumstances: When they see dollar signs or when they think the sky is falling. In actuality, the local market is merely correcting itself and weeding out the speculators and amateurs.

As I've said before, I believe in buying and holding, and that's all I believe in doing. What you have to do is find an area that has a strong growth pattern and be correct in your analysis.

LOCATION

Since the immediate, surrounding neighborhood has just as much, or more, influence on property values as the condition of the subject property itself, select a property where the neighborhood has the greatest potential for growth. Unless you just want to live in a particular neighborhood because of its charm, I would recommend going into an area that is established, that is built up, where you can see the results.

It's tremendous to buy a new luxury house in a new area if you can afford to, but if you're going to pay $400,000 or $500,000—or more—I think you could do just as well to buy into an exclusive community that's already established. In addition, if you look at the tax rates in many parts of the country, they tend to be higher in newer areas because it costs local governments more to maintain a new community.

A few years ago, I had a tenant who, when he got married and had two kids, decided to move to Palmdale, where he could buy a five-bedroom house for an affordable price. The problem was that he worked at Xerox in El Segundo, about 60 miles away. Can you imagine that? That kind of a commute is a tremendous sacrifice, and one that I don't think is a good idea, because over a period of time it's going to place a lot of stress on him and his family. I think he should have looked around here and tried to find something in a fringe area.

First-time buyers should look at property in fringe areas because the fringe area is usually the oldest. And as the greater metropolitan area grows, these fringe areas will become more valuable. In areas that have a history of growth, things tend to get better, not worse.

━━━━━━━

I did an appraisal for a redevelopment agency in Compton, California, not too long ago. The subject property was a two-bedroom, one-bath house of about 1,000 square feet that was built in the 1920s. It was in very good condition, but it was located in a rough area and was therefore only worth $50,000. Compare that house in Compton, which is about 12 miles from the beach, to a comparable two-bedroom, one-bath house on The Strand, 12 miles west, that would sell today for about $800,000 (and that's just what the land is worth). There is a range between that $50,000 and $800,000 where you will be able to find a property that fits your pocketbook.

If you plotted two-bedroom, one-bath houses from Compton to Hermosa Beach every mile or so and had 10 comparable sales to support your opinion, you would know what you could afford and the quality of the neighborhood of each subject property. Say you decide to buy a house for $150,000 in the City of Carson, about five miles from the beach. If the South Bay real estate market gets to the point where prices are going to start appreciating, that property in Carson is going to go up, too. Pretty soon, the property in Compton is going to be worth twice as much, or whatever, because it's at the lower end of the same scale, where people who can't find affordable housing in areas where they want to live *have* to live.

—————

With tract homes in outlying areas, there can be dramatic changes in the value of property over a period of a few years once the houses are built. The stabilized value of real estate can be maintained by upkeep and physical enhancements. Even financing can change the market value. I wouldn't buy a tract home, however. I would prefer to buy a house in a seasoned community where the surrounding area is already developed, where everything is established, where the schools are good, where I know what the community's like, what the people are like, and where the stores are.

With the condominiums I bought in Orange County, people can walk to restaurants, buy their groceries, even take care of their medical needs without ever crossing the street. (Table 7.3 lists some recommended distances to neighborhood facilities.) Right now, they are ideal for college students or single people. But as our population ages, there will be a tremendous demand for retirement communities. Fifteen years from now, these places will be ideal for retirees. And because the amenities are so fabulous, we'll be getting double the rent. Over the long pull, these units will do more than pay themselves off. But one of the main reasons I bought there was that the area was established.

If a developer builds a tract of houses in an outlying area, he or she has the tract next door to contend with. And that tract may extend into the desert or rural countryside for 25 or 50 miles. And there will always

TABLE 7.3
Maximum Distance and Time Recommended from a Residential Income Property to Community and Neighborhood Facilities

Facility	Recommended Distance from Subject Property
High school	3 miles
Grade school	0.75 mile
Local stores	1 mile
Church, parks, recreation	3.5 miles
Major shopping center	4.5 miles
Place of employment	35 minutes

be competition to sell and rent for a lower price than your neighbor or the seller down the street. The only thing you can count on to increase the value of that property is inflation.

The person who goes into a newly developed area and buys a new high-rise office building is making a big mistake in my opinion. They're pioneering and that's okay. But I don't think investors should do that unless they have a lot of holding power and can afford to lose money on their investment for 15 or 20 years. The opportunities for the person who isn't wealthy are much better in already established neighborhoods because you can see what directions the neighborhood is going.

I n some of these new communities, appearances are deceiving because what you may think is a jewel of an investment might be a disaster—the entire tract can go bust. Consider the example of Colorado Centre, a 3,000-acre housing development and planned community southeast of Colorado Springs. In 1985, this tract of sparkling new homes with Rocky Mountain views seemed like an idyllic place for first-time homebuyers to invest in for the future—for as little as $600 down and $730 a month.

Today, these $75,000 homes are literally worth nothing because the local municipality and tax district went bankrupt. One homeowner who was interviewed on "60 Minutes" said his home was appraised at *negative* $5,400. The hoards of people who were counted on to buy lots and build houses, along with the big companies that were supposed to relocate there and pay taxes, never came. And so the 130-odd families who *did* buy into the tract got struck with the bankrupt tax district's entire debt burden of $25 million. Some deal!

On the other hand, if you own property in an established area, you eliminate the risk of unknown variables and wishful projections. If you buy a house in San Francisco, for instance, an increase in land values can be attributed to a number of factors: the attitude and actions of the city government, which may be attempting to downzone; the regional high-tech industry may hire more people at a higher salary; or increased demand comes into the neighborhood. These are the type of pressures that create value. There are more pressures on prices to go up in areas that are already built and already have an infrastructure in place.

A friend of mind whose father lived in Philadelphia used to handle matters for Kress & Woolworth's. He was a respected attorney. Around 1910, my friend's father and his law partner each decided to build a new house. My friend's father bought a lot in the suburbs to build on for about $12,000 and his associate bought a lot in town, for which he paid $8,000. They both used the same architectural firm and built about the same size house. The guy who lived in town didn't have too far to go to the office and that was one of the great early advantages. But the guy who lived in the suburb was in a growing community with fairly nice homes.

When their estates were settled some 30 years later, the heirs of the suburbanite received $150,000, while the heirs of the city dweller, whose property was now in an industrial zone, received a pittance by comparison. After three decades, the house in the suburbs was worth 10 times more than the downtown property because the downtown site was encroached on by an industrial development, which forced the owner to tear down the house. What remained was just a vacant lot. The buildings were almost identical to begin with, it was just a matter of location. If you have the choice of buying one lot over another, you shouldn't be concerned about what they cost in today's dollars. Instead, focus on what they're going to be worth in 20 years.

Many people make the mistake of buying in the wrong location. In the above example, it took 20 years for an encroachment to occur. But when it did, there was nothing the owner could do.

But just because certain properties are high-priced doesn't necessarily mean they have some inherent advantage. One property may cost more than another today, but will it still be worth more down the line? It might be subjected to condemnation, in which the government claims the property for public use for a redevelopment or street-widening project or a new highway, school, or park. Unforeseen encroachments, such as zoning changes, can occur that alter the use and value of the property.

Real estate that is scarce is in great demand, such as oceanfront property or a property that has favorable access or scenery—whatever determines value according to the attitudes of people in the area. Some locations, such as Beverly Hills, Park Avenue, or Palm Beach, you know will never be zoned for different uses.

ANALYZING GROWTH POTENTIAL

When analyzing a property's growth potential, it is important to find out as much as you can about a community and isolate the factors that contribute to growth. You have to select the right area to start with. If you don't, you're really wasting your time. The only way to do it is to conduct research and find out what the city and regional governments are planning to do and if there are any projects on the drawing boards. If you find something unique, you might be sitting on a mountain of riches!

Another sign of growth is the addition of new area codes by the regional phone companies. The area I live in was recently assigned a new area code because of the increase of business and residential phone use created by the growing number of fax machines, computer modems, and multiple phone lines. This is a concrete sign of growth in progress. It forced me to modify all my stationery, but it's very reassuring.

―――――――――

Whmen contemplating a purchase, the best method of weighing the benefits and drawbacks is to write down everything you like about the property. Get a piece of paper, draw a line down the center, and write the property's positive attributes on one side and negative on the other. List everything about the subject property and surrounding area. This will help make your decision as objective as possible.

Start with the positive, then write the negative. If you write down everything that is negative first, you won't even get past the first step. Then cross off the things that counterbalance each other. There might be one positive quality that outweighs all the negative things put together. The three most important factors in determining growth potential are family income, population growth, and the duration of that growth. Everything else is important, but not as important.

―――――――――

You can draw all kinds of assumptions and situations from data, but it is worthless if you don't know what to do with it. The surest sign that the value of land will rise is if average income levels are on an upward trend. If you can foresee how long these trends are going to last, then you have the key to selecting the right community. All the other factors, the details, come into play when selecting the individual property that represents the best value in the community.

Essentially, our equation looks like this:

Population growth + Family income + Duration = Property values

---

As mentioned before, population on its own does not create wealth. You need population combined with industry—and the industry has to have expansion potential. Where you learn about this is in the pages of the *Wall Street Journal, Business Week, Fortune,* and the business section of your local newspaper; or you hear it on national radio programs like "Marketplace"; or you watch it on the "Nightly Business Report," "Wall Street Week," or "Adam Smith's Money World."

When I first moved to Hermosa Beach, I bought a great big street map of the city to track the local real estate activity and to become as informed as I could about the community. I hung this map on the wall and made notations with differently colored pushpins to track different developments. I used red to indicate sales, yellow for listings, blue for assessments and street improvement projects, white for new buildings, and green for other important activity, such as zone changes. I then numbered each mark, wrote a full-page explanation of it, and kept it in a loose leaf binder for easy reference.

I also used the multiple listing service and put citations from that on the map as well. If the city was planning to do something, I'd write it down in a reference book. In this way, I was able to keep very close track of what was going on in the community. I had a visual picture of the local real estate activity. When you see a property coming on the market and you know what the other properties have sold for in the last three years, you can make an informed offer.

Pick an area that you like, of say five city blocks, get a big map, and put it on the wall. Put every bit of information you know about the community on that map. When something comes along that you think you want to buy, you've got all this data to help determine what you think you can afford to pay for it. From this, you can also see what the trend is.

If you see a large number of new single family residences in an area with apartment buildings, you can probably conclude that that particular strip's been downzoned to R-1. But you should always check with the city planning department to make sure.

The important thing is to look at these factors in the form of a trend. When you see that the trends are going in the right direction, take action; when you see that they're going in the wrong direction, go on to something else.

When you're organized, it's pretty easy to figure out whether and how the community is growing. I find it useful to pencil everything out to better visualize the various pieces of the puzzle. This work is a problem for some people. It's not easy. If it were easy and took little or no effort, all the people lying on the beach in front of my building would be multimillionaires. My mother used to say that luck is 90 percent hard work and only 10 percent serendipity. It's work that makes you successful, not chance.

When I started my real estate investment program, I was working full-time as an appraiser for Marshall and Stevens and was taking care of my properties and everything else. With real estate, you have to like it or it's going to be a burden. For people who do this but hate real estate, it's probably not going to work. For me, it was always fun. I looked at it as a hobby and spent most of my spare time in some real-estate-oriented activity or discussion.

Corner Lots

A corner lot isn't worth that much in a normal single family residential area, but when you have a multiple residential situation, a corner lot becomes valuable, especially if the city is planning to change the use and require more parking per apartment unit. A corner lot becomes valuable if it is vacant and you want to build on it, primarily because of easy access. Lot orientation and use of natural lighting can also make the building look better.

Lot Size and Precise Boundaries

I mentioned before that most buyers are not aware of everything going on around a property. A lot of people aren't even informed about the zoning of the subject property—let alone the precise boundaries of the piece of real estate they're thinking about purchasing.

The size of the lot is extremely important and should conform with the neighborhood and the community. You can look for this on the tract map. If you have a larger parcel than the standard-sized lot, that's actually good. But you don't want a smaller one, unless you can buy it cheap, assuming everything is equal, because you can get into a situation where a lot is substandard. With a substandard lot, if you have two units on your property and something happened to the property, you might only be able to put one back; and if it were really small, you might not even be able to put one back.

If you're going to buy a piece of land, you ought to get a metes and bounds description of the parcel, which describes the boundary lines, as well as a survey of the land to physically locate points, so that you can go out and see what you're buying. I knew a couple who once bought a restaurant on a two-acre parcel of ground. The broker assured them that the property they were buying was two acres and came with a restaurant, an orchard, a house, and a yard. They bought the property and closed escrow, thinking they had found the deal of the century.

Well, one day the new owners (my friends) went over to the property and started working in the orchard, and the real owner told them to get off what they thought was their property! Only after this incident did they obtain a metes and bounds description, which showed the true extent of their lot, which turned out to be only $\frac{3}{4}$ of an acre. They wound up suing the former owner and the broker.

The whole thing was a disaster that could have been avoided if they had simply called and told the escrow company what they thought they were getting and the size of the lot, which they could have found out by having a surveyor physically locate the property lines from the legal, metes and bounds description before the escrow closed. If you buy a property through escrow, the seller has to give the escrow company a proper legal description. But not all states have escrow laws, so it is frequently incumbent on the buyer to obtain one independently. With real estate, you're buying the property based on the legal description, not on what you are told you're getting. To see the legal description of the lot, simply visit the county recorder's office and make a copy of the deed. If it's too complicated, have a professional read and interpret it for you. If there's any doubt, hire a surveyor while the property's in escrow, and put up some flags so you know where the property's going to be before the deal closes.

To estimate lot boundaries, look at the telephone poles. Usually, they're located on the property lines, but not always. Sometimes you can see the pins in the street or in the sidewalk where the surveyors have laid them. In California, surveyors put their numbers on their surveying pins so a record of the survey can be kept with the local City Hall.

I once bought a three-unit place and discovered that one of the units encroached on the side yard of somebody else's property. When I made an offer, I wrote on the deposit receipt what I thought the dimensions of the property were. The owners counteroffered, saying that the lot was bigger, and that they wanted more. So I said, "Okay, I'll buy it at your price if it is bigger, but I'll buy it at my price if it's smaller." Needless to say, I bought it at my price, which was 20 percent lower than theirs, because they didn't know what they were talking about. They were desperate to sell and couldn't find another buyer.

You know, there is no substitute for knowledge. Everybody has an opinion on what to do, but you have to be right on your facts. The sellers of that property were probably told what the size was when they bought the place and assumed that it was the honest truth. But it didn't matter. I did my research and proved them wrong. I even brought them a tract map to illustrate my point. If you find an encroachment, always try to make an adjustment in the price.

In 1968, my brother Paul decided to buy a four-unit building, which we spent considerable time investigating because the city claimed that it was legally a three-unit. After intensive negotiations with the owner, my brother was able to get the seller to lower his required down payment. My brother wound up buying the property for $65,000 with $5,000 down—only 8 percent of the purchase price. As my brother was strapped for cash at the time, I loaned him the down payment. In December 1970, my brother's health was failing, and he asked me to take over the property for the $5,000 debt. Eventually, I was able to prove to the city that the property was a legitimate four-unit apartment building and not a bootlegged triplex with an illegal fourth unit.

Just as you want to be sure that there are no legal discrepancies or encroachments on your property, you also want to ensure that you are not encroaching on somebody else's property. A stairway once encroached onto a property I bought in Hermosa Beach by about a foot and a half. After I made the purchase, the people who had built the stairway put their property up for sale. I didn't think it would cause much concern, so I asked the owners to remove the thing. They told me that they had a right to it and that I could go jump in the ocean. Finally, they sold their property, and the new owner and I got together: I paid him $1,500 to have it removed. That was a cheap price to pay, because after that I was able to get the necessary permits to build a new house.

The document on the following page will give you an idea of what I have been referring to. It is a legal metes and bounds description of a 54-foot by 194-foot property zoned for multiple residential building.

That portion of the Rancho Paso de Bartolo, in the County of Los Angeles, state of California, as per map recorded in Book 5, Page 318, et seq., of Patents, in the office of the County Recorder of said county, described as follows:

Commencing at the intersection of the center line of King Lane, with the Southerly prolongation of the Westerly line of Third Avenue, as said center line and said Westerly line were known on October 1, 1919; thence Northerly along the Westerly line 469.924 feet to the true point of beginning; thence Westerly parallel with said center line of King Lane, 194.35 feet, thence Northerly parallel with said Westerly line of Third Avenue, 54.481 feet, thence Easterly parallel with said center line of King Lane, 194.35 feet to said Westerly line of Third Avenue, 54,481 feet to the true point of beginning.

EXCEPT an undivided one-half interest in and to all of the oil, gas or other hydrocarbon substances, in, under or which may be produced from the herein described land for a period of 10 years from and after the date hereof, provided, however, that in case said land is under lease at the expiration of said 10 years then and in that event this reservation shall extend to such time as said lease shall be canceled and after the expiration of said period of 10 years or extended time, then said interest hereby reserved shall terminate and cease and shall ipso facto pass to and vest in fee in said grantee, her heirs, devisees and assigns forever, provided, further, that no present or future reservation is made of lease and/or land rentals or bonuses with the expiration of 6 months rental theretofore, received, which is retained in its entirety by said grantors, as reserved by John Doe and wife in deed registered on November 19, 1946, as Document No. 50010-0.

ALSO EXCEPT therefrom that portion included within a strip of land 50 feet wide, the Easterly line of which is the center line of Third Avenue, as said center line is shown on Map of Tract No. 617592, recorded in Book 424, Pages 20 and 21, of Maps, in the office of said recorder, as conveyed to the County of Los Angeles by deed recorded on February 10, 1967, as Instrument No. 5483.

8

Forecast Your Property's Market Value in 20 Years Based on Available Data

In the last chapter, we discussed how to select the right property and make an analysis of its growth potential. The next step in determining a property's growth potential is to make a long-range forecast of its market value in 20 years based on available data. Long-range forecasting basically entails making an analysis of a property's anticipated value by carefully considering the factors that influence its long-term worth. By analyzing the economic and environmental factors affecting a property, it is possible to project its future market value and, hence, its attractiveness as an investment.

Successfully investing in real estate requires a long-term outlook that isn't subject to the ups and downs of short-lived adjustment periods. By evaluating what's happened to a given market in the past and making a realistic projection based on available data, it is possible to predict future market value. In fact, it is often easier to predict the market value of a piece of real estate 20 years from now than its value next year or the year after.

An appraiser I knew was asked in the early 1920s by Northwestern Mutual Life Insurance Company to make a 50-year projection of the Stevens Hotel on Michigan Avenue in Chicago, which was at that time the largest hotel in the world. It was interesting. I talked to the guy in 1970, and, although he couldn't foresee the Great Depression, he had come very close to predicting the current market value of that property. About the only factors he didn't take into consideration were the subsequent dips in the economy, which he had no way of knowing.

Even so, he was able to predict the long-range market value of that property because he had researched the growth pattern of the area and knew that hotels were going to be popular and that commerce would be coming to Chicago in the Roaring Twenties. The second-largest city in the United States at the time, Chicago was a boom town and so it wasn't any major job to make an estimate. But the dips in between 1920 and 1970 were such that the original owner of the hotel wound up losing it in a downturn.

The first step in putting together a forecast is to gather all the information pertinent to a specific site's growth potential. There are numerous factors that are important to consider when forecasting a property's future market value. These include:

- Local population trends
- Average family income level and its projected growth or decline
- Local and regional economic trends
- Comparable property values ("comps")
- Past real estate appreciation rates
- City redevelopment plans
- Applicable zoning ordinances
- Local street-widening and public works projects
- Utility improvement plans
- School enrollment projections
- Plans for new civic and/or commercial developments that will enhance the community such as regional shopping centers, parks, schools, and recreation centers
- Plans for city or county annexations
- Plans to expand residential subdivisions
- Other relevant building, redevelopment, and real estate-related information that city and county planners can provide

A city is not going to put in more schools, parks, and utilities if it doesn't have a growth pattern. And if a city is going to expand, it must plan 5 or 10 years in advance. It can't expand without a growth plan, and such plans are a matter of public record. If you visit city hall and they don't even know what you're talking about, then you should go on to the next city.

Armed with this knowledge, you can then make an informed decision, one that is in your long-term interest. Remember, the best real estate investment strategy is the one that relies the least on chance and emotion and recognizes that patience above all else makes for profits—what you owe today you'll be worth tomorrow.

If you are willing to buy something and sit on it over the long haul, the odds of your losing are remote. But most people can't do that. They see a $500 profit and grab it. Or they think the whole thing is collapsing, so they run for it. The key is to find the right piece of property and not stick your neck out too far.

FAIR MARKET VALUE

Value is a nebulous concept that comes into play after you have inspected a property and are beginning to negotiate a deal. Fair market value is defined by *Barron's Dictionary of Real Estate Terms* as the theoretical highest price a buyer, willing but not compelled to buy, would pay, and the lowest price a seller, willing but not compelled to sell, would accept. Another definition of the market value of a building is the sum of money in which the presence of that structure adds to, or subtracts from, the value of the land it occupies, with the land being valued on the basis of its highest and best use.

As discussed in the previous chapters, there are any number of factors that affect value. Similarly, there are any number of *values* attached to a property. If you can isolate and segment the various values associated with a property, you will have the added advantage of being realistic when it comes to acquisition.

Buyers and sellers tend to cross lines: The seller usually will be sentimental, while the buyer is looking at fair market value—or less. In my experience, most sellers have some degree of sentimental attachment to their real estate, hence the reason that they price it too high when they put it on the market. But a lot of people don't know they are assigning a sentimental value to their property. Value is a personal matter. As discussed in Chapters 1 and 2, there is no absolute measure of how much a house will sell for because each property is unique and every buyer and seller brings different needs and objectives to the table.

In my opinion, the greatest gift a person can have is the ability to correctly estimate the value of things. I don't mean cost, I mean the personal value of things. Whether you're looking at a vintage automobile, a rare manuscript, or a piece of investment real estate, you have to be able to correctly estimate value.

If you're not able to estimate value, you're going to be left out in the cold. You won't be able to live in the real world if, for instance, you can't correctly estimate the value of your time. If you work for free all the time, you might go broke, end up homeless, or at the very least watch passively as your neighbor gets rich.

To reemphasize an important point, values are created and destroyed by the actions, attitudes, and thinking of people. So if the majority of people think a piece of property is valuable, it is. And that's all that matters.

Value is something in the mind. If a lot of people start thinking an area is no good, then real estate prices plummet.

Look at Germany: The biggest problem that the government has had in integrating East Germany and West Germany hasn't been the monetary system; it has been the attitudes and values of people, the way they behave and think about each other. Because the attitudes of people determine value, the value of real property, as well as business activities, in the eastern part of the country will remain low. It may take decades for people on the two different sides to get back on good terms and truly understand one another.

The following chart shows the values that may be established on a property at a given time. Values appear in the overall formula many times: during the purchasing and financing of real estate, while projecting its long-term worth and value, and then at varying intervals during the ownership period, especially for refinancing and buying other properties. Assume the subject property is a two-story residence built in 1942 and currently being used as a rooming house on a lot zoned for multiple residential building.

Property: a 50-year-old, 3,000-square-foot residence used for a rooming house on a lot zoned for multiple residential.

Land value (assumed vacant)	$150,000
Construction cost	$100/square foot
Replacement cost	$300,000
Income yield	$2,880/month
Fair market value	$240,000

Although the property might only list for $240,000 (at fair market value), there are numerous values worth considering:

Whole property:

$450,000	Replacement cost value (land and improvements)
380,000	Replacement value
330,000	Physical value
310,000	Summation value
250,000	Comparison sales value
240,000	Fair Market value
220,000	Condemnation value
200,000	Income value
190,000	Cash value
180,000	Mortgage loan value

Whole property *(Continued)* :

170,000	Forced sale value
120,000	Inheritance value
90,000	Historic cost
60,000	Assessed value

Construction only:

$300,000	Replacement cost
260,000	Replacement insurable value
230,000	Replacement value
180,000	Sound value
150,000	Sound insurable value
50,000	Book value
20,000	Salvage value

Land only:

$150,000	Vacant
130,000	Improved

Other values to consider:

Catastrophe value	Sentimental value
Going concern value	Liquidation value
Goodwill value	Nuisance value
Improvement value	Plottage value
Leasehold value	Rental value
Charity value	Leased fee value
Use value	

When I was teaching real estate courses, I used this type of example to emphasize the different values that can be applied to a property at a given time. A real estate investor should be aware of the various values associated with the subject property. The most important thing about an appraisal is its purpose. You have to know what the problem is. If an appraiser doesn't know what the problem or need is, or the type of value to be determined in the appraisal, he or she could make an improper analysis—the result could be disastrous.

When buying a property, location is the most important factor. You can't change the land or the surrounding area, but you can always replace or modify the building to counteract physical deterioration and functional absolescence, such as a poor floor plan or outdated amenities. As a property ages, economic obsolescence—the loss of value from all causes outside the property itself—becomes far more significant than physical deterioration and functional obsolescence because it affects the value of real estate more dramatically.

Economic obsolescence, or depreciation, is caused by factors that you as an individual property owner have little or no control over. These include the condition of the economy, interest rates, increased taxes, water shortages, smog, traffic congestion, crime rates, plant closings, and so on. There is more money lost because of economic obsolescence than there is from physical deterioration and functional obsolescence put together.

I mention this so that you may begin to think like an appraiser. Just as an appraiser needs to know the problem or need associated with a job, so should the investor think about a purpose for the subject property. What do you expect to do with your investment? If you buy real estate for the long term, maybe you can afford to pay a little more, especially if that property has some special, unique value.

Before I purchased the property next door to the six-unit apartment building I live in, I determined that it possessed several values above and beyond fair market value that affected me personally. To begin with, the owner of the property was an absentee landlord who let a real estate broker or property manager rent the place out. As a result, they would rent to four guys, or to two guys and two girls, just to keep the place occupied. It was an "animal house" year-round. When I moved in, I figured that I *had* to buy the building next door. It was either that or move inland. I didn't have any choice. It was an intolerable situation, even for me.

It took me a few years to acquire the property, but when I bought it, my problem was solved. Besides having control over the occupants, I can also collect the rent very easily. I've since painted the two buildings the same color scheme and have torn down the wall and made a common patio area. Because it was so ideal and easy for me to manage, I was willing to pay more for that property than I was for my original building, even though it was probably worth less.

That building is more valuable to me than it is to anybody. Considering all the added values, it was a purchase worth every penny. Not only was there nuisance value and rental value, there was also use value, improvement value, and even plottage value associated with that purchase because of the common patio area and similar design of the two buildings. Although I really couldn't afford to buy the place, I also couldn't afford not to. I just made up my mind that I had to do it and figured out a way.

Similarly, somebody can have a great interest in a wilderness cabin in Idaho, a property that is not going to particularly increase in value but that can still have an added increment of desirability and escape value to the person buying it.

The following is a list of the many attributes to consider in the analysis of a property before you make the final offer and purchase.

Physical Value

- Valuation of the land, independent of improvements
- Replacement cost of the improvements
- Depreciation of the improvements, based on age and physical condition; also, functional and economic obsolescence

Earning Value (income)

- Capitalization of net income
- Speculation
- Goodwill value of an established location

Effect of Supply and Demand

- Number of similar properties recently sold
- Number of similar properties on the market
- Advantages of good design and arrangement
- Harmony with surrounding improvements
- Any known demand for similar properties
- Any evident scarcity of similar properties

Values That Exist in the Mind of the Buyer

- General appearance of land and improvements
- Advantages of good arrangement and design
- Harmony with surrounding improvements
- Peculiarities in design (advantages or detriments)
- Sentiment in buyer
- Social advantages of neighborhood

Suitability of Improvements to Land and Location

- Whether improvements are too large and costly or too small and cheap for the location and land
- Whether land might be used for something more profitable
- Apparent trend of neighborhood development and future possibilities
- Interior and exterior design and fitting
- Extent to which district is developed and possibly changed

I once assigned an exercise to my students to make a hypothetical projection of what they thought the fair market value of a certain single family residence in West Los Angeles should be after 20 years.

Most of my students concluded that the property would be torn down and overtaken by an industrial development or a high-rise office or apartment building. It wasn't. And yet that's the way most people think—

that a property will reach a certain plateau and not go up any higher. What you have to do is make a comparison of like properties in similar areas. The best way to project what a property is going to be worth 20 years later is to find an area that had similar characteristics 20 years previously and research what happened to it from the standpoint of growth.

When I was doing appraisal work, part of my job was to do retrospective appraisals determining the market value of a property 20 or 30 years before. I once did an interesting appraisal of the Hamburger Realty Company estate at Eighth Street and Broadway in downtown Los Angeles, the site of the original May Co. department store. When the May Co. assumed the lease on the property, company executives wanted to build three stories higher.

Our job was to determine the market value of the Hamburger estate asset as of July 1, 1913, the date when federal income tax laws went into effect in the United States. They wanted to sell the estate, and in order to do so they needed to figure out their basis, or purchase price, as of July 1, 1913 to determine the amount of capital gains the Hamburgers would have to pay taxes on. The appraisal was prepared in 1960. Obviously, by that time, the building at Eighth and Broadway had been completely remodeled into a six-story department store. The Hamburger estate owned the land, plus the first three floors of the building, which is what we had to determine the fair market value of. We did it mainly by reading the classified sections of old newspapers and by looking up old grant deeds from the title company. Real estate appraising is not an exact science. Facts and data are gathered and analyzed to form an opinion of value.

Appraisers use three basic methods of estimating fair market value: the cost approach, market approach, and income approach. The cost approach is based on the depreciated replacement cost of improvements, plus the market value of the site. The market approach uses the sales prices of similar properties that have been recently sold to determine value. And the income approach bases value on the property's anticipated future net income. The three different approaches provide a framework for evaluating different properties. Table 8.1 outlines the approaches.

When making an investment decision, I consider the three approaches to the extent that they help quantify the value of the subject property. The type of approach used depends on the nature of the subject property. But, as given in Table 8.1, each method of evaluation has built-in pitfalls, or disadvantages.

The cost approach is practical if you have a building that has just been built, because you know the value of the land and the cost of construction and can separate them. If that building is the highest and best use of the land, then the cost approach can, with some degree of accuracy, determine the property's fair market value.

TABLE 8.1
Estimating Fair Market Value Using the Three Approaches

Cost Approach	Market Approach	Income Approach
Property is divided into segments (land and construction); each segment is valued separately.	Analysis of comparable sales of whole properties.	Analysis of net income, proper capitalization rate, and method of processing income.

An analysis of market data is necessary to estimate the following factors reasonably:

Land value
Construction costs
All forms of
   depreciation
	Adjustments of comparable sales	Gross income
		Vacancy and collection
		   loss
		All expenses
		Capitalization rate
		Capitalization technique

Pitfalls	Pitfalls	Pitfalls
1. Estimating land value independent of construction.	1. Locating enough similar properties that have recently sold to indicate a value.	1. Estimating future gross income, vacancy allowance, and all recurring expenses.
2. Estimating new construction costs.	2. Adjusting amenities to make them comparable to the subject property.	2. Employing the proper capitalization technique.
3. Estimating accrued depreciation.	3. Adjusting sales for down payment and terms.	3. Determining method of net income capitalization.

Correlation of the three approaches and the final demand-analysis estimate is generally a matter of experience and judgment based on factual data.

Generally speaking, though, the cost approach is the weakest of the three approaches. Excepting new developments, how can you value a piece of land independent of the improvement? The improvement, or actual building, has a direct bearing on the value of the land. Since there is no measure in the market to use for comparisons, the only thing you can do is determine the depreciated replacement cost of the improvement. (See Chapter 14 for a discussion of depreciation.) Sometimes the cost approach is the only method you can use if you are valuing a school, government building, church, or specialized industrial or commercial property.

The market approach, generally employed by buyers and realtors for single family residences, apartment complexes, commercial properties, and general purpose industrial properties, analyzes the property in relation to comparable sales that occur in the surrounding area. The only effective way of determining market value of single family residences is by analyzing comparable sales. However, as discussed in Chapter 1, every piece of real estate is unique and heterogeneous. Consequently, there are no truly comparable sales or listings.

Because of this, the market approach requires adjustments for the land and building's size, location, age, setting, and a host of other factors, including the unique circumstances and terms of sales that are comparable. However, with all the facts that go into a transaction, it's very difficult to know whether you are truly analyzing a sale that is comparable. The seller might have increased the price to get better terms or might have been motivated to sell for less for personal reasons. You can never be sure.

The income approach derives an income stream from any type of property that yields a regular flow of money, such as an apartment building, hotel, office building, restaurant or business, shopping center, or leased industrial building. The question becomes, how much net income can you get from it? The net income is then capitalized into value using a capitalization rate commensurate with market conditions.

The income approach is generally reliable when appraising large income-producing complexes, such as office buildings, shopping centers, and the like. The income approach is generally unreliable when appraising duplexes, triplexes, and small income-producing buildings.

The fundamental reason for using the three approaches is that they bracket value, leaving the appraiser to use his or her expertise and best judgment in correlating one final estimate of market value. In addition, a market demand analysis should be made to estimate present and future demand for the subject property. (For a more detailed discussion of the three approaches and how a market demand analysis is employed in the appraisal process, see Appendix B.) As a buyer, you want to pay fair market value or less. But when you start to consider what a given property will do over the long haul and what it will be worth after 20 years, current values become irrelevant.

A person with foresight has to be sure not to overpay for a property, but at the same time not let a good opportunity slip away because the property is theoretically overpriced. In my opinion, if you can get desirable terms, you can afford to pay more than market value.

In the final analysis, you should pay the present worth of contemplated future benefits, in which case you could be prepared to pay more than market value. If you are right in your analysis, it doesn't make any difference. In 1963, I bought a four-unit apartment building for $35,000. Suppose I had paid $100,000 for it. It still wouldn't have made any difference because it's worth $1.2 million today. The key is to be right in your analysis of a property's growth potential.

As we have seen, there is no way to make an exact forecast. The only thing you can be assured of is that if you buy in an area with growth potential, there will continue to be increases in land values because growth in a capitalistic economy cannot exist without inflation. You can also be assured that there will be dips in the economy, but the overall trend will inevitably be up. No doubt about it. Think how empty the term *millionaire* is becoming. It takes several million dollars cash, in the bank, to be on a par with a simple millionaire of 20 years ago.

Table 8.2 shows the percent change in median sales prices of existing single family homes in selected metropolitan areas from 1981 to 1991, including the halfway mark of 1986.

TABLE 8.2
Median Sales Prices of Existing Single Family Homes

Metropolitan Area	1981	1986	1991	Percent Change from 1981 to 1991
Albuquerque, NM	62,100	81,600	83,200	34.0
Baltimore, MD	57,700	74,000	103,000	78.5
Baton Rouge, LA	69,600	71,000	63,100	−9.3
Boston, MA	70,000	159,200	161,900	131.3
Chicago, IL	70,300	86,100	107,500	52.9
Cincinnati, OH	52,100[a]	63,500	82,900	59.1
Dallas, TX	66,500	93,800	86,100	29.5
Denver, CO	66,600[a]	86,400	83,100	24.8
Des Moines, IA	52,500	55,900	62,500	19.0
Detroit, MI	48,500	58,100	78,400	61.6
Hartford, CT	81,400	129,000	146,400	79.9
Indianapolis, IN	49,700	59,000	76,600	54.1
Kansas City, MO	46,100	65,400	73,500	59.4
Las Vegas, NV	NA	77,500	98,200	26.7[c]
Los Angeles/ Long Beach, CA	111,400	135,800	203,900	83.0
Louisville, KY	45,600	51,600	64,400	41.2
Memphis, TN	55,900	70,600	82,400	47.4
Milwaukee, WI	64,500	69,900	87,100	35.0

TABLE 8.2
Median Sales Prices of Existing Single Family Homes *(Continued)*

Metropolitan Area	1981	1986	1991	Percent Change from 1981 to 1991
Minneapolis/ St. Paul, MN	69,700	77,900	90,500	29.8
New York/ New Jersey/ Long Island, NY	73,200	160,600	165,100	125.5
Oklahoma City, OK	54,100	63,000	54,300	.004
Omaha, NE	52,600[b]	58,800	65,100	23.8
Orlando, FL	59,600	72,500	82,800	38.9
West Palm Beach/ Boca Raton/ Delray Beach, FL	82,200	92,600	105,000	27.7
Philadelphia, PA	59,200	82,400	106,100	79.2
Phoenix, AZ	70,900	78,400	84,000	18.5
Portland, OR	59,600[a]	62,600	84,800	42.3
Providence, RI	50,000	87,600	125,200	150.4
Riverside/San Bernardino, CA	79,600	92,100	133,300	67.5
Rochester, NY	45,900	68,300	78,400	70.8
Sacramento, CA	73,100	82,900	135,300	85.1
Salt Lake City/ Ogden, UT	62,900	68,500	69,400	10.3
San Antonio, TX	53,600	69,200	59,500	11.0
San Diego, CA	97,400	118,500	181,900	86.8
San Francisco Bay Area, CA	121,600	166,200	244,800	101.3
Seattle/Tacoma, WA	65,200[a]	90,100[a]	133,100	104.1
St. Louis, MO	57,000[b]	70,900	77,100	35.3
Syracuse, NY	43,200	64,300	79,200	83.3
Tulsa, OK	59,200	65,500	65,500	10.6
Wahington, DC/ Maryland/Virginia	88,300	101,600	145,500	64.8

[a] Figure used is an estimate.
[b] Figure used is for 1982, not 1981.
[c] Figure represents the percent change from 1986 to 1991.
NA = not available.
Sources: National Association of Realtors; California Association of Realtors; *Annual Housing Survey.*

As mentioned elsewhere, it is very difficult to make decisions without adequate knowledge. I recommended in Chapter 7 to buy a big map of the subject area and keep track of every development affecting the market value. This methodical system has helped me enormously over the years.

―――――――

Another important thing is to get expert advice from people you can count on. The only way you get this advice is by talking with people who are knowledgeable and have experience. But it doesn't have to cost a lot of money. When I started investing in real estate, I had just lost all of my money in the commodities market, so I couldn't afford to hire anybody. While speculating in commodities, I followed other people's advice. After losing all my money, I decided that if I was going to lose again, at least it would be my own doing, not somebody else's.

So instead of hiring a lawyer to write my contracts, I went to night school and learned from an attorney who taught the class how to write them myself. I also took classes in accounting, plumbing, electrical work, property management, just about everything that was germane to my business. When you start dealing with professionals at $135 per hour, you run out of money pretty fast. And you may not always get what you're looking for.

There are so many ways of getting informed, intelligent answers and advice from professionals that costs next to nothing. You'd be surprised how many people will give cheap or free knowledge. A friend of mine who is a fellow investor is an expert on that. He goes to a class and waits until it's over before he approaches the instructor to ask a question. He rarely enrolls in the class, but the instructors never know because there are so many students there for just one night.

―――――――

When I was teaching, I used to have my students bring in their questions, and I would do everything I could to research the answers for them. Knowledge is powerful, but I've never in my life hesitated to share my knowledge with anyone who asked. I never felt there was much that was really confidential. Everything I know I've learned from other people, so the least I can do is pass it on.

A guy who teaches school will answer any question you want because he's not teaching to make money, he's teaching to help people. In a school setting, instructors are more than willing to transmit their knowledge, which they learned from other people, to someone else. But in a business setting, there's a fee associated with giving advice.

The last thing in the world I would do is hire a bunch of consultants to tell me what to do. I don't think they know anything more about it than someone who is willing to do the homework. And if something went wrong, what would they care as long as you paid them their fee? If you hire an accountant for a real complicated tax return, the odds are 1000 to 5 that he's going to protect his interests and work out that tax return so that *he* won't get into a problem. He's not going to bend over backward for *you*. It just isn't likely to happen.

If you are going to be successful in anything, it has to be *you*, not the thinking and actions of your attorney, accountant, or broker. If you need information or advice, there is nobody in the world who won't help you if you show a genuine interest. If you show honest concern, people will go out of their way to help you, unless you're talking about taking someone's commission away, which is rarely the case. Rather than hire people to advise you, why not take a class in real estate, appraising, or property management to help get you started in buying and investing?

When I wasn't teaching one of my own courses, I'd enroll in a class. In today's world, you really have to keep studying all the time just to stay even. Not only that, I love to listen to what other people have to say. My mother used to say that the best thing you can do is keep your mouth shut and listen. If you can do that, you'll not only know what you know, you'll also know what the other person knows.

Another way to get good information is by attending all the round table discussions on real estate you can. There's always someone there to give you an idea on what to do. I used to attend real estate investment or appraisal courses, talk to the instructors, and find out how they keep up with what's going on. You can even form a discussion group yourself. It only takes two or three people to get together for breakfast or lunch every few weeks to bounce ideas off each other. You never know: the results could be astounding.

Will Rogers used to say he never met a man he didn't like. Well, I never met anybody I didn't get a good idea from.

Whenever I attend professional meetings for such groups as the Society of Real Estate Appraisers, National Association of Independent Fee

Appraisers, Certified Business Brokers Association, Certified Commercial Investment Members (CCIM), and the like, I get very enthused because the people who attend those meetings are knowledge-seekers who want to learn and get somebody else's opinion. When I was the president of the Southern California chapter of the CCIM and the president of the Independent Fee Appraisers, Southern California chapter, I would go around the room and have everybody share what they thought were good ideas and worthwhile experiences. The brokers, appraisers, and investors who attend these functions are the ones who stay up with the facts. They're in the forefront. They're the ones who have ideas.

When I was active, I always wondered why the people who attended all the meetings and seminars were always successful, and the people who were on the lower end of the spectrum, who had beer and chicken surprise for dinner rather than champagne and caviar, were the ones who never attended. Even if you only want to invest in real estate as a sideline, you can still become active as an associate member of a professional group.

The best thing you can do to develop an effective investment program is learn all you can, be willing to put yourself at some risk, use your own ingenuity, and make your decisions based on a thorough examination of the facts.

9

Time Your Investment to Get a Boost from the Economy

As mentioned in the Introduction, almost everyone I talk to both in and out of real estate has a story about how they could have made millions if they only knew 10 or 20 years ago that property values were destined to skyrocket. This familiar tale is told countless times from coast-to-coast whenever real estate experiences a boom similar to the heady price gains of the mid- to late 1980s. But rather than acting on their impulses, the vast majority of investors and real estate onlookers sit by enviously as others get rich and achieve financial security.

The right timing can enable you to buy low and in a few years' time see your property significantly appreciate in value. In 1982, during the height of the last recession, the median selling price of a single family home on the Palos Verdes Peninsula, a prime residential community in the South Bay area of Los Angeles, was $313,000. In 1989, the median price had more than doubled, to $665,000. Timing can indeed pay off. But the willingness to take some risk is equally important in deciding when to buy and how much to pay. Whatever you do, just be sure not to overextend yourself.

In a capitalistic economy, ups and downs—recessionary and inflationary spirals—are unavoidable. As an investor, you just have to hope that they're not too deep or too severe. But if you're looking at the long run, your experience, knowledge, and ability can compensate for the dips and act as a bulwark against financial ruin. Still, you have to foresee the changes ahead and put yourself in a position where you won't get knocked out of the box. I've owned my residence for 30 years, but if I wasn't able to make the payments on this house, the lender would foreclose on it just as quickly as anything.

Most people don't understand enough about investing in real estate to buy at the right time. Real estate goes in cycles. There are fantastic buys during the height of a boom and there are some terrible buys at the beginning of a recession. In general, the best time to buy is during a lull when people are anxious and prepared to bargain.

When there is a recession, the downturn doesn't affect all parts of the country in the same way. But when there is inflation, which occurs when the economy is in a growth mode, it affects all parts of the country equally. Consequently, it is easier to find a bargain during a downturn than an inflationary period because during a downturn sellers in soft markets are willing to accept less than what the market had previously borne.

Recessionary conditions that cause soft markets are really the best time for able investors to buy real estate. The reason is mainly that slow sales result in a large inventory of available properties. And when there is a glut of listings, competition forces sellers to make concessions they might not otherwise make. In a downmarket, it is easier to make a deal because sellers are eager to bargain. Such concessions might include:

- Deferring mortgage payments
- Accepting better terms
- Carrying a second mortgage
- Accepting a short-term, interest-only note
- Improving the condition of the property
- Lowering the asking price

Of all the above variables, I would worry the least about price. I figure that if I'm buying the property in the right location, I can afford to pay market value if I've done my homework. We're looking at the value of property as a long-term investment, so we're not particularly concerned about what we pay for it. We're more concerned about its growth potential and buying on the way up.

It's fine to buy property when it's available and when you can buy it, but it's a bonus if you can get an added boost from the economy by having the right timing. As discussed in Chapter 4, there are all kinds of data available to determine the health of the economy—reports by the Commerce Department, from the Federal Reserve, the trends revealed by leading economic indicators, and so on. Based on the information available at the national, regional, and local levels, you have to determine in your own mind how the economy's going to respond.

If you read the papers, every time there's a downturn you'll notice that there's a lot of gloomy prognostications of how the market is going to collapse. Those of us who have lived through the Depression and have seen all the recessions that followed know that the market has never done that and there's no reason why it will. Despite limited setbacks, the economy has adhered to a strong growth pattern since World War II and will continue to grow in the future, spurring continued investment in real estate.

How do you know when the country is reaching the end of a recession? Well, let me pose another question. How do you recognize the end of a boom? Economists, the supposed gurus of free enterprise, are always divided on these important questions, and they're all intelligent. The slowdown of the real estate market in late 1989 took a lot of people, including the industry experts, by surprise. In the final analysis, there is no exact formula for determining what is going to happen. Before the end of the Cold War, how could you have known that the Berlin Wall would collapse even six months before it did? In the summer of 1990, no one was able to predict that Iraq would invade Kuwait—not even the CIA!

Despite the unpredictable character of modern life, there still are some general rules to abide by when investing in real estate:

- Evaluate factors that affect economic strength and weakness. When you detect weakness, don't buy.
- If you detect signs of an upturn, start to invest. Acquire as much as possible—sacrifice today will be rewarded tomorrow—but don't spend money on land and improvements unless you can see a return in rent.
- When prices soar so high because of appreciation that you can't afford to buy any more, start putting money into fixing up the properties that you already own.

The best time that anybody can make a real estate investment is when you can see change, namely, when you can see change for the better. We live in a world of change and the more dramatic the changes are, the more golden the opportunities will be. Look at all the possibilities that opened up by the collapse of communism in eastern Europe and the former Soviet Union. But the more dramatic the change, the more risky it can be. Generally speaking, changes are beneficial to real estate values if they are positive in nature.

Take the 13-story Fidelity Building, an old landmark in downtown Los Angeles on the corner of Fifth and Spring streets. Around 1926, you could have purchased that building for about $2 million. But by 1932, with the Depression, most of the tenants who were occupying it had moved out. It was 65 percent vacant. Whoever held it at that time would have lost the building because they would not have been able to pay the taxes, insurance, or upkeep with such a terrible situation of office vacancies.

But if you had purchased that same building in 1944, you could have bought it for maybe $1 million with very little down because of all the vacancies. By 1946, after the war was over, the downtown business scene started booming and rents doubled and tripled. By 1948, the value of that property probably shot up to $5 million.

Timing your investment to get a boost from the economy can be very advantageous. Inflation can make a foolhardy investor look like a wise man because he has hopped on the bandwagon of ascending land values. But an investment made before or during a depression can make a wise man look like a fool, and there is nothing anyone can do about it.

If you had bought a property in 1945 at market value and benefited from the economy of the late 1940s and 1950s with our industrial buildup, you wouldn't have had to know anything. You couldn't have missed. But, if you had bought a property in 1928 and even paid below market for it, there is no way you could have held on to it because of the Depression.

The only way you can know whether the time is right or not is by doing research. But even after you gather all the data, listen to all the lectures, and do everything else, you have to go with your gut feeling of what you think is going to happen. To take advantage of what's going to happen, you have to make a decision to act. Most people are afraid to try. Yet if you act on your knowledge rather than procrastinate, you won't be watching from the sidelines as others make their fortunes.

Imagine the investor who could go to Texas today and buy a 72-unit apartment building for $10,000 a unit, or whatever the going rates are, with $50,000 or $100,000 down. If it is done right and the market starts to heat up, which it will, the property value and rents could go up with it. And if we have prosperity like we could have over the next 20 years and the investor has a structured activity in which he or she just sticks to a pattern of making the payments and fixing and maintaining the building, he or she will be wealthy in 20 years. I think the best time to take a chance is when you're young, so if it doesn't work out you can start over again and not be set back for life.

Central to an effective strategy is determining the proper time to make an investment. Do you know what the only difference between salad and garbage is? Timing. In the above example of the Fidelity Building, it wouldn't have made any difference how smart you are if you had bought that property in the early days. You would have lost it because you couldn't have made the payments. But, if you had purchased it in 1945, it wouldn't have made any difference how informed or misinformed you were. As long as you were in the right position at the right time, you would have made a killing. This is an extreme example, but there are trends like this all the time during which you can get this extra push.

It seems self-evident that the U.S. economy will experience favorable growth over the next three decades. The tremendous need for entrepreneurial services as well as all types of goods and materials available in America will put the United States in the dominant position to help stabilize the economies of formerly communist countries. The United States has an historic opportunity to take advantage of this foreseeable global economic activity. And, I believe, the cities and communities that will be the main beneficiaries of this increased activity are those with information industries, high-technology centers, and business services that can produce these results.

BEING AT THE RIGHT PLACE AT THE RIGHT TIME

M y mother was extra bright when it came to real estate. One time when I was about 18 my brother and I saved some money and were thinking of buying a new Chevrolet. We had about $500 combined. When we were ready to put our money down on the car, my mother told us, "You guys are making a big mistake." So we held on to our money. The next Sunday, we drove down to Hermosa Beach, where my parents had a summer cottage, and found a two-unit building not too far from the water, which was listed for $7,000. The seller wanted $500 down.

My mother said, "That's the thing to spend your money on. If you buy this place, in just a few years that piece of real estate will buy your car for you." So that's exactly what we did. We subsequently rented it out and in a couple of years we not only had a place of our own but a new car to drive around in as well. Our timing was superb because we bought it just before the second World War. When all the influx of population came into this area to help with the war effort, combined with the industrial base that was in place, there was a huge demand.

———————

I mentioned the advantages of buying during a recession. But, when it comes down to it, I don't think it makes any difference when you buy as long as you don't overextend yourself. Provided that your area is going to have continued growth and you don't have any balloon payments to make, you can survive through a downturn. With units that are not rentable, you may have to come up with innovative ways to find tenants.

When negotiating a real estate transaction, you're dealing with two individuals, so what the economy is like may not make all that much difference on a personal level. Pay attention to economic trends, but judge them in general terms.

———————

I n 1975, a friend of mine who was a school teacher wanted to buy a house. We found a single family residence for her for $65,000. The owner said he wanted 10 percent down, or $6,500. So my friend got the money, and we made an offer for slightly less. We decided to make an offer with a set of harsh conditions and try to extract every concession we could. We wanted the owner to carry the second mortgage for 10 years for about three points below the going market rate with no interest payments for the first two years. We asked for the range, the refrigerator, the washer, dryer, all the appliances, just about everything but the kitchen sink. From a buyer's point of view, it was perfect. But we knew the owner would have a negative first reaction.

So we put the offer in his mailbox, and I told my friend not to answer the phone for two days in order to let the seller think about the deal. At first, buyers are furious, then they're mad, then they look at their situation and realize they're not getting anybody else. After a few days he called and said, "Well, I don't know—I can't let you take my washer and dryer." That's what he was concerned about. He wasn't upset about the really important thing, the 30-year note with only 5-percent interest. We wound up buying that property for $61,000. You just never know what the other person is thinking.

———————

At some time in a person's life, real estate can become a burden; if you get there at that time, it's amazing what can happen. If, say, a couple owns some rental property in one area, and they live a distance away, and they're having trouble keeping the place up or keeping it rented, then that property has become a burden for them. A burden of that sort can easily become a bargain for you. That may not be timing your investment to get a boost from the economy, but it is being at the right place at the right time nevertheless.

———

One time we were going to buy some property, a single family residence in Sylmar, a community about 25 miles north of Los Angeles. The owner wanted $165,000 for it, but I didn't think it was worth that much, so I hired an appraiser, and he appraised the place at $100,000. I went to the owner and told him what I thought it was worth, but he was adamant and said, "No, I want to sell it for $165,000."

Sizing up my position, I said, "Okay, I'll give you $20,000 down if you agree to carry back a $145,000 first mortgage with no interest. All payments have to go toward principal." Miraculously, he agreed. Being an honest guy, I told him he was crazy because, in essence, he was selling it for the equivalent of about $75,000 with interest at eight or 10 percent. He said, "No I'm not. That's what I want." Apparently, he owned the property free and clear. He probably wanted to tell his brother-in-law in New York that he got $165,000 for the place, but his brother-in-law wasn't going to ask him what the terms were. It just goes to show that everybody has a different way of looking at things, different thinking completely.

———

It also proves that every property, and every situation, in real estate is unique. No two parcels are exactly alike, and no two buyers or sellers are exactly alike. You can never be sure of the attitudes, needs, and desires of people. What might be absolutely fantastic to one person might be unacceptable to someone else. The only way to uncover the problems is to make an offer on the property. Then you begin to understand what the sellers want out of it, why they have to leave, where they're going, and what price they need to sell for.

Making an offer is the quickest way I know of getting to the heart of the problem, learning the seller's true motives, and negotiating the best possible deal for yourself. As we'll see in the next chapter, the terms of sale and the size of the down payment are far more important than the purchase price.

PERSONAL TIMING

I think it's just awful when people are too finicky. While I was teaching, a student of mine called me up one day and said he was trying to buy a house in Newport Beach, California, which he had found for $375,000. He said he had been looking for almost two years in this particular area. He was raving about the place, the view it had, how his kids liked it. It sounded tremendous. But, he added, with his family, his monthly payments, and everything else, he couldn't justify spending more than $325,000. He was in a quandary.

So I said to him, "Why don't you sit down and just think it over for five minutes. You're quibbling about $50,000 when you know the value of that property will double in six or seven years. Why don't you work out the payments, and adjust the terms?" Price is not the most important thing at times. I know he would have lost that opportunity if I hadn't told him to buy. I've spoken to him since. He says the property's worth about $700,000 now. The problem is that most people won't take your advice unless you hold them by the hand.

About 20 years ago, I had some friends who were renting a duplex in West Los Angeles. They lived in the front unit and shared the premises with the tenants in the back unit. The owner, who wanted to sell the place, had listed the property on the market for $65,000. My friends were afraid that if he sold the place they would be forced to move. So I told them, "You have to buy this place." They said they couldn't afford to. They had managed to save up a couple of thousand dollars, but the husband had just lost his job. But I said there was absolutely no way they could afford *not to* buy it.

With a little prodding, the wife ended up borrowing some money from her mother and they managed to do it. I helped them negotiate a deal and now they send me thank you notes every Christmas. Every year they write: "Thank you, thank you! You don't know what you did for us!" Now their place is worth three quarters of a million dollars.

Whatever you do in this world is a risk, but some of these real estate deals are no more risky than things you do in your everyday life. If my friends in the above example hadn't taken that risk, they wouldn't have had a place to live in, let alone a solid investment, appreciating asset, and source of rental income. They would have had to find some other vehicle to put their kids through college and become financially secure.

10

Negotiate the Purchase Considering It to Be a Long-Term Investment

Great real estate deals are not found; they are created. Finding a good real estate investment is not a matter of luck; it's being able to act when you should. Once you have identified a neighborhood with growth potential, you can find a bargain that fits your needs. You can work maybe six or nine months to find a good bargain, but all you have to do is find one good buy a year—or not even that much. I believe that if I really put my mind to it, I could walk around the city block where I live and find a good bargain from someone who was anxious to sell.

Of course, what might be a bargain for me might not be a bargain for the guy next door. But there's probably somebody close by who wants to sell. And if you approach them in the right way, explain your position, and find a seller with the right circumstances, you probably can do very well.

You should always negotiate the terms of a transaction considering your purchase to be a long-term investment. There are various factors to consider and strategies to employ before ever making an offer on a piece of property, including, most significantly, buying properties with maximum write-off potential and obtaining seller financing.

Seller-assisted financing is the most desirable situation when buying because it enables the buyer to customize the terms and conditions of the deal. For instance, if the seller agrees to "carry paper"—accepting partial payment in the form of a promissory note—you can insert a clause on the note that allows you to pay off the mortgage at the current fair market value of the note. This can result in a tremendous savings advantage if interest rates rise dramatically during the payment period.

A deed of trust, which is used in many states in lieu of a mortgage, refers to a negotiable note that is worth cash. The note is a written instrument that places a lien on real estate as security for the payment of a specified debt. In the contract offer to purchase, the buyer can write whatever terms he or she thinks the seller will agree to.

In addition, the offer should include clauses guaranteeing that the building is legally located on the subject parcel and that it does not encroach onto adjacent property. I once bought a property and wrote into the terms of the first mortgage the option of tearing down the building on the premises without affecting the value of the note.

Certain items are not permitted, however. For instance, the buyer isn't permitted to allow the property taxes or insurance to become delinquent, to underinsure the property, to let the property run down, and so on. There is a whole series of guidelines in the trust deed or mortgage. If the borrower doesn't comply with these rules, including making the payments, the lender can call the note and initiate foreclosure proceedings. Even if you make the payments on time, the other requirements have to be complied with. When slumlords run into legal difficulties, it's more often because they haven't abided by health and safety rules, rather than the fact that they are in arrears in their payments.

When negotiating a real estate transaction, the size of the down payment and terms of sale are far more important than the purchase price. The asking price, as mentioned before, really doesn't matter that much as long as you know the area has substantial growth potential. Strive to negotiate a deal where you can live with the terms now, and grow more comfortable with them over a period of time. If the property is in the right location, eventually you won't worry about purchase price.

If, over a 40-year period, you have growth in an area that causes a property appraised at $100,000 to rise to $5 million, you can see how what you paid ceases to matter anymore. The important thing is to do your research to make sure that you've got the right location.

How the Down Payment and Terms of Sale
Are More Important Than the Purchase Price

Example: A commercial property is on the market for:

$200,000

The gross annual income on a substantial lease is:

$ 16,000

The property is owned free and clear. The owner is in the high tax bracket and also is burdened with available cash that he is required to invest. The owner asks you to make an offer on the property based on the following:

Minimum price $200,000
Minimum interest   8%
Maximum due date   9 years

Ideal Purchase
Here is the most ideal set of terms to offer:

- No down payment
- $200,000 first trust deed, carried by the owner for 9 years at 8 percent interest (a deferred mortgage loan)
- Interest to accumulate to principal and be due and payable in 9 years

The total balance due in 9 years would be:

$400,000

Undesirable purchase
A cash offer of:

$200,000

These are the two extremes. Now set the parameters for negotiation. Under the ideal purchase, you could collect substantial rents, watch property value appreciate, and in nine years refinance it and satisfy your debt to the previous owner.

AVAILABILITY OF FINANCING

Most sales are dependent on desirable financing, on whether the buyer qualifies for a loan, and the terms of that loan. Check whether financing is available from a recognized institutional lender, a lender that is solid and secure, as opposed to a fly-by-night operation or an unreliable, "hard money" private lender. Hard money lenders generally finance problem properties by extracting high interest rates in exchange for assuming risk. Hard money lenders typically offer short-term financing, which results in a balloon payment at the end of the financing term. Their loan processing fees are generally expensive as well.

If there are "clouds" in the title, such as unpaid real property taxes, unpaid street bonds, an IRS income tax lien against the property, mechanics' liens, or money judgments against the owner, financing might be hard to come by. These disputes usually must be resolved before clear title can be given to the institutional lender or new purchaser. Sometimes, the mortgage can be paid in full but its satisfaction may not be recorded. All of these claims act as encumbrances that, if valid, affect or impair the owner's title, or evidence of ownership.

While obtaining financing, be sure that you have the proper title to the property. I once bought three lots, and a friend of mine bought a fourth lot adjacent to the three that I owned. We only paid a few hundred dollars apiece for them. But I decided to pull out some title insurance on my property anyway to protect me from any loss sustained by defects that might be in the title. Title companies insure buyers against most claims to the title of the property.

About five years later, the California Department of Transportation started building a new freeway nearby and was looking for granite gravel. My hillside, which conveniently consisted of granite, was leveled. My friend had the same thing happen to his lot, but didn't have clear title to the property. When he decided to build on his land, the lender found a cloud in the title in the form of an unpaid judgment against the property, and the lender wouldn't make a construction loan until this cloud was removed. It cost my friend thousands and thousands to sue and go to court and finally get the right to do something with his property.

When you buy a property, always get a policy of title insurance. I wouldn't touch a property otherwise, because I want to know what I'm buying. Are there any liens or encumbrances against it? Are there any easements of record or any assessments against the property that you don't know about which aren't covered by disclosure laws?

But even with title insurance, you are not protected against every problem associated with a property. It only covers items of record, which may be different than actual problems. For instance, it doesn't protect the buyer of the property if the property is encroaching on the adjoining property or if there is a high voltage power line seven feet away from the property line.

Be sure to buy real estate in a comfortable way so that you don't have anything that will hurt you if you suffer a setback or decide to change careers, so it won't become a burden. You never want real estate to become a burden. It should be a pleasant experience, an asset you can enjoy and feel that you've got something that you really want and are proud to own.

HOW FINANCING AFFECTS MARKET VALUE

As mentioned, the size of the down payment and the terms of sale are far more important than the purchase price in a real estate transaction. Most people never pay off their mortgage anyway, or if they do it will be after 20 or 30 years, so it's really not important how much you pay for a piece of real estate. What matters is how much you take out of your pocket each month to make your payment.

If a seller is concerned about the price, which most are, you can offer a higher price and still not have to pay any more or make a larger down payment. In Table 10.1, notice how financing affects the purchase price.

If you can afford to buy a property at fair market value, you shouldn't hesitate if the terms are good and you know that the property will increase in value. The real estate investor does not buy merchandise (property) like other business people. The retail price of land today may be its wholesale price in the future. As far as the loan is concerned, the time it takes to pay it off really doesn't matter as long as you don't have any balloon payments. You can have a 30-year mortgage or a five-year mortgage. The lender will still foreclose on you if you don't make the payments.

On the downside, if you make a purchase in a stagnant market, you run the risk of paying more for a property than its appreciation rate will justify. If this happens, you've made a mistake in your analysis. When you do your research, make sure you've got the right location. That's the basis for the whole thing.

Interest is deductible for tax purposes, so I don't argue too much about interest rates as long as they are fair. Interest rates can fluctuate due to economic pressures, which you can't foresee, so in an unstable market I try to get a fixed rate. Sometimes a property can only be bought with a variable or adjustable rate mortgage because the lender isn't offering fixed rate mortgages. If an adjustable rate mortgage is all you can find, make sure there is a cap on the rate to protect you from large increases. Most adjustable mortgages come with a five point cap on them. You have to remain somewhat flexible as far as interest rates are concerned, but drive a hard bargain wherever you can.

———

Say you buy a property and put 25 percent down, and the owner takes back a first mortgage equal to 75 percent of the selling price. Assume your loan has a 30-year term with a 9 percent interest rate. The note should stipulate that if the seller wanted to sell the note, the buyer has the first opportunity to buy it at current market value. This is a tremendous advantage because if interest rates

TABLE 10.1
How Terms of Sale Can Affect the Sale Price

Example:

- Commercial property is listed for $230,000
- Seller will take a down payment of 40,000
- Seller will carry a first mortgage of 190,000
  15% interest per year, with the note to be amortized in full in 20 years.

Assume that the down payment of $40,000 does not change. The $2,500 per month payment on the note remains constant. If the interest rate is altered and the number of years to pay off the note is changed, the original principal sum on the first trust deed note, as well as the sales price, will change from $152,500 to $364,000 as follows:

Interest Rate (Percent)	Length of Loan (Years)	Monthly Payment	Sum of 1st Mortgage	Down Payment	Sales Price
12	5	$2,500	$112,500	$40,000	$152,500
18	10	2,500	139,000	40,000	179,000
15	10	2,500	155,000	40,000	195,000
18	20	2,500	161,000	40,000	201,000
18	30	2,500	166,000	40,000	206,000
18	40	2,500	166,500	40,000	206,500
12	10	2,500	174,000	40,000	214,000
15%	20 yrs.	2,500	190,000	40,000	230,000
9	10	2,500	197,000	40,000	237,000
15	30	2,500	197,500	40,000	237,500
15	40	2,500	199,000	40,000	239,000
12	15	2,500	208,000	40,000	248,000
12	20	2,500	227,000	40,000	267,000
12	30	2,500	243,000	40,000	283,000
9	20	2,500	278,000	40,000	318,000
9	30	2,500	310,000	40,000	350,000
9	40	2,500	324,000	40,000	364,000

rose to 12 percent, but you could still pay only 9 percent interest, that would represent a substantial discount.

─────

When negotiating, work out a payment program so that it fits into your need and financial position. If you can see that an acquisition won't be a terrible burden on you, then it's probably a good idea to go ahead with it. As long as you can hold on to the property for a reasonable period of time, inflation will take you out of the woods. Down the line, you might be able to renegotiate for a better interest rate.

The following example is used to justify the purchase price of an income property, in this case an older three-unit apartment building, or triplex, and may be used for other contemplated purchases.

Because of the long-term gains of equity buildup and appreciation (estimated at 6 percent annually, assuming the property is located in an area with growth potential) combined with immediate tax benefits, the property has an annual yield of $24,036. Since out-of-pocket costs ("losses") to own the property are $13,332, the long-term net benefits are $10,504 per year, representing a 26.3 percent return on investment in the form of a $40,000 down payment.

From an income standpoint, the property may continue to experience a negative cash flow for several years until increased rents eventually overtake the mortgage payments. Remember, though, that during this finite negative period, the property, if properly selected, will continue to appreciate and tax benefits can continue to be applied over the life of the loan and the improvements, thereby serving as a shelter.

Justifying the Purchase Price of an Older Three-Unit (Triplex) Apartment Property

(A)	Purchase price		$ 200,000
	Allocation:	Land	50,000
		Improvements	150,000
		(Life = 27.5 years at 3.64%)	
(B)	Down payment		40,000
(C)	First mortgage at 13% (25-yr. term)		160,000
(D)	Annual mortgage payment	$1,861/mo. (× 12)	22,332
(E)	Annual gross rental income	$1,200/mo. (× 12)	14,400
(F)	Annual expenses (incl. real property taxes, insurance, utilities, repairs, maintenance), vacancy allowance, and collection loss		−5,400

(G)	Annual net income		9,000
(H)	Spendable income/out-of-pocket costs:		
	(G) Total net income		9,000
	(D) Annual mortgage payment		−22,332
	Annual loss		⟨13,332⟩
	Gains to be Derived from Purchase		
(I)	Equity buildup		22,332
	Mortgage interest ($160,000 × 13%)		−20,800
	Total interest		1,532
(J)	Annual appreciation (6% × 200,000)		+12,000
(K)	Tax benefits: Buyer's tax liability = 40%		
	Mortgage interest	$20,800	
	Depreciation	+ 5,460 ($150,000 × 3.64%)	
	Total	26,260	
		× 40% =	$ 10,504
(L)	Total gains from purchase		$24,036
(M)	Out-of-pocket cost to own property		−⟨13,532⟩
(N)	Net benefits derived per year		$ 10,504
	Net benefits of $10,504 per year (N) on a $40,000 outlay		
	(B) represents a 26.3% return on investment.		

SELLER-ASSISTED FINANCING

When you buy a property, the most advantageous terms are to arrange for the seller to handle part of the financing by taking back or carrying a second, third, or fourth mortgage. Whereas the institutional lender determines the interest rate for the first mortgage, a second, third, or fourth mortgage is a negotiable instrument made between the buyer and the seller written with any terms they agree to. Second mortgages, which prolong the seller's liability on the property, are generally used when buyers don't have enough cash for the down payment.

Say you were buying a property for $100,000 and only had $10,000 for the down payment. The lender is willing to make a $70,000 mortgage loan, which leaves $20,000 difference. The seller, if cooperative, could allow you to accept the outstanding $20,000 in the form of a second mortgage, or second trust deed, which would be recorded on the property, terms to be announced. Depending on how bad the seller wanted out of the property, you might get interest-only for five years or something similar.

Sometimes brokers will agree to take a third trust deed as their commission. If there is a lot of financing, the owner might be willing to take his profit in the form of a fourth or fifth trust deed. I once did an appraisal on a vacant parcel for which the owner had a *sixth* trust deed on the land! If the sellers are flexible, write the terms however you want, whatever they will agree to. Here, you have a certain amount of latitude. The one thing that isn't allowable is a note with no interest. The tax laws state that there has to be an interest rate assigned to the note. If you don't assign one, the IRS will assume the note bears interest at the going rate.

S ay you were looking at an income property worth $200,000. The owner is willing to accept a $5,000 down payment and take back a $195,000 first mortgage. But, instead of taking the first at $1,950 a month for 30 years at 10 percent interest, suppose he raises the price to $300,000 with no interest so that you only have to pay off the principal. The payments wouldn't be any less, but the owner of the property wouldn't be collecting any interest, so the principal would be treated in the form of capital gains, which is only 28 percent taxable, as opposed to interest, which is 100 percent taxable. If you buy a property that way, you might come out ahead tax-wise. If the seller agrees to carry the mortgage, the seller has to pay the interest. It's a buyer-seller issue.

Just as no two parcels are exactly alike, no two transactions are exactly alike because you never know what somebody else is thinking. And you can never really find out until you make an offer. If people are motivated to do things, it's amazing what will happen.

The more motivated the seller is, the more flexible the terms of the deal. A friend of mine bought a residence in 1982 at the height of the recession of the early 1980s. The seller was asking $400,000, so my friend gave him $100,000 down, and the seller agreed to carry a $300,000 note on the property with no interest, no principal, no payments, no nothing for five years. At the end of this time, my friend had to make a balloon payment, but with no interest attached to it. If interest were allowed to accumulate on the principal, the balance due would have been twice as much. Consequently, my friend was able to meet his obligation.

To negotiate a fantastic deal, you need to find a motivated seller. Why do sellers become motivated? The reasons are manifold: an illness or death in the family, an all-consuming lawsuit, job loss, divorce, another property that has been bought and is ready to move into, long vacant rental units, a property that has been sitting on the market for an extended period without any takers, debts arising from a tax audit, or a small business that needs to be infused with much-needed cash. The greatest motivated sellers are those with a combination of reasons why they need to sell. Here are 10 more reasons why the owner of a piece of real estate might become a motivated seller:

1. The owner has allowed his property to deteriorate.
2. The property's rental income has dropped because the building has not been modified to keep up with the times.
3. The owners have inherited the property and can't manage it properly because no one wants to take responsibility.
4. The owners have inherited the property and are in a hurry to divide proceeds from the estate.
5. The owner is forced to sell to pay off personal debts.
6. The owners are absentee and do not keep abreast of actual rental or sale value.
7. The owner bought on speculation, became frustrated with a slow appreciation rate, and has decided to invest in another field, such as the stock market.
8. The owners are older and wish to liquidate their assets and take back the mortgage(s).
9. The owner needs to relocate because of a job transfer.
10. The owner has tired of the rat race and has decided to move to the Polynesian Islands.

———

Sometimes, negotiating a transaction takes on the dimensions of a psychological battle. In the mid-1950s, a friend of mine wanted to buy a house. The sellers of the property, some friends of his, were asking $25,000 for their residence. But he knew they were in the midst of a messy divorce, having real problems, and were about to foreclose.

So he called them up one day and said, "I want you to clear off the dining room table because I'm coming over to make an offer." He then went to the bank, took out $20,000 in $100 bills and spread these 200 C-notes around the table. The kids fingered the money and everything else. Even though the offer was $5,000 less than what they were asking—and that was a lot in those days—it didn't take much to convince them to accept.

———

NO MONEY DOWN TRANSACTIONS

I've made almost all of my real estate purchases with little or no money down. I don't think I've put more than $3,000 down on anything I've ever bought. I've done this by working with sellers. There is no way you can negotiate a good deal unless you find a person who is motivated and has a desire to sell. Finding motivated sellers is essential; the more motivated they are, the better bargain you can work out.

In 1964, I found a place on The Strand where the seller wanted $20,000 down. I was really anxious to buy it, but I didn't have enough money for the down payment he wanted. So I kept talking to him and told him what the advantages were to taking a second mortgage, including monthly payments without any tenant problems, a higher interest rate than he could get from the bank, and the sale of the property, which he was anxious to accomplish because the market was dead.

After a while, he got tired of it. There weren't many buyers around in those days, plus you couldn't rent anything. It was driving him nuts. Eventually, I got him to take a third trust deed on the property so I would only have to pay $3,000 down. It worked out well, but we probably negotiated for nine months.

Another way to get around a large down payment is by putting a second mortgage on another piece of property in which the purchaser has equity, which the seller can accept as collateral—property pledged as security for a debt.

Say you are desperate to sell your $500,000 apartment building. The buyer could go to an institutional lender and find a loan for 80 percent of the property's market value, or $400,000. This leaves the buyer $100,000 that he has to come up with. Assume he doesn't have that kind of money, but that he has a valuable house somewhere. You can accept a $100,000 mortgage on his residence in lieu of cash payment and the lender will most likely agree to the deal because the apartment building the lender is loaning on will have a $100,000 equity cushion to protect the loan.

A "no money down" transaction is a form of seller-assisted financing. It basically entails taking equity in one piece of real estate and trading the paper on that equity to the seller in lieu of cash. No money down plans usually turn out to be schemes because the lender is defrauded by not being informed that the seller—not the buyer—is really the person putting up the money for the down payment. Some banks still don't require this disclosure, but frequently some element of fraud is involved.

There are several drawbacks to no money down plans. First of all, you have to do them in an up market. Values have to be appreciating at a good clip. If there is a leveling off or if the market's dropping like it is today, no money down schemes are difficult. A lot of people try this who don't understand the problems and end up losing their shirts.

Another disadvantage to no money down transactions is that they typically result in a balloon payment of the principal balance at the end of the financing period. I think it is important to avoid balloon payments at all costs. I call them "debt bombs" because they explode in your face at a time when you least want them to.

With a balloon mortgage, you are compelled to refinance it at the will of the note rather than when you decide is the best time. That's constraining in itself. You might not be in a position to refinance when the note comes due or the market might be such that interest rates are at 20 percent, which could take all of your profit away from you.

If you do have a balloon payment, you always want an out. One escape clause that can be written in the note to postpone the satisfaction of a balloon payment may read:

> If the buyer is not able to pay off the loan in full when due, the loan will be extended for a period of time at a higher interest rate.

To illustrate how this would work, say you buy a property and the seller insists on a five-year due date for payment of the loan in full, and he gives you 10 percent interest. You could offer to pay 12 percent interest if he could extend the loan for one year, or 14 percent for two years, or 16 percent for three years. A 14 or 16 percent interest rate is still a lot cheaper than losing your investment. The market changes every three or four years anyway, so paying a little higher interest will buy you some crucial time to work on your investment and wait for property values to rise.

———————

Most of the time, people who sell for no money down are desperate. Their property either is a dog or they are about to be foreclosed on. Several "no money down" gurus went broke when the real estate market started to flatten out. A few authors of "no money down" books even had to file bankruptcy because they weren't able to prove their chalkboard theories in the real world of profit and loss. They kept floating paper, but it never panned out for them in dollars and cents.

32 ITEMS TO CONSIDER BEFORE MAKING AN OFFER

Making an offer to purchase a property and writing a satisfactory agreement are paramount in the execution of a successful real estate transaction. As a general rule, an offer should contain or consider the following:

1. How title should be taken by the buyer (joint tenants, community property, or tenancy in common).
2. The specific date and time when the offer from the buyer will expire.
3. The street address and precise lot dimensions of the subject property.
4. That the seller warrants the building(s) are located legally within the property lines.
5. That the seller warrants there are no encroachments on adjacent property.
6. That the seller warrants no other person has any right, title, or interest in the property other than what appears on the preliminary title report.
7. That the seller warrants there are no unrecorded liens against the property.
8. That the seller warrants there are no violations of building and safety laws, either pending or contemplated.
9. That the seller agrees to allow the buyer to obtain a permit of occupancy on the property. If there is any expense or corrective violations in connection with the permit, said expense shall be the total responsibility of the seller.
10. That the seller is not aware of any contemplated changes in zoning affecting the property.
11. That if the sale is contingent on a zoning change, the seller will cooperate by signing all necessary documents.

12. That the buyer shall have the privilege of approving the preliminary title report before the closing of the escrow or transaction.

13. That a termite report shall be submitted into the escrow or trust account and be dated after this agreement. And that the seller shall, at his expense, comply with all requirements of the termite report unless otherwise agreed to.

14. If the buyer's funds come from a 1031 tax-deferred exchange transaction, the seller agrees to cooperate in furthering the exchange by signing all necessary documents, provided that the seller is not affected financially.

15. That the seller warrants the property is not located in any hazardous areas, such as in a flood zone, or on an earthquake fault, an area of earth movement, sinkhole areas, tornado or hurricane regions.

16. That the buyer has authority to approve all existing leases and verify all rents. And that the seller warrants no building areas were rented by giving any concessions of any kind. Seller warrants that all rents are accurate and correct as stated and that there were no free or reduced rents given.

17. If the buyer is assuming a promissory note or deed of trust (or mortgage) of record, buyer shall be given an exact copy of said documents for his inspection and approval before the close of the transaction. Seller warrants that terms of encumbrance are exactly as stated in the offer, and that there is no enforceable acceleration clause or due date on note or notes to be assumed.

18. That the buyer and/or his broker or representative shall have the authority to inspect the exterior and interior of the structure(s) and to approve the condition of the structure as well as the roofing, plumbing, heating, electrical, and the like, before the sale is consummated.

19. If buyer disapproves of any item or items, then the escrow company or real estate attorney is instructed to return all funds to the buyer without further instructions or signature from seller.

20. Escrow or transaction officer is instructed to have all rent deposits prorated on the cash down payment and not on any trust deed(s) or mortgage(s).

21. If there are any monetary adjustments to be made, they shall be to seller's purchase money deed of trust.

22. Buyer may assume present insurance or take out a new policy at his option.

23. Seller shall pay all escrow charges in connection with the sale. All other charges shall be paid by the buyer and seller in the customary manner.

24. Buyer shall get possession of and be responsible for property after close of the transaction.

25. Seller warrants that all leases are in effect and have not been changed or modified. Seller further warrants that there are no defaults in leases, either by the lessor or the lessee.
26. Seller warrants that there is no filled ground, toxic waste, asbestos, or other hazardous materials on the premises.
27. Seller warrants that there are no loans or notes against the personal property involved.
28. Seller agrees to furnish buyer with a chattel mortgage report (pledge of personal property) at his expense. Seller agrees to list all personal property in detail that is to be included in the sale and provide a bill of sale to buyer. Buyer has authority to inspect all personal property before close of the transaction using said list and to verify the accuracy of said list.
29. If title cannot be delivered to buyer, no damage to buyer shall be incurred. Buyer shall be reimbursed for all funds deposited in escrow without further instructions or signature from seller.
30. Seller is to allow buyer two working days after close of the transaction to change over all utilities.
31. Seller is to deposit all keys to the property which are in seller's possession before close of the transaction.
32. Seller is to provide buyer with a list of all persons having keys to the property.

11

Advantages of Using
a Real Estate Broker

ADVANTAGES OF USING A BROKER

Free Expertise

Although I myself am a real estate broker, I can't recall ever buying a property without another broker representing me. When a property is sold, the buyer doesn't pay the commission; the seller does. So it's in the buyer's best interest to have a real estate agent or broker, especially one who understands your way of thinking and will negotiate the purchase the way you want it to be negotiated.

Both brokers and sales agents must be licensed by the state in which they work. The main difference between an agent and broker is the amount of education and training required. Real estate agents must work under the auspices of a broker, while a broker may be independent, work out of an office, or manage his own office and employ other realtors. In the state of California, which is recognized for having a model real estate license law, brokers must complete eight college-level courses before taking the licensing exam. To become a sales agent requires only one college-level course, although continuing education requirements must be satisfied for both brokers and sales agents.

You can never be too knowledgeable about real estate. Since realtors tend to specialize in certain areas, they are usually familiar with the local housing market, zoning laws, and tax rates, along with the reputation of school districts, and the location of churches, shopping centers, public utilities, and mass transit. They also know where to obtain financing and which lenders are active in the market.

For investors who are new to an area or new to buying real estate, a broker or agent may provide valuable assistance helping to locate the right property using the resources of the regional Multiple Listing Service (MLS). An MLS book can provide a picture of what property is currently available and at what price, along with recent sales. Sometimes, properties for sale aren't advertised as such, or are in exclusive areas that only residents and realtors with permits have access to. A competent broker should bring these so-called pocket listings to your attention.

A reputable real estate company conducts thorough research on a community, including market data and projections, and makes that information available to potential buyers. It's important to look at this information yourself, as a broker may not interpret the raw figures the way you would like to have them analyzed. A broker generally is looking for an immediate commission in buying and selling, whereas a real estate investor seeking an opportunity to buy a property for the long-term is more inclined to think in broader terms than buying today and selling in a year or two.

As mentioned, sometimes a property that is overpriced and in a run-down neighborhood might have the great potential of being a gold mine 20 years from now. That might not be obvious to a broker who is dealing in terms of yesterday and today.

I believe it is important to find a broker or agent who is active in the community, who belongs to the local Chamber of Commerce, who participates in civic affairs, who attends professional meetings and seminars, who stays informed about the community—all to keep close tabs on emerging developments and discern what the trends are. As a buyer, that gives you an edge. If, for example, the city plans to widen a certain street and you learn about it ahead of time, you have the opportunity to contact the agency involved and find out the reason behind it. Buyers who know this type of information are able to make informed decisions.

If you discover the city is widening the street for a positive reason that is beneficial to the property you are considering, then that's a valuable piece of information worth knowing well in advance. I've noted that real estate values are created by the actions, attitudes, and thinking of people. If you have a pulse on the community, you also have a pulse on the actions, attitudes, and thinking of people. An informed broker can keep you in touch with the latest developments from an insider's point of view. If, on the other hand, you are oblivious to such important developments, it's a completely different story. You're more of an outsider. It can definitely pay to have a broker.

––––––

H ow do you find a good real estate broker who is cooperative and will go along with your program and way of thinking? In my opinion, the only way is to ask questions of people who are familiar with the local market and find out who is the most active and informed in the area in which you wish to participate. Locate a broker who belongs to civic groups and stays abreast of events that are happening regionally, statewide, and nationwide. The most important thing is to be able to communicate. If you have a knowledgeable broker but you can't communicate, you might as well forget it.

Financial Assistance

Besides helping find a suitable property, flexible real estate brokers and agents are sometimes willing to help buyers finance part of the deal by lending them their commission fee, typically 5 or 6 percent of the total price of the property. On a property worth $250,000, that's $12,500 or $15,000 toward the down payment, which averages about 20 percent of the purchase price, or in this case $50,000.

A few years ago I wanted to buy some condominiums. So I found a broker and paid him a 3 percent commission for locating properties that were for sale for nothing down. He found two of them. Buyers usually don't pay any commissions, but sometimes, it's worth your while. In this case, I was essentially paying him a finder's fee. He found two units for sale for nothing down. Their list price was $60,000. Today, they're probably worth $110,000.

In another instance, I purchased 26 condominiums in a complex through a broker who had connections to an institutional lender that was foreclosing on a number of units in the area and reselling them to interested investors. I felt that the condominiums were underpriced and the terms exceptional and decided to acquire a few of these properties through a broker.

The broker cooperated by informing me when any of these properties came up for sale for little or no money down. Since I am a real estate broker, I probably could have received a partial commission on each transaction. But to provide incentive to the broker I was working with, I offered him a full commission on each sale. At times, he really went out of his way for me.

Over a period of months I had bought six of these condominiums. At one point, four more were coming on the market, so my wife, somewhat tongue in cheek, said, "If we buy 10 of them, you ought to give us one free." The lender said he had never heard of such a thing. But he came back and offered to furnish one of our units if we bought four more. We accepted the offer, so the lender gave us several thousand dollars in cash to buy furniture. This is how the place we keep for our overnight stays and weekend trips was decorated.

My broker probably made $4,000 or $5,000 on each property I bought, for a total of approximately $100,000 in commissions; but for the amount of money involved, that's peanuts. Over the next few years, I'm going to make at least a million dollars from these investments. So we were delighted that he made some money. Yet if I hadn't done this, he wouldn't have been motivated and probably wouldn't have found me all these great bargains. I was a ready market for him. All he had to do was call me up and tell me that they were available. He didn't even have to advertise.

———

Greed is a characteristic of human nature. But if you're too miserly, you're liable to let things slip by that you should have acted on because you will be too concerned about pinching pennies. Don't be afraid to pay people well. We live in the richest country on earth: There's enough to go around for everyone. Plus, if you keep an open mind and let other people make money, you'll make even more. A lot of people try to squeeze every nickel out of the deal. I like to see the other guy make a nickel, too.

The properties my broker found for me were all REO—real estate owned by a savings and loan association. I was buying these units, which had already been through foreclosure proceedings and had come back on the market, at a time when the market was difficult and there weren't many buyers. I liked the neighborhood and, once I saw what was going on there, decided to jump in with both feet because I realized it was a rare opportunity. That was only four years ago. Anybody could have done it. Our dental hygienist rushed down and bought one after I told her about it. It was probably the best investment she ever made.

I wouldn't go near a person being foreclosed on for the world, but after the institutional lender has taken it away from the previous owner and fixed it up and put it on the open market, then I am eager to buy. But I wouldn't go to someone in dire distress and offer to take their home away from them. Everybody has a different way of looking at it. I wouldn't want to be treated that way myself.

Objectivity

I get too emotional for my own good sometimes. If I'm really excited about a piece of property, I have a tendency to show that emotion to the seller and reveal my hand. When you are in the market for a property, you become a principal and as such you are biased. When you work with a broker, he or she can remain detached and unbiased. A disinterested third party can learn much more from the seller than someone who is a party to the transaction.

This is important because the only way you can really make a good decision is when you know the seller's thinking. Once you understand that, you can mold the deal to their needs and desires. You can't get that by talking directly. But a broker, because they're disinterested and detached, can ask the seller why he bought the property in the first place, why he wants to sell, and other important questions.

The broker usually presents the first offer. I always like to have my broker drop it off and let the seller consider it for a few days. Giving the seller a couple days to think it over works out well because it allows them to get over their emotions.

If you were selling a new Cadillac and someone offered you $500 for it, your first response would be to get mad. Then you would think, at least someone's talking to me. Then you would think, at least we're starting the negotiating process. What you want to do is avoid what I call a "get mad" attitude. Many times people will say things they don't mean, and if they do, they won't back down. It's better that you don't say harsh things in the first place.

If you make an offer on a property, make sure that this is what you want to do. If the seller won't even make a counter offer, at least you will be informed as to what his or her thinking is. Be aware that when a broker is involved, sellers tend to raise their prices slightly higher because they factor in the broker's commission (again 5 or 6 percent of the sales price) into their asking price.

Frequently, buyers make their offers subject to certain conditions, such as verifying that the plumbing and electrical are in good condition, that the heating works, that there are no serious cracks in the walls or foundation, that the mechanical equipment meets the present building code standards, that no flood hazard exists, and so on. If the seller agrees and accepts your offer under these conditions, you then have the right to inspect the building.. If you find anything there that is not to your satisfaction, then you can cancel the deal. Using a third party, a broker, makes negating the offer a lot easier, in my judgment.

Synergy Effect

In Chapter 2, we discussed the importance of considering what type of investment to make and determining how it fits your needs, desires, personality, temperament, and time availability. When looking for a real estate broker, find one who fits into that general framework—someone who understands your needs as well as your objective. If possible, find a broker who has the knowledge, personality, and ability to get along well with you and who understands what you're trying to do.

If you can find a broker who thinks along the same lines as you, it is possible to bounce ideas off each other and create a sort of synergy effect. It stretches your mind and enables you to understand the problem better when you can explain it to someone else. The same problem appears completely different to different people. Having a good broker is the equivalent of having a good business partner; you can do five times better than if you were operating independently.

How do you place a value on real estate brokers? As a rule, if they can contribute more than you can by yourself, then they have value to you. If you can find a full-time broker who is in the field, studying the latest trends and developments, who keeps you posted on what's happening in real estate as well as allied business activities that affect real estate, then he or she is likely to be an enormous help.

Knowledge of the area is extremely important. Usually, brokers who have been in the neighborhood for a long period of time know and understand the problems much better than those who arrived more recently, because they have lived through them.

If a person is devoting his or her professional life to real estate, he or she should be familiar with what's going on in the neighborhood, community, and surrounding area. He or she should also have a handle on what's going on at city hall, the public works department, and the school districts. Data from multiple listing services and realty boards are extremely important as well. But don't depend on your broker to do all of your work for you. I would rely on them to give you an indication of what is going on, but not a comprehensive analysis. You should do most of that research yourself.

My advice is to find a broker who isn't going to be embarrassed if you make a ridiculous offer, because it might not be ridiculous to the seller. Once, when I first started investing in real estate, I thought about making an offer on a property in the Hollywood Hills. I figured it was worth $25,000. I asked my father what he thought it was worth and he said, "Why don't you ask the seller what he wants and we'll counter." I asked the seller, but he said he wanted an offer first. I said, "You know more about the property than I do. You've lived here. You know the neighborhood." So he said. "Well, how about $22,000." So we readjusted our sights to around $18,000.

Even though the offer in the above example was made informally, that is, verbally, it would have been a big mistake to start talking about more money than I needed to. Even so, I don't think you're really doing anything serious in real estate until you have an offer in writing. That's when the broker comes in. If I was wholeheartedly interested in making an offer on that Hollywood Hills property, I would have gone through a broker and put my bid in writing. As it turned out, I never did.

DISADVANTAGES OF USING A BROKER

One of the chief disadvantages of using a broker is feeling pressured. Inasmuch as you have to be able to communicate with your realtor, it is important to have a certain chemistry. If you can't communicate, it makes the whole process very difficult. You need a broker who will keep you informed—about how the sellers are reacting to your offer, how important is it for them to sell, what kind of terms are they thinking of, and anything that might be wrong with the property that isn't obvious.

———

You also want to find a broker who doesn't talk too much. A lot of brokers will talk themselves right out of the deal. As noted above, when you're negotiating a deal, you don't want to tell the seller everything you know or are willing to concede up front. You want to know what they think first. I've known brokers who talk too much. And when that happens, they sometimes ruin the deal for you.

The worst thing a broker can do is say, "The highest figure my buyer will pay is...." That's talking too much; you don't want to tell the seller how high you are willing go until you find out what he wants. Another example of loudmouth syndrome is: "This guy wants to buy the property because he needs it for a parking lot for his business next door." When the seller finds out who the purchaser is, the price would double.

———

When the Watergate Hotel (no relation to the well-known complex in Washington, D.C.) was built in Hermosa Beach, a broker came over and told me he had a buyer for my property, which was right next door to the hotel. He said he would give me X number of dollars. I replied, "Oh, you will, huh?" He said, "Yeah, I've got a hot buyer." I told him to put it in writing. But he said, "No, I can't do that right now. The guy's going to New York but when he returns, I'll have him put it in writing." I asked if he really wanted to buy my property. He said, "Oh yeah." I could tell by the way he was talking that he represented the guy next door. He was really insistent and his was the only view that would have been blocked if I decided to build a highrise. It wasn't to anybody else's advantage to buy that property.

So I told him I didn't want to sell it. After a while, we talked and he said, "I suppose you knew that the people next door wanted to buy your property." I said that of course I knew. But I didn't tell him that I didn't want to sell because he went about it in the wrong way. If the guy who owned the property next door had said, "Look, I want to buy this place because I don't want to have my view ruined," I would have told him, "You are the first person I would sell it to." I'd even put it in writing. But I'm not going to allow somebody to go around and misrepresent the situation. Sometimes you have to be a little astute and read into what's going on.

———

M any brokers are big talkers but, when it comes down to it, are less than imaginative. When things were kind of difficult, a guy I knew put a single family residence on the oceanfront up for sale. He advertised it and had a series of brokers working on selling it but couldn't get anybody to look at it.

I went over and analyzed the situation and determined he was using the wrong approach. I told him to develop a profile of an ideal buyer. I figured it would be a husband and wife in their late 60s or early 70s who were quite wealthy, had three or four kids, and who were about to become grandparents. A couple in this situation would be ideally suited as buyers. They would derive tremendous use value from an oceanfront residence or vacation home and would have a terrific recreational facility—the beach—to attract their kids and grandkids to visit them.

———

After all, what good is a property when you have the money but can't do anything with it? This was a way to solve an emotional problem. I told him to advertise in newspapers and publications in areas where people had a lot of money, such as Beverly Hills. So he went out and did just that and eventually found someone in a very similar position to the hypothetical couple I described. He might have had 5 or 10 brokers who never thought of that idea.

It's hard to find a knowledgeable broker who really understands and is interested in what you're doing. If you find one, you don't want to let him or her get away. I think it's marvelous when you can develop a good rapport. Good brokers, if they are willing to help you, are worth their weight in gold.

A lot of people are concerned about realtors, and for good reason. Many do give poor advice and mislead prospective buyers and sellers in order to close a sale. It's totally unethical, of course. You should know who you're dealing with. Not to cast too many aspersions on brokers, but there are a lot who really aren't fair with people. They extract listings and, if something doesn't go exactly right, they'll file a lawsuit.

Oftentimes, disreputable brokers who just want to make a commission will exaggerate or not disclose all of the facts to make a property seem better than it is. Although many states now have disclosure laws that compel brokers to disclose the property's detrimental factors, not all realtors subscribe to a strict code of ethics, such as the one adopted by the National Association of Realtors® (see Appendix D). In a few worst-case scenarios, some unscrupulous realtors have been known to invest money on their clients' behalf and then skip town or declare bankruptcy.

I've never had to worry about brokers because I know as much as they do, maybe more. As mentioned, I myself am a broker. Moreover, I won't consider a real estate transaction unless I personally investigate it first. If my broker had a listing I was interested in, I would make it my business to know more about that listing than my broker by researching city records, talking to the neighbors, checking to see if there are any liens against the property, and obtaining a property profile from the title company. Most brokers don't do all this. They just take the listing and try to sell it.

I've never been surprised in a real estate deal. But then again, I don't think you can be too careful. I don't like to make snap judgments if they can be avoided, because if you give yourself enough time to think through all the ramifications of what will happen or won't happen, the right decision will usually present itself.

In the mid-1960s, a friend of mine asked if I would investigate a 25-unit-apartment building. My friend was very interested in buying it and wanted to know if he was getting a good bargain. The sellers gave me a price and told me the building was recently constructed. I went over there and found not only that it had no vacancies, but that the rents were 20 percent higher than anything else in the neighborhood. I also discovered that the contractor who built the place was also the seller.

I wondered why people would pay 20 percent more to rent in this building, even if it was new, than apartments that could be found in the neighborhood? With a little more investigation, I learned that out of the 25 people occupying the apartments, 22 were on the owner's payroll. I did this by going around and talking to people. This telling fact had a tremendous bearing on my friend's decision to pay top dollar for this apartment building.

We wrote up an offer asking for the owner to guarantee that the rent roll will remain where it is or higher for the next three years. The guy turned it down. He wouldn't even talk to us. I knew as soon as he sold that building that the new owner was going to have a 75 percent vacancy rate and a lot of debt on his hands. This explains why you can never be too knowledgeable. When considering a major investment, you have to be cautious, thorough, and hire people who know what they are doing.

———————

It wouldn't make any difference how you tried to evaluate the property if you are working with a guy who does something like that. To me, it would be enough to say I wouldn't touch that property with a 50-foot pole no matter what you did. I suppose the owner eventually sold it, but it wasn't to anybody I knew. I put in a couple of days analyzing the deal and probably saved my friend $100,000.

Do's and Don'ts to Consider When Buying Real Estate

1. Do put all terms and conditions of sale in writing.
2. Do record your deed immediately.
3. Do check property for easements or encroachments.
4. Do insist on a property inspection clause in contract offer.
5. Do verify utility bills and tax bills.
6. Don't let the seller shop your offer around to get a better offer from other buyers—put a short-term due date on the offer.
7. Don't be influenced by phantom offers.
8. Don't ever give a deposit directly to the seller—make it out to the escrow company or bank directly.
9. Don't get caught in a rezoning frenzy.
10. Never sign a contract without proper legal advice.

12

Pyramid Your Initial Investment without Overextending Yourself

When you become a property owner, it is important to decide exactly how much you can afford to pay out each month in bills and the type of cash flow you can live with. Unless you pay for an investment property with all cash, chances are you will have to absorb a negative cash flow for a while as the market catches up. During this period, it is important to maintain a long-term outlook and not overextend yourself.

As discussed earlier, owning property is a means of forced savings. With this savings, or equity, it is possible to take money out of a property in the form of a second mortgage and use it for a down payment on another property. This is "pyramiding" your initial investment. The key, as discussed, is to decide what level of debt you can live with comfortably. Some people are comfortable with considerable debt; others can't bear even a small amount.

Some people can live very comfortably with a lot of debt. They love it. They feel great about it. To them, it's a challenge rather than a burden. What one person may consider overextending financially could be a cakewalk to another person in the same income bracket. Assuming everything else is equal, the amount of debt a person can handle is as much a matter of mental attitude as anything.

S trange as it sounds, some people are scared by money. I had a friend whose girlfriend inherited around $5,000 in 1950, a significant amount of money back then. It drove her crazy. She put the money in the bank, but it bothered her there. She was afraid to leave it in the bank because she thought the bank was going to go broke, but she was also afraid to spend it. Finally, she went out and bought a car and that made her feel better. She was in debt again. She had been in debt all her life and that's what she was comfortable with.

To my way of thinking, debt is a wonderful discipline. When you buy real estate and make payments on a mortgage, it's a means of forced savings, really. It's better than putting money in the bank because, as long as you make the right investment, you are putting money into an asset that is appreciating. Your money is working for you and you can control it. Since real estate obligations place you on a structured pattern toward an objective that investing will accomplish, you can stretch your income dramatically in my judgment to pay off these loans.

Financial advisors recommend never spending more than three times your gross income when you buy your house. But if you make $25,000 a year, that's only $75,000, which isn't going to buy very much, at least in some areas.

As long as you can meet your obligations and not feel pinched, I wouldn't worry too much about debt. For virtually anyone who owns property, debt is a way of life. What you have to look at is how much your assets are appreciating.

Ideally, your mortgage payments should be about one-third or 40 percent of your monthly income, at the most. If you are speculating and have a negative cash flow, then it's probably going to be greater. If you are prudent and frugal, you may be able to get away with paying 50 or even 60 percent of your monthly income. But it takes a lot of discipline to do that. You're not going to have much disposable income to go out to the follies. If you're used to buying a new suit at a prestigious clothier every season, that would be difficult.

When I started my real estate investment program, I made major sacrifices. At least 50 percent of my income went to pay off my loans. If I had any vacancies, it was disastrous, so I intentionally kept the rents low to minimize vacancies. After a few years, however, I started to raise the rents. If you buy in an area with growth potential where the property values are on an upward trend, it doesn't take too long before you start to get a pretty significant cash flow. The right purchase in an area of appreciating land values can bring lasting prosperity.

HOW I GOT STARTED

In 1939, my mother and father decided to buy a property the family could use and enjoy together. This presented a great opportunity for my brother, Paul, and I to learn the elements of real estate investing firsthand. The subject property was a single family residence that came with a two-car garage and an apartment over the garage. Both units were old but had not yet reached the point of functional obsolescence, so we could rent them without much trouble.

For this property, my family paid $7,000 and put $500 down. Since the rental income from the two units covered our mortgage payments and the property carried itself without any appreciable out-of-pocket expenses, the land was easily worth the purchase price.

Over the next 25 years, we paid down the mortgage to zero while the land more than quadrupled in value. In 1964, my brother and I acquired the property free and clear and were able to borrow enough money on it to build two beautiful new rental units. In 1980, this property was worth about $400,000. Today, its value has increased to $550,000. Ten years from now, it probably will be worth over $1 million.

When I started investing in real estate, I didn't have a dime. I had just lost all of my money trying to strike it rich in the commodities market. But I did have a good job as an appraiser. The first real estate investment I made on my own was in 1956, when I bought a four-unit apartment building in Hollywood for $20,000 with $1,000 down. At Marshall and Stevens, the harder I worked, the more I could make. So I toiled with the objective of parlaying my initial purchases into a substantial estate.

In 1960, I bought a six-unit apartment building on The Strand in Hermosa Beach looking out over the ocean. I purchased this building, which I still live in today, for $85,000 with $3,000 down. Then I acquired the place the next door, a four-unit, for $35,000 with $5,000 down. The third property I bought, another four-unit apartment, took me months to negotiate. The seller wanted $20,000 down, but I only had $3,000. So I finally got him down. My next purchase, a six-unit building, I got for $5,000 down. With my fifth property, the broker took back the commission so I didn't have to put anything down. This was a two-unit.

From these initial investments, I have pyramided my holdings into a $15 million estate that, in addition to these five oceanfront apartment buildings, includes seven single family residences in the neighboring area and 30 condominiums in Orange County, California. The secret to an effective pyramiding program is to buy in the right location, get the best terms possible, and accumulate equity against which you can borrow to make other investments. Sounds easy, doesn't it? It can be if you are patient and disciplined.

The seller of the first six-unit building I bought couldn't get rid of it fast enough. Even though he was asking an astronomical price, $85,000, I got it on terms that were so good, it didn't make any difference. As long as I could keep the place rented, the monthly payments were low enough that I could make them without too much difficulty. Plus I knew from my analysis of the area that over a long period of time, this place would more than pay for itself. And that's exactly what happened.

One of my favorite real estate sayings is: "What you owe today, you'll be worth tomorrow." By this I mean that with the right property in an area with assured growth, inflation and appreciation will eventually render the purchase price irrelevant. To illustrate this concept, consider the beach-front property I've owned and occupied since 1960, the six-unit apartment building on The Strand in Hermosa Beach.

Purchase Price, 1960		$85,000
Cost to renovate		nominal
Down payment		3,000
Loans:	First mortgage at 6.25%	45,000
	Second at 7%	32,000
	Third at 8%	5,000
Monthly payment on first loan, including taxes and insurance		600
Monthly payment on second loan		250
Monthly payment on third loan		100
Total monthly payments		950
(all loans were paid off in 1987)		
Present market value, 1991		1,500,000
Amount owed on loans		0
Gross annual rental income, 1991	($4,500 × 12)	54,000
Less expenses		
Vacancy and credit loss		2,700
Maintenance		2,700
Loan payments		0
Taxes and insurance		3,900
Utilities		1,200
Total expenses		$10,500
Net income before taxes		$43,500

As you can see, the amount I paid for this property is now inconsequential because of the degree to which the property has appreciated in value. The property, which yields a substantial positive cash flow, generates $43,500 net income a year before taxes. I never would have been in this position had I passed on the opportunity to buy this veritable gold mine, even if it was "high-priced" back then. The value since the time of purchase has risen more than 1,000 percent.

In my opinion, it is ridiculous to quibble over $5,000 or even $50,000 in the price. If you are buying for the long term, you know that the financial structure is such that you'll be able to hold on to it. The most important thing is to have a firm idea what the property will be worth in 15 or 20 years. You have to be sure that you can foresee that growth.

It took seven years before the above property broke even. During that time, I probably lost about $500 a month, roughly 20 percent of my monthly income at the time. Today, that $500 would be equal to about $2,000 or $3,000 a month. But I had a good job and could afford to absorb some losses. Even if you have high monthly payments, you have to remember that with an income-generating real estate investment, you're going to receive income from your properties to help meet your obligations.

You can accumulate a substantial amount of debt as long as it is debt you can absorb. You can owe a creditor $10 million, but if you don't have to pay it back for 50 years, all you have to worry about is the amount of your monthly payment. When you invest in real estate, you have to assume that the income from the property will increase as the value of the real estate goes up. You also have to realize that if you have any ability in your field or area of expertise, your salary will increase, too.

By 1965, I had cumulative debt on all my real estate equal to three quarters of a million dollars, maybe more. I bought several of my original properties with multiple mortgages against them, but it wasn't the kind of debt that could hurt me because there weren't any balloon payments looming on the horizon, no "debt-bombs" that were going to detonate at some point in the future. All of my loans were long term, so I didn't have to worry about coming up with a large sum of money in a short amount of time.

PYRAMIDING TECHNIQUES

For the beginning investor, the first property, typically a house, is the most important. It establishes you as a substantial member of the community and makes it easier for you to borrow money since you can now use your property as collateral for a loan. Owning property enables you to build equity. If you have $100,000 equity in your house, you can create a $50,000 second mortgage and take that $50,000 to buy another property and use it as a down payment. Or you can borrow $50,000 from the bank and take it out and use it in other ways.

A n ideal scenario is to buy a house in a growth area, make payments for five or six years, building a sizable equity, then take that equity to buy another property using your equity as a down payment. During this initial five-year period, assume that you will receive a promotion, increase your salary or business activity, and figure out a method for expanding your holdings.

If you intend to build an estate worth $10 million, you could start by buying a single family residence for $150,000 with 20 percent down, or $30,000. Your monthly payments would be approximately $1,000. In the right location, that property could rise in value to $200,000—or more—over a five-year period. By this time, you will have accumulated a substantial amount of equity, around $60,000, just by making your monthly mortgage payments.

Typically, lenders will make first mortgage loans equal to 80 percent of the property's current market value. (In effect, your lending institution acts as your financial partner and checks your judgment.) So if your property is appraised at $200,000, you could take out a total of $160,000 loan. With that money, you could buy a duplex or small apartment building. It must be a good acquisition and you had better be able to live with the terms because in pyramiding like this, you are not only pyramiding your assets, you are also pyramiding your debt.

A ssume the apartment building costs $300,000 and you put $100,000 down. That leaves you with $200,000 in new debt and a new payment of $2,000. Because of the new loan, your mortgage payments have increased from $1,000 a month to $3,000. However, your new property may only yield $1,500 rental income per month, so you have to decide whether you can hold on until you can raise the rents or whether that is too much negative for you to absorb. In pricey areas, very few properties will generate an immediate positive cash flow unless you put 100 percent down.

Another option would be to sell your first house, buy that small apartment building, and move into one of the units like I did with my six-unit on The Strand. If the seller is willing to carry a second mortgage, you can get a tax-deferred exchange to avoid paying taxes on capital gains, provided the total property is considered to be income producing. Under Section 1031 of the Internal Revenue Code, like-kind property used in a trade or business or held as an investment can be exchanged tax-free. The scenario described here is entirely plausible, but you can't sit around waiting for opportunities to come to you. Great real estate deals don't happen on their own.

BUYING YOUR FIRST PROPERTY

In my opinion, the first property you should buy should be residential. A single family residence with a unit in the back or a duplex would be ideal. After you buy a piece of property, you become more knowledgeable, you get to know the community better, and as a result of this you become more interested. You start to see the benefits for yourself firsthand as well as how to relate these benefits to fit your particular need.

After you've bought your first property, you won't have as much trepidation. You become established and more knowledgeable as to where the trends are going in the community. Pretty soon, you'll be able to buy a second property. When the house next door becomes available, you'll be in a position to take advantage of it.

Typically, the first purchase is not that terrific because you're coming into a community you really don't know about even though you studied it. But after you've been there a while and see what's going on, you get a feel for it and ought to be able to do a good job on your second buy. Your second acquisition should be a much better purchase as far as the price and terms are concerned. But even with the second property, you may have to carry it for a while as the market catches up.

There are literally thousands of possibilities, but what you need to do is establish yourself in the community. You should be an active part of it and know what's going on. When you've got a good reputation and get to know people and start talking to them, you can find out who is interested in selling and discuss with them the fact that you're in the market for another property. You might be able to work out a good deal that way. Who knows, the guy down the street may be willing to extend favorable terms because he knows you personally.

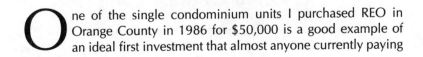

One of the single condominium units I purchased REO in Orange County in 1986 for $50,000 is a good example of an ideal first investment that almost anyone currently paying monthly rent to live in an apartment could have afforded. The low $5,000 down payment would not take anyone with a good-paying job too long to come up with, and the $375 monthly mortgage (including taxes and insurance) plus the $110 homeowner's fee is actually cheaper than renting in many areas.

Purchase price, 1986		$50,000
Down payment		5,000
Loans:	First mortgage at 8%	45,000
	Monthly payment on first loan,	
	including taxes and insurance	375
	Homeowner's Fee	110
Total monthly payments		485
Present market value, 1991		$75,000

If, instead of inhabiting the above unit, you chose to rent it out for the going rate of $600 per month, the property would immediately begin to yield a positive cash flow, albeit a modest one, because the income generated by the property would exceed the total expenses.

Gross annual rental income, 1991 ($600 × 12)	$7,200
Less expenses:	
Vacancy and credit loss (5%)	360
Loan payments, homeowner's fee,	
taxes and insurance	5,820
Total expenses	$6,180
Net income before taxes	$1,020

ESTABLISHING GOOD CREDIT

One of the questions I am frequently asked is how someone can get their foot in the door and come up with enough money for their first down payment. There are a number of ways. You could save it, or borrow from your relatives, or build up enough credit to get a loan from a bank. When you have good credit, banks are more likely to loan you money because you are perceived as a responsible individual.

When I bought my first place, I was unmarried and banks in those days thought everyone who was single was a flake. But by the time I went back for my second loan, it was a lot easier because I had made all my payments on time and had established good credit.

In addition to becoming a substantial member of the community, owning real estate improves your credit rating. By definition, you're no longer a potential fly-by-night applicant. One of the best things you can get in this world is good credit. I've always had good credit and I've always paid my bills a couple days ahead of time to establish good credit because credit is worth more than money.

I used to give my students the following advice on how to build credit. Visit a bank and become acquainted with the people there, then try to get as large a personal loan as you can. Say you can get a $5,000 loan from the bank. Take that $5,000 and deposit that money into the bank across the street and make payments from that account to pay off your original $5,000 loan. When you have the $5,000 in the second bank, borrow another $5,000 to pay off the second loan. *Do not spend any of this money.* If you discipline yourself and keep doing this three or four times, you will build up a good credit rating.

Once you prove to lenders that you are a good risk and will pay your obligations on time, you may then be able to borrow a little more money and come up with enough cash for a down payment on a piece of property. You may lose a few hundred dollars in interest payments doing this, but that isn't important. The important thing is to establish good credit.

You can use credit cards for the same purpose, but targeting a real estate lender will enhance your standing where it counts the most. Using the above strategy, you may be able to build credibility and trust with a financial institution that could finance your first property. By proving that you can make your payments on time, the lender will view you as less of a risk and will deal with you on a more substantial basis.

The biggest hindrance for many people in their twenties, thirties, and even forties is how to possibly save enough money for the down payment. These are the same people who earn a good salary, but spend their money on an expensive apartment, a new car and dining at fancy restaurants. Their assumption is that they have established a certain spending level and don't have any money to save. They don't equate having any money in the bank with reducing their consumer spending. They don't realize that in order to get ahead, maybe they should sacrifice a little and drop their spending level.

BUYING YOUR SECOND PROPERTY

It takes about a year to get a feeling for what a property can really do for you, whether it will show any short-term appreciation or income, even to tell how long you're going to have a negative cash flow. After a period of five years, you should be able to take your first property, refinance it, and buy something else. Often, when you're in a good market, you can do it in less time.

Y ou have to get it out of your head that your property value will double in two years. You have to view it with a long-range perspective and forget about what it's worth today. You should be interested in what it's going to be worth 15 years from now. For some people it's better to become passive about investment property, let someone else manage it, and then come back to it in 10 years when you can see actual appreciation. I have some friends who buy investment property, hire a property manager, and then walk away. When they return, they invariably find that their purchase was worth their while.

A duplex is an ideal second investment because one vacancy can't eat up 100 percent of your monthly return. Usually, you can get more rent from two units than you can from a single family residence of comparable value. As your family grows and your needs change, a duplex might also serve a personal need for you.

I would rather buy a four-unit because the risk is divided four ways instead of two. A vacancy in a four-unit isn't nearly as hard on you as a vacancy in a duplex or a single family residence. Plus, if you raise the rents, you're raising them in all four units so your income increases faster. The ideal situation is to charge reasonably low rents in an exceptionally good location. My smallest unit on The Strand rents for $475 a month. How long do you think it takes to find a tenant? About a minute.

A fter paying off a four-unit apartment building I purchased in the early 1960s, I decided a few years ago to sell it for $1 million and make a tax-deferred exchange, a transaction in which a property is traded for the promise to provide a replacement of like-kind property or properties in the near future with tax on the gain deferred (see Chapter 14). With the profit I received from the sale, I was able to trade my one property for three houses and a condominium.

The above example demonstrates how accumulated equity can be used to pyramid and expand your original investment. Years before I sold that apartment building, I had refinanced it for $360,000. With that money, I placed a $40,000 down payment on a $175,000 house that is worth over $500,000 today. From that one four-unit building, which I originally bought for $45,000, I was able to acquire five different income-producing, tax-sheltering properties, which may in turn yield several more. Now that's a pyramid worth climbing.

Throughout the book, I've stressed that one of the great advantages to investing in real estate is its uniqueness. There are so many ways of doing things. With real estate, you have the opportunity to use your imagination and ability like no other investment. About four years ago, I had a corner lot with four garages on it. I decided to tear that structure down and either sell the land or build something else. I wanted $150,000 for the lot, but nobody would take it. So I came up with an even better idea: to find somebody who was willing to build two condominiums on it at no cost to me.

W ith a little bit of effort, I found a contractor who was willing to build the two condos. To find a builder, I put an ad in the paper, talked to people at the local building supplies stores, and put a sign on the lot. Eventually, a guy called me. The arrangement I made with him was to give him one of the units with all the mortgages on it, and I would take the other unit free and clear for giving him the parcel of the land. I told the guy before we started that I wanted the deal to be a complete success. I wanted him to make as much money as possible. There was enough for both of us, I said—if he made a million dollars from the thing, I would be thrilled. The one option I reserved was the right to pick which unit I wanted when both were built.

It worked out great for both of us. He built his condo and sold it soon after completion for $350,000. Then he got in with some other guy on a similar deal and lost his shirt because the guy didn't treat him like I did. In my arrangement, I didn't pay for anything, but I held on to my place. It's got four bedrooms, three-and-one-half baths, and a sun deck where you can see from Catalina to Malibu. I figure it's now worth about $550,000, and I can rent it for $3,000 a month. When I originally bought that lot in 1962, I think I paid $12,000 for it and put $1,500 down. I plan to do the same thing with two other lots I own.

WHERE TO BUY

Many first-time investors make the mistake of thinking that high-priced areas are the place to buy. They really aren't the best locations for somebody to start in. You have to find an area where there's the potential for growth and fight it for a few years until the upward trend takes you out of the woods. It's important to be realistic. If you're married and the baby needs a new pair of shoes, you want to travel around the world, and you're working at Sears, you're going to have a problem—even if you *are* the best vacuum salesperson this side of Chicago!

Since neighborhoods tend to go in cycles, there is always some place you can go that has already experienced phenomenal growth where you can look back and see where your position would have been 20 years ago. This type of exercise gives you incentive. It's a way of learning without doing. It's a way of visualizing how you can pyramid yourself to the position you want to be in.

It's harder for people to buy property today than it was 20 years ago. To be sure, wages have not kept pace with housing costs. In 1973, the average 30-year-old could buy a typical house with 21 percent of his gross earnings going to mortgage payments. By 1984, he had to devote 44 percent of his income to make his mortgage payments. Today, that amount has decreased, but not by much. In my opinion, buying a house is well worth the sacrifice because houses are becoming like dinosaurs—they're getting scarce. And if you think it's hard to own property now, just think about the *next* 10 or 20 years.

Everything is anticipated. You're never certain what your need will be even tomorrow. That's what's so exciting about life. No one is willing to take a chance if they don't think they will succeed. You must have some incentive and insurance that it's going to work out for you, some motivating factor. Buy in an area with growth potential where you can afford the prices. As long as you can hold on to the property for the long pull, I can guarantee you're going to get rich.

I like to be close to my properties so I can see what's going on. When I first started acquiring real estate, I wouldn't buy anything that wasn't in walking or bicycle-riding distance. As mentioned before, I once owned a house in Hesperia about 80 miles from Los Angeles where I couldn't communicate with the people. It got to the point where I didn't want to go up there no matter what the problem was. You have to be attuned to the community. I wouldn't buy a place just because I thought I was going to make some money on it, although a lot of speculators do. To succeed in the long run, you have to know the neighborhood to really understand what's going on.

LIVING WITH NEGATIVE CASH FLOW

When you buy income property and have a negative cash flow, you can take depreciation write-offs on the improvements (the actual building) for tax purposes. The IRS allows deductions for interest, repairs, and other expenses, which helps offset your losses at the end of the year.

You want to structure a real estate transaction so you have as low a negative cash flow as possible. Say you buy a property and the owner takes back a second mortgage. You want to do what you can with that second so you don't have to make any payments on it. Take advantage and try to write favorable terms on the second because the institutional lender won't allow you to alter the first.

When I was buying my first properties, I lived with an awful lot of negative. But, like I said, I had a good job as an appraiser, so if I worked real hard, I could make my payments. Even so, many times I didn't know where the money was coming from to pay the taxes. I scraped the bottom of the barrel more than once.

It takes knowledge to accumulate real estate and the guts to put yourself on the line. You have to be disciplined and careful not to overextend yourself. But there is no way in the world you can succeed without taking a chance. It's like the turtle—he never gets anywhere if he's not willing to stick his neck out. You have to get on the bandwagon and you have to participate; otherwise it isn't going to work. A lot of people talk about what they *could* have done, but they aren't willing to put themselves at risk to take advantage of what is within their reach.

13

Manage Your Investment for Maximum Yield and Satisfaction

You don't get rich by making money. You get rich by wisely managing the money you make. The truth in this statement becomes apparent when you consider that an improperly handled investment can lose as much (if not more) as a properly handled investment can make. It therefore is in the property owner's best interest to keep the property rented at competitive rates, see that good tenants are satisfied, and ensure the building is well maintained.

A good manager will study the market constantly to see what the trends are, to observe what the competition is doing, and then raise the rents conservatively. I always try to be a couple of dollars under the market so people are happy. As long as they're paying the rent, I treat my tenants as if they own the property and do everything I can. They're buying the real estate for me. What more could I ask for?

———

On the other hand, you can't be too friendly with your tenants. But you do have to be fair with them, very fair. Whenever something breaks, I fix it as soon as possible because I don't want anybody to move. The most important thing you can do is to find a good tenant. A vacancy is profit right off the top, but believe me, a vacancy is a pleasure compared to a bad tenant.

If I can find a good tenant, I bend over backward to keep that person. I might even lower the rent if he had a problem in his job or some other major crisis, just to keep him. It costs so much money to find another tenant. If a tenant leaves and you have to redo the place, you lose a month's rent by the time you can rent it out again. It can be brutal, especially when you are just starting out.

———

A lot of good tenants have problems coming up with security deposits, plus first and last month's rent. I always try to give them the benefit of the doubt. I require a security deposit equivalent to the last month's rent, but I'm willing to work with people to get it. If the tenants are substantial, which you can determine through a credit check, I'll let them pay the security deposit over a three- or four-month period. I remember how tough it was for me, and I try to think about how other people might be in a tight situation like I was.

RETURN ON INVESTMENT

Because real estate is a wasting asset—the improvements, or building, eventually deteriorate and become obsolete—you should, as an example, get more than a standard 10 percent return on your investment because you have to put aside a certain amount of money to replace that wasting asset, so that you can get that 10 percent forever.

There are three factors that make up the income stream, or flow of money, generated by a real estate investment: quantity, quality, and duration. Quantity is obviously important. Does the property generate $200 or $3,000 a month? The quality of that income, the certainty of receiving it, also has an impact on the value of that property. Do you have a noncancelable lease with a huge corporation or have you signed an agreement with the corner shoe store? The income from the corporation is more secure than the money the shoe store will generate. Duration, the length of time the income stream from a particular property will last, is vital because it helps determine the financial viability of your investment.

Residential real estate is the best type of investment for the average person in my opinion because houses, duplexes, and apartment buildings maintain their economic viability for decades, if not centuries, while commercial properties become functionally and economically obsolete much faster owing to constant changes in the business community.

A single family residence I purchased in 1963 for $16,000 demonstrates the long duration of residential investments. The subject property is a 1,500-square-foot house with a studio apartment on the side of a single car garage. The property is zoned commercial, so it has a "mixed-use." A commercial property on an industrial lot is another example of mixed use. Mixed-use property is property zoned for a different use than the existing use. Obviously, the original zoning was residential when the house was built.

However, community influences over time acted to change the character of the area so that it is now more appropriate for commercial use. As a rule, it's difficult to finance mixed-use properties.

I put $1,000 down on this property and the owner took back the mortgage at 6 percent interest, or $95 a month. I've been very slow in paying it off. Today, because I have no due date on my loan, I continue to make my mortgage payment and collect the rent. I'm now getting $1,850 for the house and $650 for the apartment, which is $2,500 a month, or $30,000 a year. The property started to break even about four years after I bought it.

When I became interested in buying it, the owner lived in the City of Glendale, 30 or 40 miles away, and the lady who occupied the property said she didn't want me to come in because if I did, she knew I would buy the place and might make her move. I said, "Well, will you at least let me stand in the doorway?" I could tell just by doing that that the beams on the floor were solid, which was all I wanted to know.

Although I didn't ask her to, the woman moved on her own volition at the end of the escrow. That gave me incentive to upgrade the place a little. I bought a kitchen, including the counters, cabinets, dishwasher, garbage disposal, the range, and the oven, all used from another house for $1,500. It made the place more inhabitable, so I could get slightly higher rents.

COMMON INTERESTS

P eople are more tolerant of one another, and therefore more harmonious as tenants, when they have the same interests. When I was looking around for property to buy in Hollywood in the late 1960s, a lot of people were buying old apartment buildings and modifying them for cat owners. They'd put little pet doors in, cat walks along the sides of the building, a backyard for them to run around in. It was a cat lover's dream. It was a good idea because it attracted people with similar interests.

If you can alter the use of a property to cater to common interests, that will help attract tenants, keep the place rented, and stabilize the vacancy rate. Common interests apply not only to pets, such as cats, dogs, or birds, but to kids, singles, or retirees. A condominium complex I am familiar with operates a nursery near the front entrance of the complex where parents can drop their kids off before work and pick them up after. It's an ideal arrangement for a single parent or a dual-income family. They usually don't have many vacancies.

I once had an eight-unit apartment building in Los Angeles in the mid-Wilshire district. Whenever I rented an apartment there, I would ask the other tenants in the complex what they thought of the people I was renting to. I think it's important that I have a harmonious tenant mix like I do at the beach. I don't want any surprises, I want everybody to be happy, and I want to make sure they're happy—because they're buying the place for me.

A friend of mind once looked at a property on a street near a hospital that had seven one-bedroom houses on it with a large, three-bedroom house at the end. I tried to talk him into buying the property and putting up fences to divide each one of these houses for privacy. My idea was to convert the large house into a day care center and rent the other houses to nurses who worked at the hospital who had kids. They could take their kids over to the big house when they were at work and the kids could play in the yard and the owner of the big house could be a day care provider.

That would have been an interesting use of the property. I felt kind of bad the guy didn't do it because he really had a great opportunity. It was a nice piece of land with improvements already on it and he could have bought it for about what the land was worth.

If landlords would show a little more concern about finding tenants who are compatible and work together to have a desirable home and community, then things would work out much better. You show a lot of concern for your tenants by finding new renters who blend in with the existing arrangement in terms of their interests and attitudes. In my building, every tenant is compatible. If somebody moves in, I go around and introduce them to everybody else.

I also say that if they have any problem, let me know. I do this because I want my tenants to be happy. I provide tenants with every privilege I can. I always fix things as soon as possible because I don't want anybody to leave. I've always felt that was the best way to do it. They're buying the real estate for me. They can't do any more than that. At the same time, I am sure to tell them that I don't want a lot of noise and people hanging around and that if they just show concern for other people, then others will show concern back. If you put down a set of guidelines that satisfy both you and your tenants, you will be able to create a desirable atmosphere.

PERSONAL SACRIFICE

Unless you are already independently wealthy, you have to be willing to sacrifice to make a real estate investment program work. When I first started buying income property, I never thought about buying myself a new stove or refrigerator if mine was in disrepair unless all the tenants had one first because I needed the rental money to make the payment. Their comfort and satisfaction took precedence over mine.

When I started out, I lived in the cheapest apartment I had and tried to spend money on my apartments before I spent it on myself. Where I did spend money, I spent it in ways that made the rent come in. I wouldn't do anything frivolous to improve the condition of the property, but I would fix something right away if I could see that it would enhance the rental picture or make the tenants happy so they wouldn't move.

I never could pound in a nail straight. But I used to do everything I could—put in tile floors, fix stopped-up plumbing, put in a new garbage disposal, whatever it was. I had no choice, really. I couldn't afford to do anything else. The more you can do yourself, the better. It costs a bundle to hire an accountant, property manager, plumber, electrician, and handyman. When first starting out, most people don't have that kind of money. Again, look at this as a business. As the president of a company, would you hire consultants you didn't need?

If you're doing all this on a shoestring, you have to be careful. You can't always take draconian measures. When I started out, I wasn't married and didn't have much overhead. And I had a good job, so I could work long hours and make a lot of money. Oftentimes, I burned the midnight oil until 3:00 or 4:00 A.M. doing extra appraisal work to pay off some bills. Many times, I would have much preferred to go out to a square dance, but I knew what was more important. I was willing to sacrifice because I could see the opportunities were golden at the time. Now, my sacrifices have paid off. But for a while it was an exercise in discipline, perspective, and dedication.

I'm on the beach in a recreational area where tenants move in and out rapidly on a seasonal basis. Renting in this type of environment takes more effort than it would in a more stable community. Yet I've had some tenants for years and years in large part because I keep the rents down. In addition, I bend over backward for people whenever I can. As long as they don't hassle anybody, I tell them to act as if it's their apartment. No question about it.

────────

When managing your investment for maximum yield and satisfaction, you want to work out an arrangement that is enjoyable and not burdensome. The way I see it, I've got a six-unit building that has already and will again make me a million dollars. That to me is more important than the sacrifices I've made because I have an objective. Sure, it's work. But there is no way in the world that you're going to make it if you don't want to put in the effort—no matter what you do.

SELECTING TENANTS

There are several ways to determine whether you have a good prospective tenant—through a credit check, recommendations, a personal interview, and talking to previous landlords. The best thing to do is talk to people where the prospective tenant lives. Get a conversation going with the neighbors. Tell them that you understand Charlie Brown is moving out and he owes you $100. You'll hear everything you ever wanted to know. The best way to find out about other people's business is when people owe you money. Also try contacting friends, associates, former employers— whomever they put down as a reference.

But be careful about landlords; sometimes they will tell you a really bad tenant is a great person because they want to get rid of him. If you talk to people and take these extra steps, it could be worth your while, because good ol' Charlie Brown could end up owing you a lot more than 100 bucks if he's a bummer.

When I meet with prospective tenants, I basically ask if they pay the rent on time, how much were they paying before, if they have any past evictions, and if they can afford what I'm asking. The important things as far as I'm concerned are whether they will keep the place clean, abide by the rules, and pay the rent. I'm not concerned with anything else, unless it is a situation, for instance, where a tenant is physically handicapped and has difficulty getting into the place. I wouldn't want to hinder access. I've modified places for handicapped tenants. I've built ramps and decks when necessary.

═══════════

I had a friend who told her applicants that she would contact them in two days if she was interested in renting to them. She would then go to their current place of residence, unannounced, ring the doorbell, invite herself in, walk around, and make a decision on the spot whether she would rent them her house or apartment. I think that was a brilliant idea. And I'm sure it saved her a lot of money.

═══════════

A vacancy is a pleasure compared to a bad tenant. I'd rather have an apartment vacant for a month or two than have a bad tenant. It costs so much to get them out, and they wreck the place, plus you're liable to lose good tenants who are already in the building if you make a wrong selection.

Say someone rents an apartment, pays their first month's rent, and promises to pay the security deposit over a period of three months. Then they lose their job, but they don't tell you. So when rent is due, you go down there to collect it and they say they can't pay you right now, they'll have to pay you in a week. A week goes by and they say, "Oh, my dishwasher's broken and if you don't fix it, I won't pay." They might break a faucet or stuff a wad of toilet paper down the toilet. And so they maintain there are so many things wrong with the place that they don't want to pay rent. Since they refuse to pay rent, you decide to start eviction proceedings.

In many states, you start by filing a three-day notice to pay or quit and then a 30-day notice to evict. The tenant has to answer the notice, and it could take another month or so get on the court calendar. At this point, you are starting to lose money. Then, if you go to court and they can prove that you were negligent in maintaining your property, you are now in even worse shape because you are going to have to make the repairs, file eviction papers again, and then go back to court. If the judge rules in favor of the tenant, they're not going to move out, and you may not see any money from the place for several more months.

═══════════

I once had a problem with a property I owned that took almost an entire year to resolve. I lost a whole year's rent plus repair costs and legal expenses, probably $6,000, from that dispute. They didn't keep the place clean, their dog dug up the yard, they had thrown trash all over the premises, they destroyed the carpet, they didn't pay their rent, the neighbors were complaining. It was a living nightmare. After I finally got them out, I had to replace the carpet, which was brand new when they moved in! It was brutal, absolutely brutal.

When I first rented to them, they were fine. Then after a few months we started having problems. They stopped paying their rent. I had a real estate agent taking care of the place. After these tenants stopped paying their rent, the agent went over and threatened them. Plus, the lawyer I had was disorganized, so when the court issued the notice to remove these people, my attorney didn't receive the papers because he didn't provide a return envelope. I was on vacation at the time, so I wasn't there to handle it. It became a regular comedy of errors. This explains why I feel you have to be able to communicate with people, to find the type of property in an area that fits your demeanor.

When selecting a tenant, the best thing to do is tell him up front what you expect. For instance, if you don't want any dogs or loud noise or any motorcycles in the front yard, make that known. It took me a long time to learn this. I once rented an apartment to a guy from New York who rode a motorcycle. This was when I first got started. One day he decided to overhaul his bike, so he wheeled it inside and took it apart on the living room carpet!

Two weeks later I came back and there must have been about 20 motorcycles parked all over the lawn. They were everywhere. It was terrible, so I tried to get rid of him. That type of thing deteriorates the neighborhood. If you have good tenants, they won't put up with it, they'll move. If you're in a soft market and there's a bunch of vacancies, you can lose a lot of good tenants over one lousy one. That can be devastating, especially if you're working close to the bone.

When choosing tenants, try to get the best there is. Sometimes, you have to wait for the right tenant to come along, but do everything you can to keep him or her. My mother was a master of keeping tenants. Within reason, she would do anything for them—reduce the rent, fix the place up, all kinds of things. And she'd always figure out the cheapest way to do it.

I prefer to rent to a person who fits the need of the property. A single family residence is ideal for a family. I think a one-bedroom apartment is great for a couple or a single person. My studio apartments are suitable for one or two working or retired people. The property I have on the beach is not the greatest for a family—I don't think. It's too expensive. It's more suited for yuppies, single professionals on their way up who plan to be a huge success. Table 13.1 is a list of tenant arrangements I believe are suitable for different apartment sizes.

TABLE 13.1
Suitable Tenant Arrangements for Different Apartment Sizes

Size of Rental	Tenant Arrangement
Single (Studio) Apartment	Single person, any age
One-Bedroom Apartment	Young couples, middle-aged single adults and couples, senior couples
Two-Bedroom Apartment	Couples, roommates, and small families
Three-Bedroom Apartment	Larger families

CREDIT CHECKS

In addition to asking the above questions, I always obtain a credit report from a prospective tenant. A credit report is both a history and evaluation of a person's capacity to repay debts. It lets you know if they have any outstanding lien or credit delinqencies, if they make their payments on time, or if they've ever been evicted from any apartments. It's as good a sign as any that a prospective tenant is going to work out. The most important thing in a credit report is accurate information. A lot of people put down information that isn't accurate and this bogus data shows up rather authoritatively on their credit report.

As a landlord, you will encounter every kind of tenant with every type of problem there is. But it's extremely important to never, ever have a tenant submit their own credit report. If they work for a used car company or something, they can change their rating. I had a guy apply for one of my condominiums who worked for an automobile dealer that had access to TRW's credit reporting service. He was a crafty sort of fellow and found a way to insert his name onto other people's documents as they came in.

So when he applied he said, "Here's my credit report so you won't have to go through all that hassle." The property manager at the complex took the thing and it looked really good, almost too good. Well, this guy was in there for no more than two months and then we started having a terrible time. He drove a big limousine that he would park in the parking area, which was not in conformity with the rules. He wouldn't pay the rent. He was very noisy. He was a big liar, basically. We had to evict him.

With my condominiums, I have prospective tenants fill out a form and pay me $20 for the credit report in advance. On top of ensuring the veracity of the report, this method weeds out those applicants who aren't really interested. If someone pays and it doesn't work out, then they've lost the $20. If someone isn't willing to pay the fee, then you probably don't want them as a tenant anyway.

RENTAL AGREEMENTS

Most residential landlords use a standard rental agreement available through their local apartment owners association. Over the years, I have added several clauses to my rental agreement form to prevent routine problems that arise. Here is a facsimile of the rental agreement I use:

RENTAL AGREEMENT

TENANT INFORMATION   DATE: _____

Name _____   Home Phone: _____

Name _____   Employed By: _____

Name _____   Work Phone: _____

Present Address _____

MONTH-TO-MONTH RENTAL AGREEMENT

Address _____

Apartment is rented for $_____ per month. If tenant stays for a year, Rent will be increased $_____ each succeeding year due to inflation, increased costs of maintenance, taxes, utilities, etc. This provision of the Rental Agreement shall be continually in force with each succeeding tenant who occupies this rental unit.

Rent includes _____

Rent does not include _____

SECURITY DEPOSIT: Is refundable if tenant is not delinquent in rent, and
                               if no damage occurs to the building and/or furnish-
Section 1950.5:   ings, and tenant leaves the premises clean. The total
Calif. Civil Code: security deposit will be $_____. Ten-
                               ants may not, without owner's written consent, ap-
                               ply this security deposit to rent.

<u>**OCCUPANCY**</u>: Tenants acknowledge that they have examined the premises and found them to be in good and clean condition. Tenants agree to NOTIFY OWNER, <u>IN WRITING</u>, BY CERTIFIED MAIL (Return Receipt Requested), of ANY problems pertaining to the HABITABILITY of the PREMISES.

This apartment is rented to _____ person(s). No pets, no motorcycles ON OR NEAR PREMISES, no loud noises. If any additional occupants move into the apartment, then the manager has the right to request the tenants to move or adjust the rent. If Tenants are EVICTED, Tenants shall be responsible for ALL costs, including ATTORNEY FEES.

If ONE of the Tenants gives notice to move or if ONE or MORE Tenants VACATES WITHOUT GIVING NOTICE, this, in effect, GIVES NOTICE TO ALL OCCUPANTS in the Apartment that the premises ARE TO BE VACATED.

Rental starts on _____. Rent is due on _____ day of each month.

Upon signing this agreement, the Tenant(s) indicates full acceptance of all of the provisions, and further agrees that if Tenant does not inform manager, IN WRITING, at least 30 DAYS in advance of his/her intention to vacate the apartment, then the Tenant agrees to forfeit the deposit. This provision applies regardless of how long the tenant has occupied the apartment and the condition the apartment is left in. Upon receipt of written notice of Tenant's intention to move, the manager shall have the authority to show the apartment to prospective Tenants at reasonable hours. TENANTS MAY <u>NOT</u> SUB-LEASE APARTMENT FOR ANY REASON.

Amount paid by tenant as of
the date of this agreement: Signature(s)

First Month's Rent $_____   _____

Security Deposit $_____   _____

Total Paid This Date $_____   _____

Balance Due $_____   Date _____

Due Date   _____

Manager _____

Phone   _____

OWNER: DAVID T. SCHUMACHER, THE STRAND, HERMOSA BEACH, CA 90254

Occupancy Clause

With a rental agreement, you have the flexibility to stipulate whatever conditions you think are important and, of course, within the law. One item that I consider very important is my occupancy clause, which states: "Tenants acknowledge that they have examined the premises and found them to be in good and clean condition. Tenants agree to notify owner, in writing by certified mail (return receipt requested), of any problems pertaining to the habitability of the premises."

More often than not, I find that if a person can't pay the rent, they'll try to find something wrong with the apartment. They'll try to barter with you by saying, "I'll pay the rent if you fix..." the ceiling or the window or the garbage disposal. If you file a notice of default to nullify the rental agreement, they'll counter by saying the reason they're not paying the rent is that the landlord won't make certain repairs.

If you appear in front of a judge without any documentation proving the habitability of the premises when the tenant moved in, the court might rule in favor of the tenant. But, if you have a signed agreement with an occupancy clause stating that this is the way you are going to operate, the judge will be more inclined to agree with you. Without this clause, it's your word against your tenant's. And you can't even get into an occupied apartment without the tenant's permission. Believe me, this statement is invaluable.

Other times, a tenant might not inform you about legitimate problems with an apartment, except when you start filing notices. Or they won't tell you because it's something they did. Hence, the second line in my occupancy clauses states: "Tenants agree to notify owner, in writing by certified mail (return receipt requested), of any problems pertaining to the habitability of the premises." This legally obligates my tenants to inform me of any problems formally and to have proof that they sent the letter.

Nobody ever does, however. In all my time buying and managing property, I've only had one tenant who ever sent me a certified letter saying there was a mark on the wall and a little crack on the window. He didn't particularly want me to fix it, he just wanted me to know about it. I was glad he did.

Security Deposit Clause

Another important item on the rental agreement is the security deposit clause. I try to get a security deposit equivalent to one month's rent. And I stipulate in the agreement that the security deposit cannot be used for the last month's rent. When a tenant moves out, you have two weeks to decide whether to send back all of the security deposit or withhold money for repairs and cleaning expenses beyond normal wear and tear.

Rent Control Clause

I also have a clause that protects me in the event of rent control. Essentially, it states that if a tenant stays for a year, rent will be increased a certain amount each succeeding year because of inflation, increased costs of maintenance, taxes, utilities, and the like. I don't ever enforce it, but it lets people know before they come in that I reserve the right to raise rents to a certain level annually. A typical increase would be 7 percent. Depending on the exact wording of a proposed rent control ordinance, this clause may or may not hold up. But let me say this, I have a better chance of raising the rent and getting away with it than if I didn't have this clause.

KEEPING TENANTS SATISFIED

A contractor who was finishing up a remodel job for me a little while ago said, "Gee, you are going to have an awful time with your new tenant, he thinks he owns the place. He's telling everyone what to do, and he's real bossy and everything." I told the contractor that I *want* him to think he owns the place. The longer he's paying the rent and as long as he is taking pride in the place and keeps it clean and sees that nobody is stealing anything, he can go and tell the world that he owns it. I don't care. I own the deed. It doesn't hurt me any.

I feel that the tenants own the property as long as they're paying the rent because they're buying the property for me. Hence, I bend over backward to treat tenants right. One way I do this is by not raising the rents. Why squeeze your tenants like a lemon? Keep your rents reasonable. I think you should keep the rents about 10 percent lower than anyone else so you get a good tenant who stays for a while. It's cheaper in the long run. It's important to be aware of what's going on in the market, but I generally only raise the rents when people move out.

One of my beachfront properties, a lower unit, 1,000-square-foot place with two bedrooms and an oceanfront patio right on The Strand yields $2,000 a month. The upper unit, which is the same size and has an oceanfront view and a sun deck, rents for only $1,500 a month. I rented the upper unit out about 14 years ago to a woman who hasn't caused me any problems since. Everybody gets along with her. I might raise her rent eventually, but if I do, I'll only raise it to whatever she can afford.

Treat your tenants as equals, as you would like to have them treat you. Anybody who knows what they are doing can break a lease. They can just walk away, and what can you do? If you keep your tenants satisfied, they'll pay their rent on time and give you a guaranteed cash flow. I don't charge late fees. I should, but I don't. I think it's terrible to extract blood, I really do. It doesn't help any because of the spiteful mental attitude that goes with it.

On the other hand, you can't get too friendly with your tenants; otherwise, they might take advantage of the situation. If you are fair, you'd be surprised how many people they'll bring to you. If you treat a guy real nice and he moves out, sometime later you might get a friend of his as a referral and oftentimes he's a really good tenant, too.

Investigate the tenants to whom you rent first and pick people whom you like and can get along with. Ideally, the person who owns the property should collect the money. Of course, you can hire someone to do it, but when you're starting out, you probably won't be able to afford to do this. And, if you own a large complex, some people will try to take advantage of you.

A s I mentioned before, my mother was extra bright when it came to real estate. She never lost a tenant. I never in my life knew somebody who knew how to keep tenants so satisfied. She did whatever it took to keep them happy. She always said it was cheaper in the long run to be accommodating. We used to have some property in Taft, California. One tenant lived in a house we owned there for 20 years, another one for 18 years. I remember looking at my mother's tenant list one time. There wasn't one tenant who had been in a house she managed for less than 11 years!

She would do everything to keep her tenants. If someone would call up and say, "Well, we're thinking about moving," my mother would say, "Oh, don't do that. Do you want a new roof? We'll have the house painted." Or, sometimes she'd say, "I'll reduce the rent." She knew what to do and it paid off because she didn't want to drive all the way up there to fool around with vacancies.

PETS

If a tenant has a dog, I ask for a $250 pet deposit on top of the normal security deposit. Animals ruin the carpet and scratch the walls. They dig up the backyard and chew up the doors. But the worst thing is the smell. The stench they leave behind can be brutal.

My brother once had building in the north end of Hermosa Beach where he rented to a tenant who had an ocelot, a wildcat similar in appearance but smaller than a leopard. The odor that it left behind was awful! We had to tear all the carpet out, paint the place, use disinfectants, even replace some of the floorboards. Even after we did that you could still smell traces of it.

I think you should have pets in places where the pet is treated desirably. It isn't fair to keep a dog in a one-bedroom apartment where it sits in the dark barking when everybody goes to work all day. I don't think that's right. On the other hand, I don't think it's unrealistic to allow a dog if you have a two-bedroom house with a yard in the back. That's an ideal place for a dog. I don't mind cats (excepting ocelots) if they're clean.

THE BUSINESS OF INVESTING IN REAL ESTATE

If you own real estate, it's important to manage your investments as you would manage a business. When I started accumulating multiple properties, I set up a little room in the back where I kept my documents and files. I made sure to pay my bills on the 1st and the 15th of every month. Nowadays, my wife Margaret helps manage our properties out of a bedroom we have converted into an office. We make about 60 payments a month to utility companies, institutional lenders, and other creditors, and I always pay them at least two days ahead of time.

With repairs, every time a guy does a job for me, I always pay him on the spot, immediately after he finishes. Whether the plumber, the carpenter, or the electrician comes down to work on a building, they all know to knock on my door afterward to pick up their check. This way, if I want them to do something for me in a hurry, I know I can count on them. If they have to decide between two jobs, they're going to come to me first because they know they're going to get their money. I get better service than most people do, especially in times like these when people aren't paying promptly. When I call one of my repairmen on the phone, they're here in 20 minutes. And I know they won't overcharge me because they don't want to lose my business.

———————

Some people like to collect stamps or play volleyball on the beach. But for me, real estate is a sort of hobby. If you have another job, as I did when I started my investment program, you have to feel that real estate is a hobby. Otherwise, you might not enjoy it, and eventually you might get burned out. I really love the business, and I think that you have to enjoy it to be successful at it.

In addition to being dedicated, you have to be organized. You don't have to have a separate room for an office, but it helps. I keep at least one file for each property. We currently have 66 units that we collect rent from. Each time someone pays, I put an "X" by the month. The ledger I keep is good for three years. I have another three-ring binder where I keep all correspondence, leases, and rental agreements. I then assign each of my 66 tenants a number and write that number on any and all documents and correspondence that pertains to them or their unit.

At the end of the year, I add up the tallies for tax purposes and income reporting. And at the end of three years, I start a new ledger. I never made my bookkeeping system into a big deal, although now there are computerized accounting programs that streamline this whole process. I figure the best way to do it is to make it as simple as possible.

I also keep a folder (actually a photo album) of 5 × 7 cards for tenant records—who to contact in an emergency, where they work, when they moved in, what they're paying, things like that. It also lists repairmen. I also keep a list of all their bills from properties. Finally, I maintain a separate notebook of all my properties, their current market values, their tract map parcel numbers, the dates the escrows closed, the purchase price, recording document, square footage, the escrow number, type of property, zoning designation, and estimated value.

MANAGING PROPERTY

When you purchase properties, buy them close together so they're easy to take care of. When I started, my time was very valuable then because I was working a steady job as an appraiser and, at the same time, had to rent these places, maintain them, and do everything required, including cleaning, repairs, and renting out the units, so I confined my efforts to a small area. I didn't have any choice because I didn't have the money to pay somebody else to do it. Even so, you have to figure that your time is worth something and plan accordingly.

A person can have a job and manage a four-unit building without any trouble. But in my opinion, it's much easier to buy five single family residences that are close together than to buy a large apartment building. Once you get over 10 or so units, it becomes quite involved. In Los Angeles, apartment buildings with more than 16 units require an on-site property manager to handle rent collection, maintenance and repairs, and bookkeeping. The larger the complex, the more variables involved. If you own a 50-unit apartment building and you have an on-site manager, there are lots of ways a conniving person could take you to the cleaners, and you have to be aware of that. It's just like any other business.

As discussed in Chapter 2, with condominiums and townhouses the homeowner's association takes care of most outside maintenance and assists with renting. Inside repairs are generally simple because the units have a uniform building design. But with a custom duplex or unique single family residence, maintenance and upkeep can get complicated.

With people moving in and out of the 66 units I currently own and manage, some more frequently than others, it's virtually impossible to keep every unit rented 100 percent of the time. Today, that isn't a burden. I can afford a vacant apartment for a month or two and it won't hurt me. But when you're counting on the rent to make your payments, it's a different story. You have to be really diligent when you first start out because every nickel is important to you.

Say you own six units, and two of your six tenants aren't paying rent, or they write checks that bounce. That can be a real challenge. Some landlords insist on cashier's checks. When times were tight and I received bounced checks, I'd ask my tenant when he got paid. When payday came around, I would be the first person there to collect the money. Other times I would accept postdated checks.

HANDLING VACANCIES

In one condominium complex I have 26 studio apartments, so there are always one or two vacant there. Whenever I have a vacancy, I put some of these $50 flyers on the doors of my current tenants and manage to find new tenants pretty fast.

$50 $50

You can receive $50.00 for helping us find a satisfactory tenant to occupy our vacant Costa Mesa studio condominiums, located directly adjacent to the South Coast Plaza mall.

Just call...(714) 555-1234 or (213) 555-1234 and register your prospective tenant. Certain conditions apply.

Thank you. David T. Schumacher, Owner

$50 $50

W hen I bought the six-unit apartment building I live in, the whole thing was vacant. The entire neighborhood was characterized by vacancies. The person who owned the property before me couldn't handle it. When I moved in, I got the names and addresses of all the real estate brokers in the area and had cards printed up. The cards stated that if the broker contacted me, registered his or her name, and referred to me a tenant, I would give him or her 25 percent of the first month's rent. I mailed these cards out until I got every one of my units filled.

A good manager will study the market constantly to see what the trends are, note what the competition is doing, and then raise his rents conservatively. I have found that it takes about a year to feel comfortable with a property in terms of finding good tenants, making necessary repairs, and setting the right rents. As mentioned, I always try to be a few dollars under the market so that people are happy. It works out well.

Here is another flyer I use to rent my studio apartments. I place these 5 × 7 cards on bulletin boards, at the market, in laundromats, or wherever prospective tenants might congregate. The units I own there turn over pretty fast, but with these cards and the help of the on-site property manager, I usually have no problem renting them out.

FOR RENT

LARGE STUDIO APARTMENT

$_____ per month

FABULOUS LOCATION
Walk to South Coast Plaza Shopping Center, supermarket, restaurants,
medical facilities, etc.

SECURITY GROUNDS
Park-like setting, locked gates, swimming pools, jacuzzi, tennis courts,
exercise rooms, laundry facilities.

APARTMENT UNIT FEATURES:

500 square feet (approx.)
Enclosed patio with sliding glass door
On-site parking for two cars
Laid carpet, drapes, range, refrigerator
Dishwasher, wall heater, air conditioner
Pulldown queen-size Murphy bed
Built-in nightstand, desk, breakfast bar
Mirrored wardrobe closets

CALL TODAY FOR A WALK-THROUGH APPOINTMENT!

(213) 555-1234

COMMON MISTAKES

Many landlords make costly mistakes that cause no end of aggravation. These include inadequate oversight, sloppy bookkeeping, failing to run credit checks, and holding grudges. Some property owners get annoyed if they are called by tenants to repair things. They explode if they receive a check that bounces or, at two o'clock in the morning, a renter calls because a water line breaks and there's water running all over the floor.

No matter what you do, you're going to be disappointed. People aren't going to show up or pay you when you want them to. They're going to trash the place and break things. You can't let these kind of things anger you because you'll lose sight of the objective. It's hard when tenants move ut and you discover that they have ransacked the place. You just have to say to yourself, "Well, I have their security deposit and this property is really going to be worth something in 20 years." I admit, it's not easy to do.

S ome of the biggest mistakes I've seen landlords make in terms of managing their investments is getting mad at tenants for no good reason, or being too nit-picky. Why be overly concerned about whether a tenant ruined the screen door or spilled grape juice on the carpet? This kind of aggravation is trivial when you think about it. I don't have a real affection for the buildings. If something is damaged, I can get it fixed. If somebody busts the window, I'm not going to lose my appetite for dinner. I'm not going to have a bad night's sleep over it.

If a tenant calls me up with a mechanical problem, such as a backed-up sink or power outage, I get somebody out to fix it as soon as possible. I don't think you can expect to receive the rent on time if you wait two weeks to fix a clogged toilet. That's not being fair with people.

If you have a few good tenants and you establish a rapport with them, they'll keep you informed about everything going on at your apartment(s). I love being informed about my apartments, I really do. I don't mind being contacted. It's lots of fun. When people start to tell me what to do, how to run my business, I get fired up. I enjoy the tenants; I get a big bang out of them. I think the most important thing a landlord can do is listen to what your tenants have to say. When you listen, it calms people down. You can avoid a lot of problems that way.

When I taught night school, I got into a lot of challenging conversations. I thrived off that exchange and that rhetoric. I loved it. I ate it up. If it had been somebody else, they might have gone through the roof. Your personality has a lot to do with the type of landlord you are.

An adventure is defined as an unusual and suspenseful experience. If you enjoy spontaneous excitement, the problems you sometimes encounter as a property owner can make being a landlord adventurous and interesting.

O ne time a police officer knocked on my door at 2:00 A.M. and said, "You own the place, don't you?" I said, "Yes." He said, "Well, you have a flood out there." Some guy had apparently

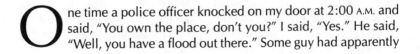

taken a sledgehammer in the wee hours of a Sunday morning and had broken my water spigot. It was shooting across The Strand. I said, "Oh my gosh, what am I going to do?" And the officer said, "You have two choices—either you call a plumber at triple time or you turn the water off."

I called my plumber, but he was in Lake Tahoe. So, mindful of costs, I turned the water off and wrote a note to all the tenants saying we couldn't get anybody out to fix the thing until Monday. People were screaming, they couldn't take a shower, wash their dishes, flush the toilets, anything. It was pandemonium at first, but when the tenants realized what had happened, they calmed down and accepted the situation in good spirit.

Another time, I got a call one night about 8 P.M. from a county health inspector who said he had found some hazardous waste in the trash bin of one of my Strand properties. The inspector said he was going to have to cordon off the area and call a hazardous waste removal team. The inspector had gotten a call from one of my tenants who, when taking out her trash, noticed a bunch of hypodermic needles in a box that had fallen open. So the health department came down and made a big scene.

When I got down there, he told me that I had to get rid of this hazard right away. I told him I would talk to a tenant of mine who works for the hospital. But the guy from the health department was adamant. He said, "Nobody's touching this. We've got to get a hazardous team out here." He handed me a list of five companies that handle hazardous materials and told me to call. Finally, I got a hold of a guy in Long Beach who said he would come out for $2,500, but it had to be cash or a cashier's check. I said, "It's 9 P.M., what do you expect me to do?"

So I told the health inspector that I thought he was being absolutely unreasonable. Then, I gathered up some bicycle chains and chained the container so nobody could get into it. In the morning I called up the waste disposal company that owned the bin, and they got their hazardous materials guys to come out with their gloves and hat and whole bit to remove this little box of needles. I had to pay them $650 to do it.

By taking pictures of the box and looking at it closely, they discovered that it had originated from a plastic surgeon in Los Angeles. Apparently, the doctor or someone from her office had dumped it into my trash bin. Since the origin of the syringes could be traced back to this particular doctor, the waste disposal company took her to court and the judge ordered her to pay my $650 back. I found out later that it was the health inspector's first case and that he wanted to make a big deal out of it to look good.

If the tenant who originally spotted the problem had just called me, I could have taken care of it by chaining up the trash container and having the fire department pick it up the next day. They do that kind of work all the time. This whole incident was much ado about nothing, really. But it was kind of exciting, too. It was a nice evening out, there was a challenging problem to solve, and I got to meet a few extra people. How you react to potential landlord problems like this is a matter of mental attitude.

Inadequate Oversight

If you agree to rent a two-bedroom apartment to two single guys, you want to make sure that it doesn't become a crash pad for a fraternity house. Most cities have ordinances limiting the number of occupants per unit. I'm tolerant of most situations, but I do care if renters disturb other tenants or infringe on their neighbors' rights. The minute they do, they're going to hear from me.

I used to have a tenant who ran his stereo out onto the beach. I told him he had an inferiority complex, that he did this to attract attention. There was no other reason I could come up with why he did it. I told him that if he had a charming personality, he could attract the girls some other way. We talked about it for a while and came to the conclusion that he should see a therapist, which he did, and it worked out. He didn't play his stereo anymore.

I like my tenants to be considerate and adhere to and respect other people's wishes. That's the way I would act if I was renting, and I expect them to be the same way.

Hasty Move-Ins

When renting to a prospective tenant, you don't want to have them sign a rental agreement today and have them move in later that afternoon or the morning after. Even if you've interviewed friends and former neighbors, you may not know why they're so anxious to get in, or where they were kicked out from. Usually, people are more than willing to give their previous landlord notice and go apartment hunting at least a few weeks in advance of their move date.

If, on the other hand, a renter gives notice in the morning and moves out in the afternoon, they might do the same thing to you—without even telling you. In some states, the law stipulates that tenants have to give two weeks' notice before they vacate, but what are you going to do if they don't—hire a private detective to track them down? You can't get blood out of a turnip. One of the things you *can* do is demand a cashier's check when a new tenant moves in. As a rule, I never accept an out-of-state check.

Sloppy Bookkeeping

Most people don't like bookkeeping, but without an orderly system, you won't be able to keep track of who's paying the rent on time, who's late, who's coming and going, and who your renters are. Many times, you may have two or three people sharing an apartment who each pay their rent separately. It can get really complicated, especially when some of the checks start bouncing.

Even if you only look at real estate as a sideline, you still need to be very careful to keep accurate records. With a sloppy bookkeeping system, you can lose track of things. A friend of mine once owned a 20-unit apartment building, which his wife would not have anything to do with. She refused to collect the rent, even if a tenant brought it by. She would say, "I'm sorry, that's not my department. Bring it back tomorrow when my husband's here." They probably lost a few month's rent because of that.

Holding Grudges

If you're bothered by quirks, nuances, and relatively minor things, then you're not going to be able to keep tenants for any length of time. My mother never held a grudge against anybody. If something happened she didn't like, she had this way of dismissing it from her mind. She didn't believe in gossip, either. She felt that if you didn't have something good to say about someone, then you shouldn't say it. It's very easy to find fault in people; we can look in the mirror and find fault in ourselves. Nobody is perfect.

If you hold people in low esteem on account of their failings, that attitude will certainly be reflected onto your interaction with tenants because they're anything but perfect. It doesn't work to get into grudge matches as a landlord because if you irritate your tenants, and they annoy you, everyone is going to be unhappy. Life's too short for that kind of aggravation. Happiness is a journey, not a destination. The journey should be filled with rich and rewarding experiences, rather than pet peeves, grudges, and other things that make people upset.

Both of my parents were positive thinkers. They always looked at the bright side of what was going on. For me, things always work out better when I think about the good. If you look at the bright side, it's easier to adjust to life's setbacks. And most everything does have a bright side.

EVICTIONS

I n my 35 years of renting houses and apartments, I've developed a method of ejecting tenants that could help people tremendously. I sometimes offer problem tenants money to leave; dismiss the back rent if they move out immediately; or help them find an apartment at a more reasonable price to expedite their departure.

W hen I bought my first six-unit apartment building by the beach, I rented out the penthouse suite to a couple who wrote me a check that bounced. I kept after them. But one night about two weeks after they moved in, they decided to move out. I figured they left about 2:00 A.M. because I couldn't hear them, and none of the neighbors saw them leave. They took my barbecue and all kinds of other things. I should have called the police because it was illegal, but I felt sorry for them. I knew that they were in worse shape than I was. I figured that in a few days I would forget them and have someone else to worry about, but they would carry their problems with them and probably suffer for the rest of their lives.

I generally don't file judgments against current and former tenants and go after them for back rent. Most of the time, you can't collect anyway. If they couldn't pay you when they lived in your place, why should they be able to pay you now? To my way of thinking, when somebody cheats you out of something and it's not of terrible consequence, the best thing you can do is to try to adjust to it and forget about it. Besides, if you pursue it, you might ruin their credit and that wouldn't be fair to the next person they tried to cheat!

One tenant of mine who lived in one of my beach apartments couldn't pay his rent and knew that he had to pay or quit, but couldn't adjust to the fact that he had to move out. He ended up living in his car for six months. That was much worse than anything I could have ever done to him. I could have sued him and maybe taken his car away from him, but what good would that have done?

Another tenant who wouldn't pay his rent stayed until the moment the sheriff came and told him he couldn't go back in. Then he wanted to cut some kind of deal with me. Lots of times people just don't want to accept reality. We all have problems. Life's just that way. So I don't view someone who doesn't pay his rent as a vindictive person who is hateful toward me. I see it more as that person's problems playing themselves out on a financial level.

Many people bite off more than they can chew. For them, life is just one darned problem after another. It's kind of sad really. But as long as their delinquency doesn't hurt me; as long as I can absorb the extra expense, I'm not going to raise a fuss over it. I figure there's enough in the world to go around for everybody. I really feel sorry for people who get into circumstances like that. And then I say to myself, well, maybe I made a mistake by accepting them as tenants in the first place.

When it comes to evicting tenants, there are important differences between residential and commercial properties. Residential property is someone's home. There's a different feeling about it than a commercial property. There is an emotional or sentimental attachment to shelter, whereas commercial real estate is a business and you deal with people like you would with any other type of business. One of the difficulties associated with buying real estate is not realizing what you're getting into, the humanity that comes into play.

When you're dealing with a family living in a residence, they might have a baby and haven't been able to sleep for two nights. You have to be sympathetic and understanding toward that, even if they are late on their rent. Commercial property is a horse of a different color; if someone doesn't pay their rent, you kick them out, no questions asked. It's more cold blooded. I would be more inclined to let a person who told me their problems slide along with the rent in a residential setting than in a commercial arrangement. I wouldn't want somebody to kick me out of my house, but I would understand if I was running a business and wasn't meeting my obligations and got the boot.

14

How to Make the System Work to Your Benefit: Refinancing and the Tax-Deferred Exchange

REFINANCING

After the great economic boom of the mid- to late-1920s, the crash of the stock market and the Depression that ensued virtually crippled the financial industry. These two events rocked money markets all over the world. Prior to the Depression, the typical homebuyer with adequate credit would take out a short-term, one- or two-year loan from a bank. The loan was usually interest-only. At the end of the financing term, the bank would renew the loan, enabling the borrower to defer payment of the principal balance almost indefinitely.

When the Depression came, banks could no longer afford to extend these one- or two-year "roll over" loans, so many properties were foreclosed because property owners could not come up with the cash required to meet their obligations. After congressional legislation restructured the Federal Reserve Bank, lending institutions were allowed to place amortized mortgages on real estate, on which borrowers could make equal payments of both interest and principal over 15 to 30 years.

Because amortized mortgages prevented serious financial hardships created by the one- and two-year mortgages, building became a gigantic industry in America. The new method of debt satisfaction allowed investors to accumulate huge debt loads without painful consequences as long as the payments were met. Refinancing of equities soon became a prudent way to take out cash from these investments.

Refinancing basically involves paying off the old loan with a new loan and getting a new, preferably lower, interest rate. Refinancing works out the best when property values appreciate because you can take out a new loan for up to 80 percent of the current appraised value. So if you bought a place for $100,000, and its market value had doubled to $200,000, you would be able to refinance for up to $160,000. That $60,000 above and beyond the purchase price is yours to do what you want with, although there might be some tax liability.

Property owners refinance their property for various reasons. They may need the money for a down payment on another property, for an addition or remodel of their current home, to sustain their small business, or to finance their children's college education. Some owners refinance their property every few years, some may never refinance. If the value of the property keeps going up, refinancing is advantageous. It's better than having money in the bank, really, because when your real estate increases in value it allows you to draw out a percentage for other uses.

When a better interest rate is available, there are financial advantages to refinancing your mortgage. It generally becomes advantageous to refinance long-term loans when interest rates fall two points below the fixed rate of the original loan. A new loan with an interest rate three points lower than your original loan would be fabulous. You can save real money in a deal like that.

Other times, refinancing is done for a specific, personal reason. A friend of ours refinanced his condominium once to take a vacation. He was paying 18 percent on his new loan, but for him, it was a question of going or not going. Luckily for him, interest on loans is deductible.

When you refinance a mortgage, you can often pick up cash, which is nontaxable because it is not considered income. I know a woman who, by refinancing her first mortgage, was able to take out a $1 million loan on her property, which she had purchased for $20,000 in the early 1960s. Of course, she could be subject to a hefty IRS tax on the loan depending on what she did with the money.

Usually, refinancing a first mortgage will enable you to get better terms, including a lower interest rate and a longer duration loan. With junior liens, such as second, third, or fourth mortgages, the risk involved generally demands a higher interest rate and a shorter due date on the loan.

———

In 1965, I acquired a four-unit building for $45,000. Today, the four units produce $4,000 a month in rental income, or $48,000 a year. My monthly mortgage payment, however, is only $350 a month. In 1985, 20 years after I bought it, that property was worth about $500,000. Today, it's worth $650,000. I know for a fact that the people I bought it from thought I would refinance the place and pay them off.

I still have about $15,000 outstanding on the mortgage, but I receive $4,000 a month in income from the property, so worrying about paying off the loan is a moot point. At only $350 a month with 6 percent interest, I have no need to pay it off. Today, I couldn't get

6 percent somewhere else. And for $15,000, where else could I find this type of write-off?

═══════════

When I first started buying, most of my loans had a 6 to 6.5 percent interest rate. Once, I had a 5.5 percent rate. We consider these rates low today, but they weren't then (see Table 14.1). Over the years, interest rates have fluctuated dramatically. During the recession of the early 1980s, interest rates peaked at around 20 percent. Today, the Federal Reserve discount rate to institutional lenders is at its lowest level in almost 30 years—3.5 percent. Mortgage rates, currently around 6 percent for adjustable mortgages and 8 to 8.5 percent for fixed-rate loans, are at their lowest levels since the 1970s, so many property owners who still have high interest rates are refinancing.

TABLE 14.1
Average Interest Rates of Conventional First Mortgage Loans on Single Family Homes from 1970 to 1991

	Existing Homes	New Homes	Federal Reserve Discount Rate
1970	8.2%	8.3%	5.5–6.0%
1975	9.0	8.8	6.0–7.75
1980	12.5	12.3	10.0–13.0
1981	14.5	14.1	12.0–14.0
1982	14.8	14.5	8.5–12.0
1983	12.3	12.1	8.5
1984	12.0	11.9	8.0–9.0
1985	11.2	11.1	7.5–8.0
1986	9.8	9.7	5.5–7.5
1987	8.9	8.9	5.5–6.0
1988	9.0	8.3	6.0–6.5
1989	10.3	10.1	6.5–7.0
1990	9.8	9.7	6.5–7.0
1991	8.4[a]	8.4[a]	3.5–6.5

[a] As of November. Figures represent national averages for all major lenders.
Source: Federal Housing Finance Board.

U nless I could get an incredible interest rate or had some other solid reason for refinancing, I would refrain from it because refinancing usually results in a higher payment. The publisher of the local newspaper refinances his property regularly to get cash for his business. That's marvelous. But I think it's better if you have low interest loans to try to pay the loans down and work with the income from rents rather than borrowing on the property and creating heavy debt. I've had second, third, and fourth mortgages, but I've only ever once refinanced a property.

The property was a single family residence in Hollywood that I bought for $24,000 in 1973. The seller accepted $5,000 down and carried the first mortgage for four years. At the end of three years, I refinanced that property for $24,000 and paid off the loan. So I don't have a penny in it now. I'm paying about $230 a month on the note from the refinance, but I'm renting the place for $1,200 a month, or $14,400 a year. The property is now worth about $375,000.

If you have to rely on refinancing a property in a certain amount of time to pay off your loan or to make a balloon payment, you might not be able to do it unless something dramatic happens to real estate prices— inflation, appreciation—or you enhance value through your own improvement efforts, such as remodeling or rebuilding. Again, you have to be in a growth neighborhood so that the property goes up in value.

An example of how refinancing can benefit an investor was demonstrated to me recently. An intrepid friend of mine owned a residence and four separate houses on the same block or within a short walking distance. He understood the area completely and had studied it knowing that the values would increase over a period of time because there was tremendous growth potential. He would refinance one house every fourth year and thus have one refinancing project every year. By doing this, he was able to pick up close to $50,000 each year in tax-free cash to spend on other investments.

A nother example is a young man whose father owned a used furniture store. The father wanted his son to continue with the business, but the son didn't take to his father's business and decided he wanted to become a real estate investor. To establish himself as a good risk, he took a job as a mailman. Over the next five years, he purchased over 35 small houses in the suburbs, many for nothing down. They were mostly foreclosures, so lenders were happy to sell them to him since his credit was good.

Once he had acquired all this real estate, he decided to quit his job and devote himself to fixing up, renting, and maintaining his properties. Twenty years later, his combined assets totaled in the millions because he had purchased his properties for dirt cheap in a down market that rebounded fantastically.

One of the main advantages to refinancing is that you can take out a loan for more than the original mortgage or purchase price. Say you purchased a property five years ago for $200,000 and took out a $120,000 loan. Now you want to refinance because the value has risen to $320,000. So you visit your lender and obtain a loan for $220,000. Because you are now $20,000 above the basis, or purchase price, you have to pay tax on it because it's added income. Before the Tax Reform Act of 1986, you didn't have to pay tax on the amount that was over basis.

The drawback of refinancing to get a lower rate is that it costs money to go through the process. When lenders agree to refinance a loan, they charge a few points in transaction costs. So refinancing may cost a little money. The tax laws haven't been too favorable toward refinancing, which is one of the reasons the real estate market has not been as active as it used to be. Whereas before the 1986 tax reforms all home mortgage interest was fully deductible, now mortgage interest is deductible only on your place of permanent residence.

In order to tap the equity in a property, some owners would rather put another lien on their real estate than refinance the first mortgage. In general, it's not a good idea to disturb the first mortgage to put on a second. You might decide to take out a second mortgage from a "hard money" lender—a private lender who gets funds from private parties and loans it for individual properties.

As mentioned before, hard money lenders demand a higher rate of interest than institutional lenders because they assume more risk and don't have to comply with regulations as strict as those governing lenders who deal with public funds. Hard money lenders usually require a balloon payment as well. I would avoid a hard money lender if at all possible.

TAX-DEFERRED EXCHANGE

Although never selling is my rule of thumb for successful real estate investing, there are rare instances when selling after an extended period of ownership is advantageous, particularly when a tax-deferred exchange can be made. Under Section 1031 of the Internal Revenue Code, like-kind property used in a trade or business or held as an investment can be exchanged tax-free. The tax system, through the tax-deferred exchange, encourages sellers to buy similar properties of equal or greater value by making them tax exempt.

Many residential income property owners choose to make an exchange when, after owning a piece of real estate for over the 27.5-year depreciation period, they can no longer take a tax write-off because the paper value of the building for tax purposes has reached zero. (Prior to 1986, the depreciation period for residential income property was 19 years.)

After owning the four-unit apartment building described in Chapter 12 for 25 years and seeing its real value soar from $45,000 to $1 million (while its paper value dropped to nothing because of depreciation), I decided to sell it and make a tax-deferred exchange. With the profit I received from the sale, I traded my one property for three houses and a condominium.

I can now take the depreciation on those four properties and use it as a tax shelter—an investment that produces after-tax income that is greater than before-tax income. The old property, although worth a great deal, was only yielding a 5 percent annual return. Because the depreciation period had expired, it was in my best interest to exchange other properties that I could take depreciation on.

By selling one property and buying four others, I increased my assets without paying taxes on capital gains. If you buy enough property, the depreciation you can take will offset the taxable income you receive. It works out so you don't have to pay as much tax.

If you bought a property in a mediocre location with a huge structure on it, a higher dollar value would be allocated for the improvements, the actual building, than the land. Say you pay $100,000 for a property. For tax purposes, you make an allocation of the depreciable assets compared to the nondepreciable assets. Depreciable assets include the building, utilities, underground plumbing, sidewalks, fixtures, contents, everything except the vacant land, which isn't depreciable.

The higher the building-to-land ratio, the more depreciation you can take. For this reason I decided to buy apartment buildings on the oceanfront rather than single family residences. With apartments, you can allocate more for the buildings.

T he most desirable thing is to find a property that is overbuilt, for instance, a multiunit legal nonconforming apartment building where you can't put back a building of similar density because of city downzoning. By buying the nonconforming building, you get a better depreciation write-off because you can allocate more for the building. In some instances, it is wiser to put money into improving a legal nonconforming building than investing in a teardown property or new development.

Industrial and commercial buildings have a longer depreciation period than residential dwellings. But an advantage to buying, say, an apartment building is that you can take many of the things that aren't considered construction items and put them in a separate category of furnishings and equipment. Items such as carpets, drapes, refrigerators, drop-in ranges, window air conditioners, portable heaters, swag lamp fixtures, gardening equipment, and pool and patio equipment can all be valued and depreciated over a short term.

For tax assessment purposes, I always segregate the purchase price into the land, the improvements, and the equipment. Assume you paid $100,000 for a property, say $90,000 for the real estate (including land and improvements) and $10,000 for the equipment that came with the building. For tax assessment purposes, that $10,000 for equipment should not be assessed with the building. It should be a separate category.

I do this to achieve a lower assessed value. If you start at a lower base, your taxes are going to be lower. The mistake accountants make at the time of acquisition is that they take the assessed value ratio of the land and improvements for depreciation instead of going to the site and studying the problem. And when most county assessors establish property values for tax purposes, they distinguish between land and improvements, but they don't isolate the equipment value. It's important to be honest with everything you do. But if you know your facts and what to do, you can save some money here and there. If you own real estate, it's important to manage your investments as you would manage a business.

W hen you buy real property, the allocation for improvements is depreciable over a 27.5-year period. As the value of the physical building depreciates, some of the net income is sheltered for tax purposes. It's a loss, but a paper loss. Actually, the building will probably appreciate in value if the market goes up.

In the above example, say the land was allocated at $20,000, the improvements at $70,000, and the personal property at $10,000. Assuming you can take $10,000 off the value of the building improvements attributable to depreciation over a few years, your basis will then be $60,000. At the end of the fourth year, you decide to spend $20,000 on an addition.

Your basis then rises to $80,000 on the improvements, plus $20,000 on the land, plus whatever amount you have not depreciated on the personal property, for a total of, say $105,000. Now, assume you trade up for a like property for an equal or greater value. You wouldn't have to pay any federal income tax on it; you simply exchange the basis to the new property and continue on. When you trade up, you change your basis—the purchase price less the depreciation taken on the improvements and the personal property, plus any added monies you put into the property.

A tax-deferred exchange is a way of extending your wealth and achieving your goal. It's not a tax-*free* exchange, it's a tax-*deferred* exchange. You're deferring your payment of taxes until the time you're through with all your exchanges. In a tax-deferred exchange, you sell your property and put it into an accommodator account. You then take the money from the sale and purchase another like-kind property of equal or greater value.

The IRS looks at an exchange as if you were extending your first investment onto the next property as it increases in value. Say you buy a duplex for $100,000, which has a $60,000 loan against it with $40,000 equity. If you trade that duplex for a $200,000 triplex or four-family flat, you're trading your equity into a new property. As long as you keep extending your investment and the price goes up, there's no tax to pay. But if you make the exchange and have to put in boot to make the payment—cash, rare coins, jewelry, cars, anything of value that isn't considered like-kind property—that's added cash, which you as the seller will have to pay tax on.

Say you have $60,000 in equity in a duplex worth $100,000, which you trade for a $200,000 duplex that the seller only has $40,000 equity in. You're assuming his or her $160,000 loan. But if you have $60,000 equity to trade, he or she has to give you $20,000 boot to make the deal. That's money the buyer has to pay taxes on.

Although I have used it, the tax-deferred exchange was never much of a consideration for me because I always planned to never sell the property I bought. If you pick the right piece of real estate in a good location, you want to retain the property, not exchange it for something else. The best time to make an exchange is when you want to buy something better or consolidate your properties.

When you are involved in making any kind of real estate exchange, it is essential that you consult a competent tax attorney and accountant to be sure that you are complying with the current rules and regulations of the IRS. Tax laws change rapidly and rules that are appropriate today might be drastically different tomorrow. It is therefore important to stay current and make adjustments that reflect changes in the tax laws.

15

Protecting Your Investment and Accomplishing Your Objective

PROTECTING YOUR REAL ESTATE
INVESTMENT FROM NATURAL DISASTERS

There is a natural human instinct to protect family, home, and personal belongings against disasters of all kinds. One of the reasons that casualty insurance companies have been so successful in past generations is that they have played on the fears of people and stressed how a loss would affect their lives. Casualty insurance is a business based on fear. People are afraid that they are going to lose something.

———

S ome close friends of our family never carried any insurance, except on their automobile. They had no life insurance, health insurance, or fire insurance. Since they owned their residence free and clear, they were not required to carry fire insurance on their home. If they had a mortgage on the property, the lender would have insisted on adequate fire loss protection. This family insured themselves by having sufficient revenues in the bank, plus other debt-free income property.

The husband lived to be 89 years old and his wife died at the age of 87. Neither of them ever spent a night in a hospital, and they seldom went to the doctor. I often thought about how much money they saved in the form of insurance premiums during their lifetime.

On the other hand, my father and his business partner had about every kind of insurance imaginable. In later years, when my father became ill, the insurance company refused to pay for his medical bills a few months into his illness. When I complained to the office of the Insurance Commissioner, the insurance company promptly canceled his policy. Wasn't my father fortunate to have investment real estate with sufficient income so that the loss of his insurance policy was unimportant?

Fire Losses

A fire insurance policy is very difficult for a layperson to thoroughly understand. Fortunately for the insurance company, the policy does not require strict interpretation until a loss occurs. All reputable institutional lenders require adequate fire insurance on real property improvements if a real estate mortgage is in force. The insurance policy may be written to cover replacement cost of the building or it may be written to cover the *depreciated* replacement cost of the building. The difference is in how the costs are arrived at.

Replacement cost is defined as the cost to replace a structure with one having utility equivalent to the subject structure but built with modern materials according to current standards, design, and layout. Depreciated replacement cost is defined as replacement cost, less accrued depreciation based on age, use, and condition. Another method of calculation used by insurers is reproduction cost, or the cost of reproducing the subject structure with one that is an exact replica in quality of workmanship, design, and layout.

Most fire insurance policies are written using the replacement cost method because it measures depreciation (the loss in value of a structure due any cause) in dollar amounts. As an investor, it is very important for you to be fully aware of the type of insurance you are carrying, how your assets will be calculated in the event of a loss, and if your policy carries adequate protection.

When I worked for Marshall and Stevens, I used to appraise real and personal property for fire insurance purposes. With real property, my job was to write a report describing in great detail the physical structure of the building and all of the components, including the foundation, frame, floors, ceilings, exterior walls, interior layout and design, plumbing, electrical, heating, air-conditioning, roofing, and exterior features such as porches, balconies, and fire escapes. I would also list in detail the personal property, such as carpets, drapes, kitchen appliances, lobby furnishings, and other types of portable equipment necessary and pertinent to the operation of an apartment building. Each component was priced showing replacement cost and depreciated replacement cost. In addition, the furniture and equipment was priced showing present and replacement value.

The benefits of a fire insurance appraisal to the investor are enormous. The most important benefit is that a fire loss is virtually settled before the fire happens. The appraiser is an unbiased, third party who has described in detail and placed a value on each of the characteristics of the construction and personal property in sufficient detail to support the property owner's claim of loss. It should be pointed out that it is the policyholder's responsibility to provide the insurance company with a proof of loss statement listing and valuing all items affected by the fire.

With a replacement cost appraisal in hand, the proof of loss settlement is, in effect, prepared in advance by a competent, disinterested third party who is qualified to testify in court on the validity of his or her appraisal report.

Under certain circumstances, this report could be invaluable. I remember many years ago, one of the appraisers working in our company prepared an appraisal of the construction and equipment of an industrial building for fire insurance. The industrial plant's main process was metal plating. About two years after the appraisal was completed, a tremendous explosion occurred in the plant, actually blowing the building and equipment into oblivion. The explosion was so severe, it catapulted chunks of concrete in the air, hitting buildings one and two blocks away from the scene of the accident.

As I recall, a number of people perished in the explosion. Afterward, there was nothing left. Only some parts of the concrete foundation from the building could be seen around the deep hole created by the blast. The only copy of the appraisal report prepared two years earlier was in our office. The other two copies were tucked away in the company's fireproof safe. No trace of the safe could be found anywhere.

The copy of the original appraisal report that we had in our office became essentially priceless. Criminal charges were filed against the owner. Lawsuits were filed by homeowners and commercial property owners in the surrounding neighborhood whose buildings suffered damage in the explosion. People affected by the disaster were up in arms. It was a terrible tragedy.

The property owners used the appraisal report to construct on paper exactly what activities were performed on-site, what type of equipment was used, and what condition the items were in before the loss. Using that as a basis, the owners proved that they were not negligent in maintaining the plant premises and operating the business. I was later informed by a reliable source that the insurance company had no recourse but to pay up in full. I bet it cost them millions.

If no surviving appraisal had existed after the explosion, the final outcome for the property owners would have been altogether different. A fire loss or any kind of catastrophe can be devastating. I periodically check my property for hazards, such as an accumulation of junk in basements, attics, garages, and storage areas. Also, it is extremely important to have working smoke detectors installed as well as fire extinguishers and garden hoses.

One of my buildings has an outdoor fire escape with a drop ladder to the street. A few years ago, one of the large trucks that pick up trash in the area hit the fire escape and bent the ladder. I wrote several letters to the trash company explaining what a serious hazard was created by not having the ladder completely operative. I asked them to repair the damage. After nine months of getting nowhere with letters, phone calls, and personal interviews, I figured out what to do.

The trash company collected trash from five of my buildings. So when the bills came in, I held them for two months. Then I made out the checks for the five accounts but did not sign them. I sent the unsigned checks to the trash company, along with a letter explaining the fire escape problem and how disturbed I was. I told them if they wanted the checks signed, to bring them along when they came out to repair the fire escape. They had a man out within two weeks and performed the repairs to my satisfaction.

Most insurance policies covering investment-type properties are written with a coinsurance clause in the policy rather than as a stipulated amount. A stipulated amount policy is one where the value of the improvements are specifically stated in the policy for a given period of time. With this type of insurance, the policyholder usually pays a higher premium than for carrying coinsurance.

Over 90 percent of all the fire losses throughout the United States are partial (not total) loss claims. The insurance industry realized many years ago that if you owned a commercial building that would cost, say, $150,000 to replace but only insured it for $50,000, the odds were 9 out of 10 your $50,000 policy would cover any damage resulting from a partial loss. The odds would be in your favor of having the building restored, provided the insurance company paid for the loss. You can see from this example how an insurer could lose valuable premiums by not having buildings insured to full value.

T he insurance companies concluded this was not good for business and decided to correct it by issuing coinsurance policies. For a reduced premium rate, the insured policyholder with a coinsurance policy agrees to insure his building for the full value. If a coinsurance policy is in force and a fire occurs, and it is determined that the building is underinsured, the policyholder becomes a coinsurer and must make up a portion of the loss.

For example, say you own a commercial property. The market value is $300,000. The land is estimated to be worth $200,000 and the building, or improvements, to be worth $200,000. Through negligence or an oversight, you only have the building insured for $100,000. If a fire occurs causing $50,000 damage to the building, the insurance company will penalize you by 50 percent for not having adequate coverage under the terms of the policy.

When a Fire Loss Can Be Advantageous

S ometimes a fire loss can result in a decided advantage. An interesting case occurred to a property owner in downtown Los Angeles. Many years ago, a widow owned a two-story commercial building on a valuable corner lot. She inherited the property from her father's estate. The building was leased to a commercial tenant on a fixed rental of $1,500 per month for 30 years. The tenant paid all expenses, including real property taxes, insurance, and maintenance. The fair market value of this burdensomely leased property was $225,000. The property owner had the building appraised for fire insurance by a qualified appraiser. The insurance company stipulated the full value at $185,000. About two-and-a-half years later, the property owner traveled to Europe.

While she was in Europe, the building burned down. It was a complete loss. She came home, collected her $185,000 from the insurance company and sold the vacant land to a parking lot operator for $200,000. She ended up with $385,000, all cash, for a property that a few years before was worth only $225,000. Before it burned to the ground, the building was a burden on the land because the land wasn't being put to its highest and best use.

Contingent Liability

If an investor owns a property in an area where the construction does not comply with the present zoning laws, the investor must be sure to carry special coverage to protect against contingent liability. Contingent liability insurance covers a situation where if a structure is partially destroyed to the point where the city or county won't permit reconstruction to its original use, the insurance company will consider the structure a total loss.

If a fire loss occurs and the company's adjuster and the insured cannot agree on a settlement, the case usually goes to arbitration. This means that the insurance company selects a representative and the insured selects his own representative. The two representatives then meet and mutually select a third person. The three people become the arbitration board. After hearing all of the evidence, two out of the three arbitrators agree on a settlement.

═══════════════

A number of years ago, I represented the owner of a restaurant in arbitration after a serious fire damaged his kitchen. The insurance company offered the insured $20,000 to settle his claim. During this period of my appraisal career, I appraised many of the fine restaurants along La Cienega Boulevard in Los Angeles. I was very familiar with kitchens, so the first thing I did was to draw a floor plan of the burned-out kitchen with the ashes from the fire. With the help of the employees, I was able to plot the location and sizes of all the equipment in the area before the loss.

We were then able to determine all of the items on the countertops, racks, and shelves that were necessary to operate the business. During the course of my analysis, I was able to discern the extent of fire damage to the building. When the case went to arbitration, I represented the property owner and with all of the factual data, agreed on a settlement in excess of four times the original offer from the insurance company. If you ever have a need for someone to represent you in a fire loss settlement, be sure to get a person who understands the problem and has experience in that type of case.

═══════════════

Hurricanes

Technically, a hurricane is an atmospheric disturbance characterized by masses of air rotating around a low pressure center with heavy rains and wind reaching beyond 75 mph. Hurricanes that affect coastal areas of the United States generate their wind velocity in the Atlantic Ocean, the Gulf of Mexico, or the Caribbean Sea. During the early and mid-1900s, hurricanes created devastation without adequate warning to coastal communities, killing scores of people and destroying almost everything in their paths.

Since the onset of the space age, satellites have traced weather patterns, enabling scientists to predict the course of hurricanes well in advance of a disaster, thus allowing evacuation plans to go into effect, saving money and lives and protecting property. Today's improved construction standards take into consideration hazards from high-velocity winds and severe rainstorms.

Obviously, for the investor, it is best not to purchase property in the path of hurricanes. Before you purchase a property, study the history of the area to determine what has happened in the past. Remember, history often repeats itself, especially where nature is concerned.

ACCOMPLISHING YOUR OBJECTIVE

Henry Ford, John D. Rockefeller, Andrew Carnegie, and Thomas Alva Edison all rose from poverty to become multimillionaires, great innovators, and catalysts who helped spark our nation's tremendous economic growth in the late nineteenth and early twentieth centuries. Each of these industrial giants is credited with setting and accomplishing monumental goals during their distinguished careers. These men must have taken countless risks before achieving great success. And their willingness to take chances paid tremendous dividends when combined with perseverance and commitment.

We can apply the experiences of these towering figures in American history to long-term real estate investment. The importance of developing the qualities that helped make them successful, namely patience and dedication to a task (or objective), cannot be over-emphasized.

When you buy real estate, a strong sense of what you hope to achieve through investing is paramount. As with a college education, you should know what's involved and what kind of return you expect to get from the efforts you put into it. You never want real estate to become a burden. You want it to be a pleasant experience, and you want it to be something you can always enjoy and feel you really want and are proud to own.

As realtors are so fond of saying, location is everything. You'll always make money if you buy the cheapest property in the best location, but you'll almost always lose money if you buy the most expensive property in a lousy location. Most importantly, you must identify an area that has growth potential.

Everything we do in life is a risk. I don't care what you do. Walking out the front door is a risk. Putting your money in the bank is a risk. Speculating in the stock market is a risk. But the odds of investing in real estate the way I have outlined are a great deal better than the odds of winning the lottery.

The thing you should never do is overextend yourself. You have to take a chance, but you have to take a chance that's in your favor. The risk is commensurate with the return, but taking a risk doesn't mean putting everything on the line.

American financier and statesman Bernard Baruch used to say that a guy is rich if he has a dollar more than he needs. In real estate, success comes to those who make smart decisions, are willing to take a certain amount of risk, and can wait it out.

I felt like I was starting to accomplish my objective after I had acquired five buildings on the oceanfront, which was about five years after I started on my real estate program. I felt that I was on the road. It probably took me a few more years to realize my first significant cash flow, however. At that point, I felt I was accomplishing something. I was building an estate, creating some wealth. That gave me incentive to continue buying.

When I first started, I bought everything I could with the money I had. I knew that after prices went out of sight I would not be able to afford to buy any more and would have to concentrate on improving my existing properties. A lot of people hold a ceremony when they burn their paid off mortgage. Whenever I pay off debt, I immediately think about new possibilities. It frees me up to start thinking about making other investments. Opportunities do not come in real estate if you stop buying.

Patience is Virtue

A lot of people are easily upset because they can't see the end result when they embark on a project. But you can't think about real estate that way. If you own an apartment building, you have to fight it until the time comes when the area improves and you achieve a positive cash flow. There are always people who have a negative outlook—far more people in this world have a negative outlook than have a positive way of seeing things. They hate getting up in the morning to go to work, they don't like their community, their city council, the way their kids are treating them, the smog, the congestion, the way Congress is acting.

I say: Change your attitude. There is no other solution. My mother had this way of only remembering the good things in life. She used to tell me it was too much trouble to remember all the terrible things in life, probably because there was so much of it. She regarded all the bad little things, especially gossip, as so much trivia that didn't do any good for anybody. The worst thing you can do is worry about things you have no control over. That will destroy you more than anything. If you can do something about it, then great. Take action. Otherwise, why dwell on it?

With real estate, you've got to find property that fits your need, attitude, desire, and personality. If it isn't for you, don't meddle with it. It probably isn't worth fighting. I don't know too many people who would have bought in Hermosa Beach when I did in the early 1960s, when motorcycle gangs used to blare up and down the main street and rumble down the alleyway. Sometimes, they would stop outside my door at 3:00 A.M., open up the throttle, and rev their motors, driving me crazy.

Yet thousands of people who lived in this area during the 1940s and 1950s who sold their property wished they hadn't. That goes for so many areas across the country. I had a friend who owned a house on The Strand who tried to sell it in 1972 for $60,000. He did everything he could: advertised it, sat on it, told people about it. Finally, he found a buyer. Today, that house is worth $1.3 million. I talk to him all the time. Now he feels real bad about selling. He said he needed the money at the time to help his kids, but his kids are in worse shape now than they were before.

In real estate, you shouldn't sell when the market is good. You have to look beyond the short term. I know if my friend had his Strand property now, he could borrow a half a million on it without any problem, as long as he had the income to support the loan. It's not easy to distinguish between today's reality and what a property will be worth 20 years from now, but this is the way you should start thinking about real estate.

I knew a woman who had a couple of kids and wanted to sell her house. I told her that if she sold that house, she would never have another one. She would always be renting. No matter what her difficulties were, I told her she should hang on to it. She was divorced, living on her own. The fact that she didn't have enough income to qualify for a housing loan would have prevented her from buying another property. But I'm sure a broker came along a few years later and persuaded her otherwise.

Selling is tempting. It endows you with a bundle of cash to pay off your bills, buy a new Ferrari, a yacht, or RV, whatever it is. But you're really in worse shape when you sell property for that reason. I always hate to see that happen to families because it's always so hard for the kids. They have to move into a rented apartment or house and never experience from their parents the stability and security that ownership provides.

If you locate a true growth area, prices will rise rather dramatically, so if you sell today for $120,000 and over a few years prices increase to $265,000, you're going to have a hard time qualifying for a new loan, unless you've hit a jackpot in the meantime. Rents will rise in proportion to land values, so it's much better to hold on to property than sell.

You're looking at real estate to do you some good over the long term. Everyone who sells property too soon loses the farm. Anyone who builds a house and sees a small profit ahead and lets go by selling, unless they are stretched, also loses. If they could have held on to their land, taken the benefits, and kept it for a period of time, they would have come out much better.

When I moved to Hermosa Beach, every Halloween there were hundreds and hundreds of kids who walked up and down The Strand. It was fantastic. Last year, there wasn't one trick or treater. The spiraling price of real estate has taken young families out of the market. It's sad, really. But it's also a firm indication of what the trends are in a community.

I'm amazed at the number of people who come up to me and say, "The price of that lot over there is $1 million. How can that possibly go up? How can it get any higher? That place used to sell for $20,000." And I say to them, "It hasn't started to go up yet. You're dreaming. You're talking about 5-cent beer." Do you think the market will ever revert, that housing prices will start going down instead of up? That's like saying the horse and buggy will one day replace the automobile. Prices may fluctuate from time to time, but I don't foresee any drastic downturn.

For genuine perspective, you should travel to other parts of the world, if you ever have the opportunity, and see what houses are selling for in major metropolitan areas. Try pricing real estate in the center of Tokyo, where a three-bedroom house sells for about $12 million. There isn't any major city in the world in a desirable area where the prices aren't out of sight: London, Paris, Tokyo, Hong Kong, Geneva.

In the United States, look at Houston, Dallas, Phoenix, Seattle, or Portland compared to Los Angeles or New York. Prices are bound to go up in these areas, but I'd have to have a reason to go to one of these cities and invest. If you have studied the community and are correct in your analysis and buy real estate for the long haul, you're going to get rich. I know you are.

Appendix A: Schumacher's Real Estate Axioms

- If you own real estate, it's important to manage your investments as you would manage a business.
- Strange as it sounds, some people are scared by having money.
- You don't get rich by making money. You get rich by wisely managing the money you make.
- If you're smart enough to have some money, you're smart enough to use it wisely.
- There's only one, positive guarantee of security, and that's a life term in Leavenworth maximum security prison!
- When money is involved in a transaction, you have to have it in writing; otherwise, it doesn't carry much weight.
- You can buy a man a fish dinner and feed him for the evening. But if you teach him how to fish, he can survive for a lifetime with that knowledge.
- Everybody has a right to their opinion, but to make a good decision, you have to get your facts straight.
- Debt is a wonderful discipline.
- My mother never held a grudge against anybody. If something happened that she didn't like, she had this way of dismissing it from her mind and not remembering.
- A vacancy is a pleasure compared to a bad tenant.
- Investing in real estate can be like a trip through the looking glass with Alice in Wonderland. If you don't know where you are going, it doesn't matter which way you turn.
- Like they say, a penny saved is a congressional oversight.
- Bogus advice has always been around. But advice that is bogus for one person might be good for someone else.
- I never met anybody I didn't get a good idea from.
- Great real estate deals are not found. They are created.
- Finding a good real estate investment is not a matter of luck; it's being able to act when you should.

- Opportunities do not come in real estate if you stop buying.
- All you have to do is find one good bargain a year.
- You can rest assured that values will increase because a capitalistic economy cannot exist without inflation.
- Don't make snap judgments if they can be avoided.
- If you're going to be successful in anything, it has to be you making the decisions—not your broker, attorney, or tax adviser.
- With real estate, you have to like it, or it's going to be a burden.
- When making a purchase, it's more important to consider economic obsolescence than physical deterioration and functional obsolescence.
- Get the best terms possible when buying because if you buy it right, it's easy to keep. On the other hand, don't miss your chance by haggling over a few thousand dollars.
- There's always a price at which a property is worth purchasing.
- For the right property, you can afford to pay top dollar.
- The real estate investor does not buy his or her merchandise (property) like other business people. The retail price of land today is its wholesale price in the future.
- How much should you pay for an income property depends on the anticipated present worth of contemplated future benefits.
- There's no way in the world you can succeed without taking a chance. A turtle never gets anywhere until it sticks its neck out.
- Scores of books have been written on how to sell property, but the most important aspect of real estate is how to buy.
- A good buy will sell itself.
- The down payment and terms of sale are more important than the purchase price.
- Don't ever buy a piece of real estate without knowing the subject property's growth potential. Ask yourself what it will be worth in 20 years.
- Spend time studying neighborhood trends.
- Think back 20 years—if only you had held on to that property!
- If you think it's hard to buy property now, just wait 10 or 20 years.
- The dips in the 20-year cycle are what take you for a ride, but the only way to get rich is to hold on for the long pull.
- Don't get caught up in the trivial or let short-term adversities get you down.
- Residential property, including houses, apartments, and condominiums, is the smartest investment for the average investor because everyone knows something about housing.
- Today's best investment is the single family residence.
- Houses are becoming like dinosaurs; they're getting scarce.
- When demand is high, severe restrictions from the city, such as zoning changes, will increase the value of existing property.

- In a densely populated area, downzoning a land parcel on which an apartment building sits from multiple residential to single family residential will generally increase the value and help eliminate rental competition. That's why some of the best real estate buys are legal nonconforming buildings.
- Be sure not to buy a 22-unit motel when a Holiday Inn is being built two blocks down the street.
- If you can't afford to buy a large apartment building, buy a few smaller buildings in a clustered area that are easy to manage. In order for this to work, you must be familiar with the area you are investing in.
- Avoid the loss of income by performing a periodic rental analysis of the area to keep up with what is happening in the market and adjust the rents accordingly.
- You can never be too knowledgeable.
- Read the morning paper. Pay attention to news affecting the real estate market. Governmental actions, defense contracts, and economic conditions all affect real estate values.
- Keep abreast of how legislation in your city, county, state, and region will affect your real estate.
- Evaluate factors that affect economic strength and weakness. When you detect weakness, don't buy.
- If you can detect signs of an upturn, start to invest. Acquire as much as possible.
- When prices go so high you can no longer afford to buy, start putting money into fixing up your existing properties.
- You should look at real estate as a vehicle to accomplish an objective, whether it's a place to live, a source of retirement income, a tax shelter, or an estate to leave behind to your kids.
- Your objective must be realistic and suit your abilities, interests, personality, and finances.
- Buy real estate to fill a need.
- You're bound to make money if you buy the least expensive property in the best location.
- Location is everything. When you buy property, you want to get a sweeping view, not a view of the sweepings!
- Quality is a key word in acquiring real estate, quality of the neighborhood, the construction, and the condition of the building.
- Don't be afraid of debt; what you owe today you'll be worth tomorrow.
- Think big. You have to think high to rise.
- Treat your tenants as if they own the place. In paying the rent, they are buying the property for you.
- If you have a good tenant, do everything you can to keep him or her; it costs too much to rehabilitate wear and tear caused by people constantly moving in and out.

- Sometimes it's cheaper to keep a tenant at a lower rent than to lose money on a vacancy and repairs.
- Try to stay out of potential rent-control areas.
- An ideal location to get started is in an area with growth potential that has hit bottom and can't go anywhere but up.
- A depression can make a wise man look like a fool.
- Inflation can make a fool look like a wise man.
- Timing is the key factor. The only difference between salad and garbage is timing.
- Wherever possible, enhance a property's value by rehabilitating it to a higher and better use.
- Save money by using your know-how and resourcefulness to fix up and maintain your property.
- Don't spend money on property unless you can see the return in rent or better tenants.
- When you first start out, do all the work yourself, including collecting the rents, to make as much profit as possible.
- Keep good records for cost control.
- Increase the value of your property by buying and improving the place next door, around the corner, and across the street.
- Most people don't know how to invest for the future. If you buy real estate in growth areas and let it ripen, no more decisions are necessary— just patience.
- Good credit is essential. Pay your bills two days before they are due. Always pay the plumber and the electrician on the spot.
- Never overextend yourself. If you are not able to control your finances, you are not able to control your destiny.
- The sooner you realize that there is no easy way to get rich, the better off you are going to be.
- Consult a competent real estate attorney and accountant on all important matters.
- You can sum up success in real estate in one word: perserverance. If you don't make it the tenth time, try the eleventh.

Appendix B:
The Appraisal Process

When buying real estate, the investor should try to estimate the fair market value of the proposed purchase so that he or she will be in an informed position to negotiate the transaction and know approximately how much money can be financed in the form of a first mortgage.

A qualified real estate appraisal of the subject property by a competent, unbiased appraiser could be money well spent. The cost of a competent narrative appraisal for, say, a 10-unit apartment building located in a desirable blue collar district in a major metropolitan area ranges from $1,500 to $2,500, or more, depending on the amount of detail required to prepare the report. The cost also depends on such factors as accessibility to the property, availability of good supporting data, previous commitments of the appraiser, and so on.

I believe it is essential for the first-time investor, as well as the seasoned professional, to be familiar with what a comprehensive narrative appraisal should contain. The following, beginning with a report outline, is a discussion of the elements found in a narrative fair market value appraisal of an apartment property.

REPORT OUTLINE

Preface

Statement of Limiting Conditions

Summary of Important Facts and Conclusions

Location Map

Photograph of Subject Property

Site Plan

Construction Plan

General Information

Identification of the Property

Purpose of the Appraisal

Definition of Fair Market Value

Approaches Considered in Valuing the Property

- Cost approach
- Market data approach
- Income approach
- Demand analysis

Date of Value Estimate

History of the Property

Property Rights Appraised

Trends Affecting the Value of the Subject Property

- Nation
- Region
- Metropolitan area
- Community
- Neighborhood

Present and Future Market Demand for Subject Property

- Present competition
- Future competition

Land or Site Data

- Legal description
- Zoning
- Restrictions
- Easements
- Highest and best use
- Real property tax data
    Assessed values
    Tax rate
    Current real property taxes
    Trend of future taxes

Physical Factors Affecting Site

- Frontage
- Shape
- Area
- Topography and soil conditions

- Landscaping
- Available utilities

Relationship of Site to Surrounding Area

- Corner influence
- Rear or side alley influence
- Detrimental influences
- Advantageous influences
- Street

Description of the Construction [Improvements]

- Buildings
- Yard improvements
- Construction

Valuation of the Property

Cost Approach

- Land value
    Land sales analysis
    Discussion of land sales
    Correlation of land sales
    Land value estimate
- Construction value [Improvements]
    Replacement cost
    Depreciation
      physical deterioration
      functional obsolescence
      economic obsolescence
    Construction value estimate
- Cost Approach value estimate

Market Data Approach

- Comparable sales analysis
- Gross income multiplier method
- Per room comparison basis
- Correlation of the methods
- Market data approach value estimate

Income Approach

- Stabilized annual gross income
- Vacancy and collection loss
- Annual operating expenses
- Interest/capitalization rate
- Useful life of construction
- Method of capitalization
- Income capitalization process
- Income approach value estimate

Market Demand Analysis

- Summary of present and future demand considerations
- Demand factor

Correlation of the Value Estimates and the Demand Analysis

Fair Market Value

Certification of the Appraiser

Addenda

City Map [including subject property]

Neighborhood Map [showing land sales and comparable, whole property sales]

Land Sales Data

Construction Data

Construction Cost Form

Comparable Sales Data

Include: Plot plan, maps, pictures, charts, and factual data pertinent to the value estimate and necessary as supporting evidence that are not included in the body of the report.

Appraiser's Qualifications

PREFACE

Statement of Limiting Conditions

1. All facts and data set forth in this report are true and accurate to the best of your appraiser's knowledge and belief.

2. Your appraiser has made a personal inspection of the property appraised.
3. Your appraiser has no present or contemplated financial interest in the property appraised.
4. The fee for this appraisal report is not contingent on the values reported.
5. No land survey has been made by your appraiser. The legal description and land dimensions given in this report are taken from available records and your appraiser assumes no responsibility for the accuracy of such data.
6. Maps and plot plans, which are a part of this report, are included to assist the reader to visualize the property and its surrounding area. They should not be used for any other purpose.

[Any other item that is important to clarify the parameters of the appraisal report should be stated here. For example: "The value estimate assumes that the subject property has no liens, encumbrances, or assessments against the property." Another example would be: "Your appraiser has not taken into consideration any mineral rights that may be under the surface of the subject property."]

Summary of Important Facts and Conclusions

Name of Subject Property

Location of Subject Property [address]

Purpose of the Appraisal [to form an opinion of fair market value]

Property Rights Appraised [unencumbered fee ownership]

Land Data

- Lot size [frontage, depth, square foot area, shape, contour]
- Zoning [present zoning, probably future zoning]
- Current assessments [land, improvements]
- Current real property taxes
- Highest and best use

Improvement Data

- Construction and yard improvements [including materials and type of construction]
- Size of building [gross square foot / cubic foot area]
- Net rentable area
- Number of stories

- Number of apartments

    Bachelors
    One bedroom
    Two bedroom

- Total number of rentable rooms
- Age of building [actual age, effective age]
- Garage [size and capacity]
- Yard improvements
- Quality of construction
- General condition

Value Indicated by the Three Approaches:

Cost Approach
  Replacement cost of all construction $_____
  Total accrued depreciation $_____
  Indicated value of all construction $_____
  Land value $_____
  Total indicated value by the cost approach $_____
Market Data Approach
  Value indicated by the market data approach $_____
Income Approach
  Estimate of potential annual gross income $_____
Vacancy and collection loss   _____%
Net income $_____
Method of Capitalization
  Interest/capitalization rate   _____%
  Useful life of construction   _____yrs.
  Value indicated by the income approach $_____
Market Demand Factor
Final Estimate of Fair Market Value of the Subject Property $_____
Date of Value Estimate   _____

LOCATION MAP

(Indicate subject property in red)

PHOTOGRAPH OF SUBJECT PROPERTY

(Front view; others may be included)

Date of photograph(s)

SITE PLAN

(Draw lot to scale, showing dimensions as well as street,
alley, distance to corner, etc.)

CONSTRUCTION PLAN

(Draw exterior plan of buildings
and improvements to scale)

[Note: The above items may occupy one to four pages of the report.]

GENERAL INFORMATION

Identification of the Property

The property appraised in this report consists of the land and construction
of the

[Name of Apartments]
Located at
[Address]

Purpose of the Appraisal

This appraisal was prepared for the purposes of forming an opinion as to the fair market value of the subject apartment property under conditions prevailing as of the date of this appraisal.

Definition of Fair Market Value

The value estimated in this appraisal is the fair market value of the subject property. Fair market value for purposes of this appraisal is defined as follows:

> The highest price estimated in terms of money that a property will bring if exposed for sale in the open market allowing a reasonable time to find a purchaser who buys with the knowledge of all the uses for which it is capable of being used, neither buyer nor seller being compelled to act.

The definition of fair market value is sometimes interpreted as follows:

> The price a willing seller would sell and a willing buyer would buy, neither being under abnormal pressure to act.

Approaches Considered in Valuing the Property

The fair market value of the subject property was estimated after giving due consideration to the following approaches to value as developed in this appraisal:

> Cost approach: Land value, exclusive of improvements, is added to the depreciated replacement cost of the construction to give an indication of the value of the subject property by the cost approach.

> Market Data Approach: Sales of similar apartment properties are analyzed and used to form an opinion as to the value of the subject property by the market data approach.

> Income Approach: The estimated annual potential net income is capitalized into value as an indication of the value of the subject property by the income approach.

> Demand Analysis: Present and future demand for the subject property is correlated with the approaches to value to form a final opinion of fair market value.

Date of Value Estimate

The fair market value as set forth in this appraisal report is as of _____ and is based on conditions prevailing as of the date.

History of the Property

[Discuss in narrative form the history of the subject property. Include historical factors that might have a bearing on the present and future market value of the property.]

Property Rights Appraised

The property rights appraised in this report consist of the fee ownership in the land and construction.

Trends Affecting the Value of the Subject Property

Nation	[Brief narrative indicating how the present and probable future actions of the federal government will likely affect the market value of the subject property.]
Region	[Brief narrative indicating how the present and probable future actions of the state government will likely affect the market value of the subject property.]
Metropolitan Area	[Brief narrative indicating how the present and probable future actions of the county and/or city government will likely affect the market value of the subject property.]
Community	[Brief narrative indicating how the present and probable future actions of the community will likely affect the market value of the subject property.]
Neighborhood	[Complete narrative description of the neighborhood. Physical, economic, social, and governmental characteristics that presently affect the amenities of apartment living in the area should be considered. Also includes present and probable future trends of the neighborhood that will likely affect the market value of the subject property.]

Present and Future Demand for the Subject Property

Present Competition: Requires a complete narrative of the present competition affecting the subject apartment property.

Future Competition: Requires a complete narrative including statistical data on proposed future competitive apartment properties.

Land or Site Data

Legal Description: The land appraised in this report is legally described as: [complete legal description, including lot, tract, book, page, county, and state].

Zoning: [Discuss present and probable future zoning, if a probability exists. Description of permitted uses.]

Restrictions: [Discuss public and private restrictions that presently exist on the property and the probability of future changes.]

Easements: [Discuss any easements affecting the site and their affect on the value of the property.]

Highest and Best Use: [Discuss present use and indicated trends toward other uses, if any. Definitive statement as to the highest and best use of the site, considering existing zoning. Reasons for opinion stated.]

Real Property Tax Data:

Assessed values: The current assessed value of the land and improvements is as follows:

Land	$_____
Construction	$_____
Total	$_____

The previous year assessed value of the land and improvements is as follows:

Land	$_____
Construction	$_____
Total	$_____

Tax rate: The current real property tax rate for this area is [amount] per $100 of assessed valuation:

Current real property taxes: The current real property taxes for the subject property are:

Trend of future taxes: [Discuss of future trends of real property taxes in the area and their likely effect on real estate values.]

Physical Factors Affecting the Site

Frontage: The subject site has _____ feet frontage on [street name].

Shape: The subject site is [rectangular] shape with an average width of _____ feet and depth of _____ feet.

Area: The subject site is approximately _____ square feet.

Topography and Soil Conditions: [Brief discussion of topography and contour of the site, as well as type of soil and the possible and probable effects of erosion and drainage. Also includes detailed discussion of any known subsoil conditions, such as toxic waste.]

Landscaping: [Discuss landscaping that exists on the subject site.]

Available Utilities: The subject site has the following utilities available and connected; [such as domestic water, electricity, sanitary sewer, natural gas, telephone, cable television.]

Relationship of Site to Surrounding Area

Corner Influence: [If any.]

Rear or Side Alley Influence: [If any.]

Detrimental Influences: [Discuss whether the site is adjacent to commercial or industrial property and what affect that has on the value of the subject site.]

Advantageous Influences: [Discuss desirable factors affecting the site, such as proximity to parks, mass transit, schools, churches, and so on, and whether the property has a desirable view.]

Street: [Discuss the width of the street, type of street surface, curbs, sidewalks, if any, type of lighting, and location of nearest fire hydrant. Also includes discussion of neighborhood traffic pattern and its effect on subject site.]

Description of the Construction

[Brief description of the important factors of each separate improvement on the site. An example follows.]

Main Building: A two-story wood, frame, and stucco structure containing the following apartment units: 6-one bedroom; 4-two bedroom, or a total of 10 units. The building is approximately 26 years old, of average quality workmanship, and in average condition. Total floor area of this structure is 11,000 square feet.

Annex Building: A one-story, wood, frame, and stucco structure, etc.

Garage: A one-story wood, frame, and stucco structure providing space for 20 cars, laundry facilities, swimming pool, filtering, maintenance equipment, etc.

Yard Improvements: Consist of concrete walks, steps, curbs, asphalt driveways, flagstone patio, swimming pool, brick barbecue, concrete block and wood fence, lawn sprinklers, landscaping, etc.

Discussion of Construction: Details of the construction, together with the appraiser's estimate of the present replacement cost new of each improvement, is set forth in the Addenda.

[Note: The above statement should appear in the report and a detailed description of the construction should appear in the addenda. All cost information should also appear in the addenda.]

VALUATION OF THE PROPERTY

Cost Approach

The value estimate developed by the cost approach considers the replacement cost of the construction, less depreciation from causes, added to the value of the land. The land is as if vacant and ready for development to its highest and best use.

Land Value

The appraised value of the land is based on:

1. Sales of similar sites in the area.
2. Interviews with active real estate brokers and knowledgeable property owners in the area.
3. Consultation with other informed services in the area, including banks, lending institutions, and the like.

Land Sales Analysis: Sales that are considered as an indication of the subject property's land value are summarized on the following page. More complete information regarding each sale may be found in the addenda of the report.

[Note: The above statement should appear in the report and a detailed description of each comparable land sale used should appear in the addenda of the report.]

Summary of Land Sales: [percentage or dollar adjustments are made for each varying characteristic.] (See table on next page.)

Discussion of Land Sales: [Discuss each land sale in relation to the subject site, for which it is necessary to justify the basis for arriving at the adjustments used in the analysis.]

Correlation of Land Sales: [Discuss in narrative form estimate of market value of the subject land parcel and the reasons for arriving at the value.]

Land Value Estimate: Based on the foregoing factors and after consideration of the present and probably future highest and best use of the site, in [the appraiser's] opinion the fair market value of the subject land, exclusive of all improvements, is the sum of:

$_____

Sale Price
of Vacant Land

$_____ $_____ $_____ $_____ $_____

Sale Number

Characteristics	#1	#2	#3	#4	#5
A. Zoning B. Restrictions C. Easements D. Tax Rates E. Assessments	[Note: It is desirable to have sales with items A, B, C, D, and E similar to the subject site; otherwise, many complications may arise in adjusting the sale to the subject site.]				
F. Frontage G. Shape H. Area I. Topography J. Soil Condition K. Utilities (availability)	[Note: Physical characteristics of vacant land sales can be more easily detected and adjustments verified.]				
L. Location in neighborhood M. Street, alley, corner N. Factors affecting surrounding area O. Time adjustment P. Terms of sale	[Note: When making adjustments for characteristics, it is important the appraiser be consistent in applying value differences.]				
Total Adjustments					
Indicated Value of Each Sale (as it relates to subject property)					

Construction Value

An analysis of the construction was prepared. Detailed information pertaining to the construction, together with replacement costs, may be found in the addenda of this report.

Replacement Cost: The replacement cost of all construction described in the addenda is as follows:

Total Replacement Cost $\$$_____

Depreciation: Depreciation from all causes is deducted from the total replacement cost to develop the depreciated replacement cost of the construction

Depreciation factors considered are as follows:

Physical Deterioration (curable and incurable)	[Discussion of how the subject construction is affected by each type of depreciation. A dollar amount is assigned for each depreciation category.]
Functional Obsolescence (curable and incurable)	
Economic Obsolescence	

Construction Value Estimate: A summary of the depreciation factors, together with the appraiser's estimate of the Depreciated Replacement Cost of the construction, is as follows:

Total Replacement Cost		$\$$_____
Depreciation		
Physical Deterioration	$\$$_____	
Functional Obsolescence	$\$$_____	
Economic Obsolescence	$\$$_____	
Total Depreciation		$\$$_____
Replacement Cost		
Less Depreciation of Construction		$\$$_____
Round Figure		$\$$_____

Cost Approach Value Estimate:

Based on the conclusions set forth, the value estimate as indicated by the Cost Approach is as follows:

Land Value	$\$$_____
Construction Value	$\$$_____
Total Indicated Value by the Cost Approach	$\$$_____

Market Data Approach

The value estimate developed by the market data approach considers comparing apartment properties that have sold and are of a comparable nature to the subject property.

Your appraiser has gathered other information pertaining to apartment property values from active real estate brokers in the vicinity of the subject property as well as knowledgeable property owners and officials in banks and other lending institutions active in the subject area.

Comparable Sales Analysis

Sales that are considered to be an indication of value of the subject property are summarized. More complete information regarding each sale may be found in the addenda of this report.

[Note: The above statements should appear in the report, and a detailed description of each comparable whole property sale used should appear in the addenda of the report.]

Summary of Comparable Sales

Sale # Address	Price Paid	Sale Date	No. of Units	No. of Rooms	Gross Rent per Month	Gross Floor Area (sq. ft.)
1						
2						
3						
4						
5						
6						

Gross Income Multiplier Method

Comparison by gross income multipliers. The gross income multiplier is obtained by dividing the annual gross income into the sale price of each property.

Comparable Sale No.	Sale Price	Annual Gross Income	Gross Income Multiplier	Degree of Comparability
#1				
#2				
#3				
#4				
#5				
#6				

Correlation of Gross Income Multiplier: [Discuss in narrative form the appraiser's estimate of the Gross Income Multiplier selected and reasons for arriving at estimate given.]

Indication of Value by the Gross Income Multiplier. The value estimate developed by the Gross Income Multiplier is calculated as follows:

Subject property's estimated annual
potential gross income $_____

× Gross Income Multiplier   ×_____

Indicated value of property by
the gross rent multiplier method $_____

Per Room Comparison Basis

This method of comparison considers the number and size of rentable rooms. [Note: An analysis per apartment may be substituted for the room basis if proper adjustments are made.] (See table on next page.)

Sale Number

Sale Price	#1	#2	#3	#4	#5
Date of sale No. of Rooms Price per Room Sq. Feet per Room	[Note: Room counts must be consistent in each sale property as well as the subject property.]				
Adjustments: Factors to consider affecting each sale property	[Appraiser relates each factor to the subject property. (Percentage adjustments are recommended.)]				

Time of Sale:
  Terms
  Reliability
Neighborhood
Location
Land Parcel
Construction:
  Size of Rooms
  Functional Layout
  Quality
  Condition
  Effective Age
  Mechanical
    Equipment
  Exterior Appearance
	[Note: When making adjustments for characteristics, it is important to be consistent in applying differences.]				

Total Adjustments (composite of adjustments for each sale)	[Correlation of the results of each sale.]				
Indicated Value of Subject Property by this Method	[Arrived at by multiplying the number of subject rooms by the correlated sales room value.]				

Correlation of the Methods

The value estimates developed by the market data approach are as follows:

Gross income multiplier method $_____
Per room comparison basis $_____
(Per apartment unit comparison) $(_____)

[Discuss here in narrative form the merits and adversities of each method. Appraiser makes a determination of one figure to be used as the estimate of value of the subject property by the market data approach.]

Market Data Approach Value Estimate

Based on the conclusions as set forth, the value estimate as indicated by the market data approach is in the sum of:

[Note: Net rentable square-foot area of the subject building and other comparable apartment building sales may be used as a basis for this approach.]

Income Approach

The value estimate as indicated by the income approach considers the stabilized annual net income that the property is capable of producing capitalized into value.

The building (land or whole property) residual method is used because the supporting data for the land value estimate is more reliable than the calculations used to estimate depreciation of the construction from all causes.

[Note: The above statement must be changed if the land or whole property residual technique is employed.]

The process of capitalizing net income into value is as follows:

[Note: This statement considers the capitalization of net income using the building residual technique. If another technique is used, this statement must be altered to conform.]

The estimated annual gross income with an allowance for vacancies and collection loss deducted from the gross income gives the effective gross income estimate the subject property is capable of producing during the remaining useful life of the construction. Annual operating expenses are deducted from the annual effective gross income to produce the annual net income before capital charges. Annual net income is then capitalized into indicated value of the property.

A fair rate of return on the value of the land is deducted from the net income to produce the residual income attributed to the construction. Residual income attributed to the construction is then capitalized into construction value. The land value added to the construction value (developed from the residual income) becomes the indicated value of the whole property by the income approach.

Stabilized Annual Gross Income (assume no leases exist)

The estimated annual gross income the subject property is capable of producing is derived from the rental of apartments (and garages) with other income from miscellaneous sources (coin-operated laundry equipment and the like).

The estimated annual gross income affecting the subject property is as follows:

[It is necessary to study the present rental income from the subject property and relate it to previous rental schedules for a minimum period of five years, if possible. Appraiser converts present and past rental data into workable elements—per room, per apartment, per square foot of floor area, and the like. Appraiser also analyzes income data from comparable apartment properties and relates comparable rental data with actual and historical rents from the subject property. Finally, a projected future gross income that the subject property might be expected to produce is assigned.]

[Note: A complete explanation should appear in the report as to how the gross income was estimated. If rental schedules, charts, and the like are necessary to support the explanation, they should appear in the addenda of the report and referred to in this section.]

Vacancy and Collection Loss

Detailed discussion of projected vacancy and collection loss estimate. Appraiser justifies estimate and provides reasons. If long-term vacancy rates are apparent, they should be reflected in the market demand analysis.

Annual Operating Expenses

Annual operating expenses affecting the subject property's effective gross income are estimated as follows:

[Discuss in detail the projected annual operating expenses that are likely to affect the subject property's estimated effective gross income. Expenses must be realistic. Expenses should include an allowance for: fixed charges, taxes, insurance, operating expenses, management, maintenance and repairs, and reserve for replacement of short-lived capital assets. Forecasting operating expenses entails an analysis of present and historical data affecting the subject property as well as comparable properties. Possible future factors that are likely to affect the expenses of the subject property are also considered.]

Interest Rate (Capitalization Rate)

The rate used to process income into value is developed as follows:

[Detailed discussion of the method used to estimate the interest and/or capitalization rate employed. Selection justified with data and reasons. The interest and/or capitalization rate should be in harmony with the method of capitalization.]

Useful Life of Construction

After giving consideration to the many factors affecting the subject construction, your appraiser has estimated that the remaining useful life of the construction to be _____ years. The basis for this estimate is as follows:

[Detailed discussion of the process used to estimate the useful life of the construction. Estimate justified with data and reasons.]

Method of Capitalization

The method of capitalizing the annual net income into value is as follows:

[Detailed discussion of the method to be used. Selection justified with data and reasons.]

Income Capitalization Process

The income capitalization process using the building (construction) residual process:

Stabilized annual gross income		$_____
Vacancy and collection loss	_____%	
Effective annual gross income		$_____
Annual operating expenses		
Fixed charges		
Real estate taxes	$_____	
Insurance premiums	$_____	
Operating expenses		
Utilities	$_____	
Trash renewal	$_____	
Gardening	$_____	
Services	$_____	
Management	$_____	
Maintenance and repairs	$_____	
Reserve for replacement of		
short-lived capital assets	$_____	
Total estimated annual operating expenses		$_____
Estimated annual net income		
available for capital charges		$_____
Interest rate employed _____%		
Recapture rate _____%		
Capitalization rate _____%		
Income required to support land value		
($_____ × _____%)		$_____
Residual income attributed to construction		$_____
Construction value by residual process		
($_____ × _____%)		$_____

Income Approach Value Estimate

Based on the conclusions set forth, the value estimate as indicated by the income approach is as follows:

Land value (by analysis) $_____

Construction value (residual) $_____

Total indicated value by the

  income approach $_____

Rounded $_____

Market Demand Analysis

It is apparent that the process of estimating the current fair market value is based on historical facts and data. Market trends either up or down influence values. The inclusion of a market demand (or lack of demand) analysis is essential to the valuation conclusion.

Summary of Present and Future Demand Characteristics

[Discussion in narrative form of the present and future demand characteristics and how they affect the present fair market value of the subject property.]

Demand Factor

Based on the data and conclusions, your appraiser is of the opinion that a demand factor should be applied to the correlation and final estimate of fair market value. To arrive at the final estimate of fair market value, your appraiser estimates a plus (or minus) factor of _____.

[Detailed discussion appears justifying the conclusion and why the appraiser selected the demand factor.]

Correlation of the Value Estimates with the Demand Factor

The value estimates developed by the appraisal procedures used are:

Cost Approach Value Estimate $_____

Market Data Approach Value Estimate $_____

Income Approach Value Estimate $_____

[Discuss in narrative form the merits and adversities of each approach. Explanation of any wide discrepancies that might exist between approaches. Estimate of market value given, along with reasons for the conclusion.]

Demand Factor   _____

Calculation of Fair Market Value

[Estimate of Market Value × Demand Factor = Fair Market Value]

Fair Market Value

Based on the data and conclusions as set forth in this appraisal, in my opinion, the fair market value of the subject property, if offered for sale on the open market, allowing a reasonable time to find a purchaser, under the conditions prevailing as of the date of this appraisal, is the sum of _____ (thousand) dollars.

$ _____

Certification of the Appraiser

I hereby certify that I have no interest, present or contemplated, in the subject property and that neither the employment to make this appraisal nor the compensation is contingent on the value of the property. I certify that I have personally inspected the property and that, according to my knowledge and belief, all statements and information in this report are true and correct, subject to the underlying assumptions and contingent conditions.

Based on the information contained in this report and on my general experience as an appraiser, it is my opinion that the Fair Market Value as defined herein, of the subject apartment property, as of (date of value), is in the sum of _____ dollars.

$ _____

_____
[Appraiser's Signature]

Addenda

[Includes one or more pages for each of the following:]

- City Map
- Neighborhood Map (showing land and comparable, whole property sales in relation to subject property)
- Land Sales Data
- Comparable Sales Map
- Construction Data
- Square Foot/Cubic Foot Cost Form
- Comparable Sales Data
- Appraiser's Qualifications

[Other items that might be included in the Addenda, which are necessary to support the value estimate and are *not* included in the body of the report are:]

- Plot Plans
- Maps
- Pictures (subject property and comparable sales)
- Charts

Land Sales Data

Sale Identification

Sale Price $ _____

Grantor _____

Address _____

Grantee _____

Address _____

Assessor's Identification:

    Book   Page   Parcel

   _____   _____   _____

Address of Property _____

Legal Description _____

_____

_____

_____

_____

_____

Land Size _____

Zoning _____

Improvements on Property at the
   Time of Sale _____

_____

_____

Sale Confirmed by:

Name _____

Address _____

Date of Confirmation _____

Remarks _____

_____

Recording Data

Date of Recording _____

Book _____ Page _____

Document No. _____

Date of Transaction _____

Revenue Stamps on Deed $ _____

Documentary Transfer Tax $ _____

Amount of Concurrent Deeds of
   Trust Recorded with this
   Document:

Amount   In Favor Of

_____   _____

_____   _____

Amount and Date of Deeds of
Trust Assumed by Grantee:

| | Date | In |
Amount	Recorded	Favor Of
_____	_____	_____
_____	_____	_____

Real Property Assessments

Year	Land	Improvements
_____	_____	_____
_____	_____	_____

Tax Rate

Year	Rate
_____	_____

[Note: This represents information for one comparable land sale. A separate page should be filled out for each comparable land sale.]

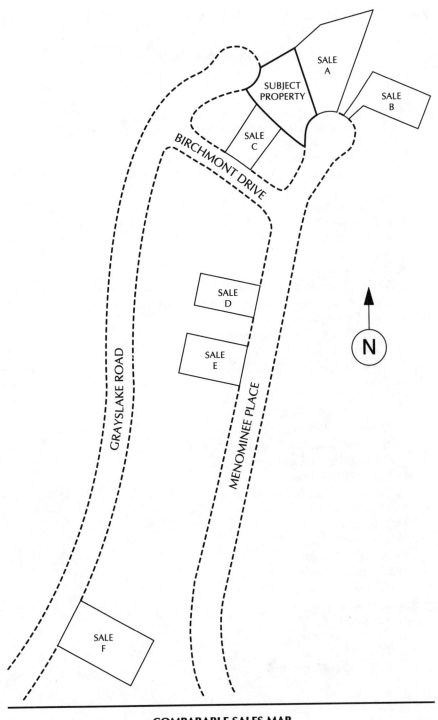

COMPARABLE SALES MAP

Construction Data

1. Basic Description
   A. Type and age of construction
   B. Architectural style
   C. Number and size of apartments
   D. Number of rooms
2. Summary Square-Foot/Cubic-Foot Areas
   A. Apartment building(s)
      i. Ground floor
      ii. Second floor
      iii. Porches
      iv. Basement
   B. Garages
   C. Other structures
3. Quality of Construction, General Condition, and Estimate of Remaining Useful Life of Construction
4. Exterior Description
   A. Foundation and substructure
   B. Exterior treatment
   C. Roof design and cover
   D. Porches
5. Interior Description
   A. Room descriptions
      i. Space allotment
      ii. Floor, walls, and ceiling finish
      iii. Built-ins and fixtures
6. Mechanical Equipment
   A. Heating and air-conditioning
   B. Electrical
   C. Plumbing
   D. Elevator
   E. Fire Protection
7. Yard Improvements
   A. Fencing
   B. Paving
   C. Landscaping
   D. Swimming pool
   E. Patio area
   F. Miscellaneous grounds

Construction Costs

Construction cost data is obtainable from:

Local Builders and Developers.
Jurisdictional Government Building departments.
Experienced Cost Estimators, Architects, Real Estate Agents, Entrepreneurs, and the like.
Building Cost Publications, such as Marshall and Swift Nationwide Construction Cost Service.

The best method of gathering cost information is to make a thorough analysis of actual construction projects of the type being appraised that have been built in the area of the subject property.

Square Foot/Cubic Cost Form

Identification	Total Square Feet or Cubic Volume	Estimated Cost Per Square Foot/ Cubic Foot	Replacement Cost
Main Building	_____	_____	$_____
Other Structures	_____	_____	$_____
Garages	_____	_____	$_____
Yard Improvements	(Lump Sum Amount)		$_____
_____	_____	_____	$_____
_____	_____	_____	$_____
		Total Replacement Cost	$_____

Comparable Sales Data (Whole Property)

Sale Identification

Sale Price $ _____

Grantor _____

Address _____

Grantee _____

Address _____

Assessor's Identification:

Book	Page	Parcel
_____	_____	_____

Address of Property _____
_____

Legal Description _____
_____
_____
_____
_____
_____

Land Size _____

Zoning _____

Improvements on Property at the
Time of Sale _____
_____
_____

Sale Confirmed by:

Name _____

Address _____
_____

Date of Confirmation _____

Remarks _____
_____

Recording Data

Date of Recording _____

Book _____ Page _____

Document No. _____

Date of Transaction _____

Revenue Stamps on Deed $_____

Documentary Transfer Tax $_____

Amount of Concurrent Deeds of
Trust Recorded with this
Document:

Amount	In Favor Of
_____	_____
_____	_____

Amount and Date of Deeds of
Trust Assumed by Grantee:

Amount	Date Recorded	In Favor Of
_____	_____	_____
_____	_____	_____

Real Property Assessments

Year	Land	Improvements
_____	_____	_____
_____	_____	_____

Tax Rate

Year	Rate
_____	_____

[Note: This represents information for one comparable whole property sale. A separate page should be filled out for each comparable sale used in the report. All of the above information (except confirmation of sale and description of improvements) can usually be obtained from official public records.]

Other data required for each comparable sale includes the building square foot/cubic foot, age, condition, quality of construction, number of rooms/apartments, configuration, gross annual income, vacancy allowance, expenses, and other pertinent data.

Appraiser's Qualifications

[A concise statement generally in outline form containing information pertaining to the appraiser's education, background, employment, and type of assignments performed, which render him or her qualified to make an appraisal of the subject property.]

Appendix C: Outline of Factors Influencing the Value of Residential Property

I. **The Nation:** The national economy and the actions of the federal government can have a profound effect on every usable piece of real estate in the nation.
   1. Population Growth
      a) Present trend
      b) Anticipated trend
   2. Fiscal Policies
      a) Federal spending
      b) Attitude toward taxation
   3. Cost of Government
      a) Increasing
      b) Decreasing
   4. Inflationary or Recessionary Trend
      a) Shortage or surplus of labor and materials
      b) The effect on housing
   5. Federal Participation in Housing
      a) Subsidized housing programs
      b) Insured mortgages
      c) Redevelopment plans
      d) Money supply

II. **The Region:** Generally, a segment of the nation set apart from other areas by geographical boundaries that typically comprises a cluster of states, such as New England, the South, Southwest, Midwest, Atlantic Seaboard, Pacific Northwest.
   1. Population Growth
      a) Present trend
      b) Anticipated trend
   2. Economic Considerations
      a) Natural resources
      b) Labor supply
      c) Interest rates
      d) Tourist attractions (the beach, mountains, and so on)

3. Legislative Actions
   a) Existing laws
   b) Proposed legislation
   c) Attitude toward property owners
   d) Environmental restrictions
4. Climatic Conditions
   a) Effect on health and welfare
   b) Effect on the social and economic climate
5. Agricultural Production
   a) Growth and expansion
   b) Spin-off activity
6. Government Actions
   a) Subsidized industries and installations
      i. Aerospace and defense
      ii. Military bases
   b) Taxation policies

III. **The Metropolitan Area:** A large center of population including one or more central cities and the adjacent satellite communities.
   1. Population Trends
      a) Increase
      b) Decrease
      c) Migration
   2. Economic Activity
      a) Active versus dormant industries
      b) Labor Market
         i. Employment trend
         ii. Unemployment and prolonged strikes
         iii. Factors affecting these developments
            a.) Influx or flight of industry
            b.) Current labor-management relations
            c.) History of previous job actions
            d.) Natural disasters
         iv. Possibility of future occurrence
      c) Recreational facilities
   3. Construction Costs
      a) Skilled labor supply
      b) Adequacy of materials
   4. Civic Government Policies
      a) Tax increase
      b) Assessments
         i. Utilities
         ii. Maintenance

5. Major Improvement Programs
   a) Redevelopment projects
   b) Major construction projects
   c) Highway and freeway development

IV. **The Community:** That part of the metropolitan area composed of a number of neighborhoods that have a tendency toward common interests and problems.
   1. Geographical Pattern
      a) Natural terrain
         i. Level areas; Unimproved land
         ii. Mountainous regions
         iii. Natural barriers: Hills, valleys, rivers, forests, lakes, ravines, and the like
         iv. Natural beauty
         v. Hazards
   2. Satellite Communities
      a) Suburban areas
      b) Residential districts
      c) Regional shopping centers
      d) Industrial complexes
   3. Civic Government Policies
      a) Tax increases
      b) Assessments
         i. Utilities
         ii. Maintenance
      c) Rent control

V. **The Neighborhood:** A residential area with distinguishing characteristics comprised of people with similar interests. Numerous factors and trends affect the quality of the neighborhood.
   1. Physical Characteristics
      a) Overall trend of the area
      b) Quality, convenience, and availability of facilities
         i. Public schools
         ii. Public transportation
         iii. Shopping centers
         iv. Churches
         v. Cultural and recreational
      c) Land and improvement characteristics
         i. Street patterns
         ii. Availability of utilities

        iii. Similar land uses; Size and shape of lots
        iv. Percentage of area developed
        v. Harmony of development
           a.) Similar types and quality of improvements
           b.) Monotonous housing tracts
           c.) Cohesiveness of original designs (size, quality, price range)

    d) Manmade attributes
        i. Freeways
        ii. Boulevards
        iii. Railroad tracks
        iv. Industrial and commercial complexes
        v. Zoning designations

2. Economic Characteristics
    a) Family income traits
        i. Occupations
        ii. Wage levels
        iii. Employment stability
        iv. Percentage of families on public assistance
    b) Degree of home ownership
    c) Number of rentals
    d) Range of rental income
    e) Number of vacancies

3. Social Characteristics
    a) Density and composition of population
    b) Average family size and ages
    c) Prestige/Social status
    d) Attitudes of the inhabitants
        i. Civic pride
        ii. Participation in community activities
        iii. Pride of ownership
    e) Existence and use of educational and cultural institutions
    f) School enrollments
    g) Absence or presence of vice

4. Real Estate Sales Activity
    a) Number and price of homes for sale
    b) Availability of office space

5. Sales Conditions
    a) Availability of financing
    b) Size of down payments made on purchases
    c) Willingness of lenders to participate in the area
    d) Number of foreclosures

6. Governmental Characteristics
   a) Taxation policies
      i. Property taxes
      ii. Other taxes; City license fees
      iii. Delinquencies
   b) Municipal fees and assessments
   c) Zoning ordinances
   d) Building codes
   e) Health and fire regulations

Appendix D:
Code of Ethics and Standards of Practice of the National Association of Realtors®

Where the word REALTORS® is used in this Code and Preamble, it shall be deemed to include REALTOR-ASSOCIATE®s.

While the Code of Ethics establishes obligations that may be higher than those mandated by law, in any instance where the Code of Ethics and the law conflict, the obligations of the law must take precedence.

PREAMBLE...

Under all is the land. Upon its wise utilization and widely allocated ownership depend the survival and growth of free institutions and of our civilization. REALTORS® should recognize that the interests of the nation and its citizens require the highest and best use of the land and the widest distribution of land ownership. They require the creation of adequate housing, the building of functioning cities, the development of productive industries and farms, and the preservation of a healthful environment.

Such interests impose obligations beyond those of ordinary commerce. They impose grave social responsibility and a patriotic duty to which REALTORS® should dedicate themselves, and for which they should be diligent in preparing themselves. REALTORS®, therefore, are zealous to maintain and improve the standards of their calling and share with their fellow REALTORS® a common responsibility for its integrity and honor. The term REALTOR® has come to connote competency, fairness, and high integrity resulting from adherence to a lofty ideal of moral conduct in business relations. No inducement of profit and no instruction from clients ever can justify departure from this ideal.

In the interpretation of this obligation, REALTORS® can take no safer guide than that which has been handed down through the centuries, embodied in the Golden Rule, "Whatsoever ye would that others should do to you, do ye even so to them."

Accepting this standard as their own, REALTORS® pledge to observe its spirit in all of their activities and to conduct their business in accordance with the tenets set forth below.

Articles 1 through 5 are aspirational and establish ideals REALTORS® should strive to attain.

ARTICLE 1

REALTORS® should become and remain informed on matters affecting real estate in their community, the state, and nation so that they may be able to contribute responsibly to public thinking on such matters.

ARTICLE 2

In justice to those who place their interests in a real estate professional's care, REALTORS® should endeavor always to be informed regarding laws, proposed legislation, governmental regulations, public policies, and current market conditions in order to be in a position to advise their clients properly.

ARTICLE 3

REALTORS® should endeavor to eliminate in their communities any practices which could be damaging to the public or bring discredit to the real estate profession. REALTORS® should assist the governmental agency charged with regulating the practices of brokers and sales licensees in their states. (Amended 11/87)

ARTICLE 4

To prevent dissension and misunderstanding and to assure better service to the owner, REALTORS® should urge the exclusive listing of property unless contrary to the best interest of the owner. (Amended 11/87)

ARTICLE 5

In the best interests of society, of their associates, and their own businesses, REALTORS® should willingly share with other REALTORS® the lessons of their experience and study for the benefit of the public, and should be loyal to the Board of REALTORS® of their community and active in its work.

Articles 6 through 23 establish specific obligations. Failure to observe these requirements subject REALTORS® to disciplinary action.

ARTICLE 6

REALTORS® shall seek no unfair advantage over other REALTORS® and shall conduct their business so as to avoid controversies with other REALTORS®. (Amended 11/87)

- **Standard of Practice 6-1**
  REALTORS® shall not misrepresent the availability of access to show or inspect a listed property. (Cross-reference Article 22.) (Amended 11/87)

ARTICLE 7

In accepting employment as an agent, REALTORS® pledge themselves to protect and promote the interests of the client. This obligation of absolute fidelity to the client's interests is primary, but it does not relieve REAL-TORS® of the obligation to treat fairly all parties to the transaction.

- **Standard of Practice 7-1**
  Unless agreed otherwise in writing, REALTORS® shall submit to the seller all offers until closing. Unless the REALTOR® and the seller agree otherwise, REALTORS® shall not be obligated to continue to market the property after an offer has been accepted. Unless the subsequent offer is contingent upon the termination of an existing contract, REALTORS® shall recommend that the seller obtain the advice of legal counsel prior to acceptance. (Cross-reference Article 17.) (Amended 5/87)
- **Standard of Practice 7-2**
  REALTORS®, acting as listing brokers, shall submit all offers to the seller as quickly as possible.
- **Standard of Practice 7-3**
  REALTORS®, in attempting to secure a listing, shall not deliberately mislead the owner as to market value.
- **Standard of Practice 7-4**
  (Refer to Standard of Practice 22-1, which also relates to Article 7, Code of Ethics.)
- **Standard of Practice 7-5**
  (Refer to Standard of Practice 22-2, which also relates to Article 7, Code of Ethics.)
- **Standard of Practice 7-6**
  REALTORS®, when acting as principals in a real estate transaction, cannot avoid their responsibilities under the Code of Ethics.

ARTICLE 8

REALTORS® shall not accept compensation from more than one party, even if permitted by law, without the full knowledge of all parties to the transaction.

ARTICLE 9

REALTORS® shall avoid exaggeration, misrepresentation, or concealment of pertinent facts relating to the property or the transaction. REALTORS®

shall not, however, be obligated to discover latent defects in the property or advise on matters outside the scope of their real estate license. (Amended 11/86)

- **Standard of Practice 9-1**
  REALTORS® shall not be parties to the naming of a false consideration in any document, unless it be the naming of an obviously nominal consideration.
- **Standard of Practice 9-2**
  (Refer to Standard of Practice 21-3, which also relates to Article 9, Code of Ethics.)
- **Standard of Practice 9-3**
  (Refer to Standard of Practice 7-3, which also relates to Article 9, Code of Ethics.)
- **Standard of Practice 9-4**
  REALTORS® shall not offer a service described as "free of charge" when the rendering of a service is contingent on the obtaining of a benefit such as a listing or commission.
- **Standard of Practice 9-5**
  REALTORS® shall, with respect to the subagency of another REAL-TOR®, timely communicate any change of compensation for subagency services to the other REALTOR® prior to the time such REALTOR® produces a prospective buyer who has signed an offer to purchase the property for which the subagency has been offered through MLS or otherwise by the listing agency.
- **Standard of Practice 9-6**
  REALTORS® shall disclose their REALTOR® status when seeking information from another REALTOR® concerning real property for which the other REALTOR® is an agent or subagent.
- **Standard of Practice 9-7**
  The offering of premiums, prizes, merchandise discounts or other inducements to list to sell is not, in itself, unethical even if receipt of the benefit is contingent on listing or purchasing through the REALTOR® making the offer. However, REALTORS® must exercise care and candor in any such advertising or other public or private representations so that any party interested in receiving or otherwise benefiting from the REALTOR®'s offer will have clear, thorough, advance understanding of all the terms and conditions of the offer. The offering of any inducements to do business is subject to the limitations and restrictions of state law and the ethical obligations established by Article 9, as interpreted by any applicable Standard of Practice. (Adopted 11/84)
- **Standard of Practice 9-8**
  REALTORS® shall be obligated to discover and disclose adverse factors reasonably apparent to someone with expertise in only those areas re-

quired by their real estate licensing authority. Article 9 does not impose upon the REALTOR® the obligation of expertise in other professional or technical disciplines. (Cross-reference Article 11.) (Amended 11/86)

- **Standard of Practice 9-9**

REALTORS®, acting as listing brokers, have an affirmative obligation to disclose the existence of dual or variable rate commission arrangements (i.e., listings where one amount of commission is payable if the listing broker's firm is the procuring cause of sale and a different amount of commission is payable if the sale results through the efforts of the seller or a cooperating broker). The listing broker shall, as soon as practical, disclose the existence of such arrangements to potential cooperating brokers and shall, in response to inquiries from cooperating brokers, disclose the differential that would result in a cooperative transaction or in a sale that results through the efforts of the seller. (Amended 11/91)

ARTICLE 10

REALTORS® shall not deny equal professional services to any person for reasons of race, color, religion, sex, handicap, familial status, or national origin. REALTORS® shall not be parties to any plan or agreement to discriminate against a person or persons on the basis of race, color, religion, sex, handicap, familial status, or national origin. (Amended 11/89)

ARTICLE 11

REALTORS® are expected to provide a level of competent service in keeping with the standards of practice in those fields in which the REALTOR® customarily engages.

REALTORS® shall not undertake to provide specialized professional services concerning a type of property or service that is outside their field of competence unless they engage the assistance of one who is competent on such types of property or service, or unless the facts are fully disclosed to the client. Any persons engaged to provide such assistance shall be so identified to the client and their contribution to the assignment should be set forth.

REALTORS® shall refer to the Standards of Practice of the National Association as to the degree of competence that a client has a right to expect the REALTOR® to possess, taking into consideration the complexity of the problem, the availability of expert assistance, and the opportunities for experience available to the REALTOR®.

- **Standard of Practice 11-1**

Whenever REALTORS® submit an oral or written opinion of the value of real property for a fee, their opinion shall be supported by a memorandum in the file or an appraisal report, either of which shall include as a minimum the following:

1. Limiting conditions
2. Any existing or contemplated interest
3. Defined value
4. Date applicable
5. The estate appraised
6. A description of the property
7. The basis of the reasoning including applicable market data and/or capitalization computation

This report or memorandum shall be available to the Professional Standards Committee for a period of at least two years (beginning subsequent to final determination of the court if the appraisal is involved in litigation) to ensure compliance with Article 11 of the Code of Ethics of the NATIONAL ASSOCIATION OF REALTORS®.

- **Standard of Practice 11-2**
  REALTORS® shall not undertake to make an appraisal when their employment or fee is contingent upon the amount of appraisal.
- **Standard of Practice 11-3**
  REALTORS® engaged in real estate securities and syndications transactions are engaged in an activity subject to regulations beyond those governing real estate transactions generally, and therefore have the affirmative obligation to be informed of applicable federal and state laws, and rules and regulations regarding these types of transactions.

ARTICLE 12

REALTORS® shall not undertake to provide professional services concerning a property or its value where they have a present or contemplated interest unless such interest is specifically disclosed to all affected parties.

- **Standard of Practice 12-1**
  (Refer to Standards of Practice 9-4 and 16-1, which also relate to Article 12, Code of Ethics.) (Amended 5/84)

ARTICLE 13

REALTORS® shall not acquire an interest in or buy or present offers from themselves, any member of their immediate families, their firms or any member thereof, or any entities in which they have any ownership interest, any real property without making their true position known to the owner or the owner's agent. In selling property they own, or in which they have any interest, REALTORS® shall reveal their ownership or interest in writing to the purchaser or the purchaser's representative. (Amended 11/90)

- **Standard of Practice 13-1**

  For the protection of all parties, the disclosures required by Article 13 shall be in writing and provided by REALTORS® prior to the signing of any contract. (Adopted 2/86)

ARTICLE 14

In the event of a controversy between REALTORS® associated with different firms, arising out of their relationship as REALTORS®, the REALTORS® shall submit the dispute to arbitration in accordance with the regulations of their Board or Boards rather than litigate the matter.

- **Standard of Practice 14-1**

  The filing of litigation and refusal to withdraw from it by REALTORS® in an arbitrable matter constitutes a refusal to arbitrate. (Adopted 2/86)

- **Standard of Practice 14-2**

  The obligation to arbitrate mandated by Article 14 includes arbitration requests initiated by REALTORS®' clients. (Adopted 5/87)

- **Standard of Practice 14-3**

  Article 14 does not require REALTORS® to arbitrate in those circumstances when all parties to the dispute advise the Board in writing that they choose not to arbitrate before the Board. (Adopted 5/88)

ARTICLE 15

If charged with unethical practice or asked to present evidence or to cooperate in any other way, in any disciplinary proceeding or investigation, REALTORS® shall place all pertinent facts before the proper tribunals of the Member Board or affiliated institute, society, or council in which membership is held and shall take no action to disrupt or obstruct such processes. (Amended 11/89)

- **Standard of Practice 15-1**

  REALTORS® shall not be subject to disciplinary proceedings in more than one Board of REALTORS® with respect to alleged violations of the Code of Ethics relating to the same transaction.

- **Standard of Practice 15-2**

  REALTORS® shall not make any unauthorized disclosure or dissemination of the allegations, findings, or decision developed in connection with an ethics hearing or appeal or in connection with an arbitration hearing or procedural review. (Amended 11/91)

- **Standard of Practice 15-3**

  REALTORS® shall not obstruct the Board's investigative or disciplinary proceedings by instituting or threatening to institute actions for libel, slander or defamation against any party to a professional standards proceeding or their witnesses. (Adopted 11/87)

- **Standard of Practice 15-4**

  REALTORS® shall not intentionally impede the Board's investigative or disciplinary proceedings by filing multiple ethics complaints based on the same event or transaction. (Adopted 11/88)

ARTICLE 16

When acting as agents, REALTORS® shall not accept any commission, rebate, or profit on expenditures made for their principal, without the principal's knowledge and consent. (Amended 11/91)

- **Standard of Practice 16-1**

  REALTORS® shall not recommend or suggest to a client or a customer the use of services of another organization or business entity in which they have a direct interest without disclosing such interest at the time of the recommendation or suggestion. (Amended 5/88)

- **Standard of Practice 16-2**

  When acting as agents or subagents, REALTORS® shall disclose to a client or customer if there is any financial benefit or fee the REALTOR® or the REALTOR®'s firm may receive as a direct result of having recommended real estate products or services (e.g., homeowner's insurance, warranty programs, mortgage financing, title insurance, etc.) other than real estate referral fees. (Adopted 5/88)

ARTICLE 17

REALTORS® shall not engage in activities that constitute the unauthorized practice of law and shall recommend that legal counsel be obtained when the interest of any party to the transaction requires it.

ARTICLE 18

REALTORS® shall keep in a special account in an appropriate financial institution, separated from their own funds, monies coming into their possession in trust for other persons, such as escrows, trust funds, clients' monies, and other like items.

ARTICLE 19

REALTORS® shall be careful at all times to present a true picture in their advertising and representations to the public. REALTORS® shall also ensure that their status as brokers or REALTORS® is clearly identifiable in any such advertising. (Amended 11/86)

- **Standard of Practice 19-1**
  REALTORS® shall not submit or advertise property without authority, and in any offering, the price quoted shall not be other than that agreed upon with the owners.
- **Standard of Practice 19-2**
  (Refer to Standard of Practice 9-4, which also relates to Article 19, Code of Ethics.)
- **Standard of Practice 19-3**
  REALTORS®, when advertising unlisted real property for sale in which they have an ownership interest, shall disclose their status as both owners and as REALTORS® or real estate licensees. (Adopted 5/85)
- **Standard of Practice 19-4**
  REALTORS® shall not advertise nor permit any person employed by or affiliated with them to advertise listed property without disclosing the name of the firm. (Adopted 11/86)
- **Standard of Practice 19-5**
  Only REALTORS® as listing brokers, may claim to have "sold" the property, even when the sale resulted through the cooperative efforts of another broker. However, after transactions have closed, listing brokers may not prohibit successful cooperating brokers from advertising their "cooperation," "participation," or "assistance" in the transaction, or from making similar representations.

  Only listing brokers are entitled to use the term "sold" on signs, in advertisements, and in other public representations. (Amended 11/89)

ARTICLE 20

REALTORS®, for the protection of all parties, shall see that financial obligations and commitments regarding real estate transactions are in writing, expressing the exact agreement of the parties. A copy of each agreement shall be furnished to each party upon their signing such agreement.

- **Standard of Practice 20-1**
  At the time of signing or initialing, REALTORS® shall furnish to each party a copy of any document signed or initialed. (Adopted 5/86)
- **Standard of Practice 20-2**
  For the protection of all parties, REALTORS® shall use reasonable care to ensure that documents pertaining to the purchase and sale of real estate are kept current through the use of written extensions or amendments. (Adopted 5/86)

ARTICLE 21

REALTORS® shall not engage in any practice or take any action inconsistent with the agency of other REALTORS®.

- **Standard of Practice 21-1**
  Signs giving notice of property for sale, rent, lease, or exchange shall not be placed on property without the consent of the owner.
- **Standard of Practice 21-2**
  REALTORS® obtaining information from a listing broker about a specific property shall not convey this information to, nor invite the cooperation of a third party broker without the consent of the listing broker.
- **Standard of Practice 21-3**
  REALTORS® shall not solicit a listing which is currently listed exclusively with another broker. However, if the listing broker, when asked by the REALTOR®, refuses to disclose the expiration date and nature of such listing; i.e., an exclusive right to sell, an exclusive agency, open listing, or other form of contractual agreement between the listing broker and the client, the REALTOR® may contact the owner to secure such information and may discuss the terms upon which the REALTOR® might take a future listing or, alternatively, may take a listing to become effective upon expiration of any existing exclusive listing. (Amended 11/86)
- **Standard of Practice 21-4**
  REALTORS® shall not use information obtained by them from the listing broker, through offers to cooperate received through Multiple Listing Services or other sources authorized by the listing broker, for the purpose of creating a referral prospect to a third broker, or for creating a buyer prospect unless such use is authorized by the listing broker.
- **Standard of Practice 21-5**
  The fact that a property has been listed exclusively with a REALTOR® shall not preclude or inhibit any other REALTOR® from soliciting such listing after its expiration.
- **Standard of Practice 21-6**
  The fact that a property owner has retained a REALTOR® as an exclusive agent in respect of one or more past transactions creates no interest or agency which precludes or inhibits other REALTORS® from seeking such owner's future business.
- **Standard of Practice 21-7**
  REALTORS® shall be free to list property which is "open listed" at any time, but shall not knowingly obligate the seller to pay more than one commission except with the seller's knowledgeable consent. (Cross-reference Article 7.) (Amended 5/88)
- **Standard of Practice 21-8**
  When REALTORS® are contacted by owners regarding the sale of property that is exclusively listed with another broker, and REALTORS® have not directly or indirectly initiated the discussion, REALTORS® may discuss the terms upon which they might take a future listing or, alternatively, may take a listing to become effective upon expiration of any existing exclusive listing. (Amended 11/86)

- **Standard of Practice 21-9**
  In cooperative transactions REALTORS® shall compensate cooperating REALTORS® (principal brokers) and shall not compensate nor offer to compensate, directly or indirectly, any of the sales licensees employed by or affiliated with other REALTORS® without the prior express knowledge and consent of the cooperating broker.
- **Standard of Practice 21-10**
  Article 21 does not preclude REALTORS® from making general announcements to property owners describing their services and the terms of their availability even though some recipients may have exclusively listed their property for sale or lease with another REALTOR®. A general telephone canvass, general mailing or distribution addressed to all property owners in a given geographical area or in a given profession, business, club, or organization, or other classification or group is deemed "general" for purposes of this standard.

  Article 21 is intended to recognize as unethical two basic types of solicitations:
  First, telephone or personal solicitations of property owners who have been identified by a real estate sign, multiple listing compilation, or other information service as having exclusively listed their property with another REALTOR®; and
  Second, mail or other forms of written solicitations of property owners whose properties are exclusively listed with another REALTOR® when such solicitations are not part of a general mailing but are directed specifically to property owners identified through compilations of current listings, "for sale" signs, or other sources of information required by Article 22 and Multiple Listing Service rules to be made available to other REALTORS® under offers of subagency or cooperation. (Adopted 11/83)

- **Standard of Practice 21-11**
  REALTORS®, prior to accepting a listing, have an affirmative obligation to make reasonable efforts to determine whether the property is subject to a current, valid exclusive listing agreement. (Adopted 11/83)
- **Standard of Practice 21-12**
  REALTORS®, acting as agents of buyers, shall disclose that relationship to the seller's agent at first contact. (Cross-reference Article 7.) (Adopted 5/88)
- **Standard of Practice 21-13**
  On unlisted property, REALTORS®, acting as agents of buyers, shall disclose that relationship to the seller at first contact. (Cross-reference Article 7.) (Adopted 5/88)

- **Standard of Practice 21-14**
  REALTORS®, acting as agents of the seller or as subagents of the listing broker, shall disclose that relationship to buyers as soon as practicable. (Adopted 5/88)
- **Standard of Practice 21-15**
  Article 21 does not preclude REALTORS® from contacting the client of another broker for the purpose of offering to provide, or entering into a contract to provide, a different type of real estate service unrelated to the type of service currently being provided (e.g., property management as opposed to brokerage). However, information received through a Multiple Listing Service of any other offer of cooperation may not be used to target the property owners to whom such offers to provide services are made. (Adopted 2/89)
- **Standard of Practice 21-16**
  REALTORS®, acting as subagents or buyer's agents, shall not use the terms of an offer to purchase to attempt to modify the listing broker's offer of compensation to subagents or buyer's agents nor make the submission of an executed offer to purchase contingent on the listing broker's agreement to modify the offer of compensation. (Adopted 2/89)

ARTICLE 22

In the sale of property which is exclusively listed with a REALTOR®, REALTORS® shall utilize the services of other brokers upon mutually agreed upon terms when it is in the best interests of the client.

Negotiations concerning property which is listed exclusively shall be carried on with the listing broker, not with the owner, except with the consent of the listing broker.

- **Standard of Practice 22-1**
  It is the obligation of the selling broker as subagent of the listing broker to disclose immediately all pertinent facts to the listing broker prior to as well as after the contract is executed.
- **Standard of Practice 22-2**
  REALTORS®, when submitting offers to the seller, shall present each in an objective and unbiased manner.
- **Standard of Practice 22-3**
  REALTORS® shall disclose the existence of an accepted offer to any broker seeking cooperation. (Adopted 5/86)
- **Standard of Practice 22-4**
  REALTORS®, acting as exclusive agents of sellers, establish the terms and conditions of offers to cooperate. Unless expressly indicated in offers to cooperate made through MLS or otherwise, a cooperating broker may not assume that the offer of cooperation includes an offer

of compensation. Entitlement to compensation in a cooperative transaction must be agreed upon between a listing and cooperating broker prior to the time an offer to purchase the property is produced. (Adopted 11/88)

ARTICLE 23

REALTORS® shall not knowingly or recklessly make false or misleading statements about competitors, their businesses, or their business practices. (Amended 11/91)

The Code of Ethics was adopted in 1913. Amended at the Annual Convention in 1924, 1928, 1950, 1951, 1952, 1955, 1956, 1961, 1962, 1974, 1982, 1986, 1987, 1989, 1990, and 1991.

EXPLANATORY NOTES
(AMENDED 11/88)

The reader should be aware of the following policies which have been approved by the Board of Directors of the National Association:

In filing a charge of an alleged violation of the Code of Ethics by a REALTOR®, the charge shall read as an alleged violation of one or more Articles of the Code. A Standard of Practice may only be cited in support of the charge.

The Standards of Practice are not an integral part of the Code but rather serve to clarify the ethical obligations imposed by the various Articles. The Standards of Practice supplement, and do not substitute for, the Case Interpretations in *Interpretations of the Code of Ethics.*

Modification to existing Standards of Practice and additional new Standards of Practice are approved from time to time. The reader is cautioned to ensure that the most recent publications are utilized.

Articles 1 through 5 are aspirational and establish ideals that a REALTOR® should strive to attain. Recognizing their subjective nature, these Articles shall not be used as the bases for charges of alleged unethical conduct or as the bases for disciplinary action.

NOTE: The Delegate Body at the 1990 Annual Convention approved numerous amendments to the Code of Ethics and Standards of Practice to ensure gender neutrality. However, only areas with content change reflect a 1990 revision date.

Index

Adjusted sale price, 46
Appraisal:
  cost, 246
  cost approach, 143, 144, 253, 256–259
  demand analysis, 253, 266
  elements of a narrative fair market
    value appraisal report, 246–273
  of fair market value, 143–145, 246–273
  income approach, 143, 144, 145, 253,
    263–266
  market data approach, 143, 144, 145,
    253, 260–263
  purpose of, 140, 253
  replacement cost, 233–234
Arbitration, 237
Assessment, 94, 114, 229
Axioms, 242–245

Bookkeeping, 220
Brokers, 175–184
  advantages of using, 175–181
  agents, compared with, 175
  disadvantages of using, 181–184
  financial assistance provided by,
    177–178
Building codes, 117–118, 278
Bureau of the Census, 81

Capital gains tax, 46
Capitalization, 263–266
CC&Rs, 30
Civic government policies affecting real
    estate, 94–95
  assessment, 94
  rent control, 94–95
Clean Air Act of 1990, 74
Commercial property:
  industrial buildings, 36–37
  landlord responsibilities, 41–42
  location of, 40
  office buildings, 33–34
  redevelopment projects and, 88–89

vs. residential, 27
  shopping centers, 35–36
  specialty investments, 34–35
  taxation and, 229
  traffic regulations, 104
Community, 91–94, 276
  definition of, 91
  geographical pattern, 91–93
  satellite, 93–94
Condemnation, 90, 91
Construction costs, 13, 85
Cost approach, 143, 144, 253, 256–259
  construction value, 259
  land value, 257, 258
  value estimate, 259
Credit, 192–194
  reports, 206–207

Deed of trust, 160
Demand analysis, 253, 266
Demarcation lines, 103
Depreciation:
  depreciated replacement cost, 233, 259
  economic obsolescence, 140–141
  straight-line method, 18
  taxation and, 228–229
Down payment, 161–162, 170

Environmental Protection Agency (EPA),
    75
Eviction, 221–222

Fair market value:
  cost approach, 143, 144, 253, 256–259
  definition of, 138, 253
  demand analysis, 253, 266
  estimating, 143–145, 246–273
  income approach, 143, 144, 145, 253,
    263–266
  market data approach, 143, 144, 145,
    253, 260–263

Family income:
  as determinant of growth potential,
    130, 131
  neighborhood analysis and, 107
Federal Home Loan Mortgage
    Corporation ("Freddie Mac"), 71
Federal Housing Administration (FHA),
    21, 70, 71
Federal National Mortgage Association
    ("Fannie Mae"), 71
Federal participation in housing, 69–71,
    274
  insured mortgages, 70–71
  money supply, 71
  subsidized housing programs, 69–70
Financing:
  availability of, 162–163
  effect on market value, 164–167
  refinancing, 223–227
  seller-assisted, 160, 167–169
Fiscal policies, 63–68
  federal spending, 63–65
  free trade agreements, 65–67
  taxation, 67–68
Foreclosures, 113

Government National Mortgage
    Association ("Ginnie Mae"), 71
Gross domestic product (GDP), 56, 66

Income approach, 263–266
  building residual method, 263, 265
  income capitalization process, 263–266
  stabilized annual gross income, 264
Income property, 15–16, 18, 26, 121, 228
  benefits of owning, 15–16
  factors affecting value of, 121
  taxation and, 18, 228
Inflation:
  buying real estate during inflationary
    periods, 152, 154
  depression versus, 57–58
  effect on real estate values, 56–58
  rates from 1960 to 1988, 124
  real estate as hedge against, 20
Insurance, 232–238
  coinsurance policy, 236
  contingent liability, 237
  fire, 233–236
  hurricanes, 237–238
  stipulated amount policy, 235

Interest rates, 164, 165
  effect on real estate market , 58–59
  for mortgages, 225
Internal Revenue Code, 228
Internal Revenue Service, 230, 231

Joint tenancy, 48

Location of property, 125–129, 140,
    196–197
Lots:
  boundaries of, 133
  corner, 132
  legal description of, 133
  metes and bounds description of, 132,
    135
  size of, 132

Market data approach, 143, 144, 145, 253,
    260–263
  comparable sales analysis, 260
  gross income multiplier method, 260–261
  per room comparison basis, 261–262
Metes and bounds description, 132,
    135
Metropolitan area, 81–91, 126, 146–147,
    275–276
  active vs. dominant industries, 81, 83
  fringe areas, 126
  improvement programs, 86–91
  labor market, 83–85
  median sales prices of single family
    homes, 1981–1991, 146–147
  population trends, 81, 82
  recreational facilities, 85
Miniwarehouses, 34–35
Mortgages, 160–161, 167
  adjustable rate, 164
  balloon, 171
  insured, 70–71
  interest rates, 225
  payments, 186
  refinancing of, 223–227
  second, 16
Multiple Listing Service, 175

National Association of Realtors, 38, 183,
    279–291
  code of ethics and standards of practice
    of, 279–291

Natural barriers, 91–92
Negative cash flow, 197
Neighborhood:
  building codes, 117–118, 278
  crime rates, 111–112
  definition of, 96
  demarcation lines, 103
  economic characteristics of, 106–107, 277
  facilities, 99, 276
  family income characteristics of, 107
  governmental characteristics of, 114–119, 277
  health and fire regulations, 118–119
  land and improvement characteristics of, 99–102, 276
  municipal fees and assessments, 114–116
  physical characteristics of, 96–99, 276
  population composition and density, 108–09
  pride of ownership, 110–111
  real estate sales activity, 112–113, 277
  rehabilitation, 117
  sales conditions, 113, 277
  social characteristics of, 108–110, 277
  street patterns, 99–100
  taxation policies, 114
  traffic regulations, 104
  zoning ordinances, 105, 116–117, 277, 278
No money down transactions, 170–172

Obsolescence:
  economic, 140–141
  functional, 141
  infrastructure, 91
Offers, 160–161, 172–174

Population:
  metropolitan areas, 81, 82
  neighborhood analysis and, 108–109
  real estate values and, 59–62, 131
  regional growth and, 72–73
Price:
  adjusted sale, 46
  median sales price of single family homes, 146–147
  purchase, 161–162, 165–167
Probate, 49

Property:
  analyzing growth potential of, 130–135
  buying, 191–192, 194–197
  commercial, 27, 33–37, 40, 41–42, 88–89, 104, 229
  community, 48
  highest and best use of, 28
  income, 15–16, 18, 26, 121, 228
  location of, 125–129, 140, 196–197
  lot characteristics, 132–135
  management of, 198–222
  mixed-use, 199
  non-income-producing, 26
  physical deterioration of, 141
  residential, 27, 29–33, 37–40, 40–42, 228, 229
  title to, 48–49
  vacant land parcels, 28–29
Property management, 198–222
  bookkeeping, 220
  common mistakes in, 216–221
  evictions, 221–222
  pets, 211–212
  rental agreements, 207–210
  tenants, 198–199, 200–207, 210–211
  vacancy notices, 214–216
Property values, *see* Real estate values
Pyramiding, 185–197
  techniques of, 189–197

Real estate investment:
  advantages of, 10–13, 16–25, 45–47, 49–53
  advice on, 238–241, 242–245
  vs. financial investments, 10–13, 19–20, 22–25
  heterogeneous nature of, 20–22
  objectives of, 43–55
  pyramiding, 185–197
  return on, 199
  tax benefits of, 18–20
  timing, 151–159
  types of, 10, 26–42
Real estate values:
  active *vs.* dormant industries, 81–83
  assessment, effect on, 94
  civic government policies affecting, 94–95
  climatic conditions and, 77–78
  construction costs and, 85
  cost of government and, 68–69, 274

Real estate values *(continued)*
  economic obsolescence and, 140–141
  economic trends affecting, 56–71,
    73–74, 81, 83–85, 151–156, 274
  environmental regulations affecting,
    75–77
  expansion and, 123
  fair market value, 138–146
  federal government actions affecting,
    79–81, 274
  federal participation in housing, 69–71,
    274
  fiscal policies affecting, 63–68
  functional obsolescence and, 141
  improvements and, 142
  inflation, effect on, 56–58, 152, 154,
    274
  infrastructure obsolescence and, 91
  interest rates and, 58–59
  labor market and, 83–85
  location, effect on, 125–129, 140,
    196–197
  long-range forecasting of, 136–150
  outline of factors affecting, 73–74,
    274–278
  population and, 59–62, 131
  recession, effect on, 56–58, 152, 274
  supply and demand, effect on, 142
  types of, 139–142
Recession:
  buying real estate during, 152
  effect on real estate values, 56–58
Redevelopment projects, 86–91
Refinancing, 223–227
  advantages of, 224–227
  drawbacks of, 227
Regional growth, 72–81
  agricultural production and, 78–79
  climatic conditions and, 77–78
  economic considerations, 73–74
  government-subsidized industries,
    79–80
  legislative actions affecting, 74–77
  population and, 72–73
  taxation policies and, 80–81
Replacement cost, 233–234, 259
Residential property:
  apartment buildings, 31–33
  vs. commercial, 27
  condominiums and townhouses, 30
  duplexes, triplexes, and fourplexes,
    30–31

  financing of, 40–41
  landlord responsibilities, 41–42
  location of, 37–40
  single family residences, 29, 146–147,
    199
  taxation and, 228, 229
  traffic regulations, 104
Resolution Trust Corporation, 73

Sellers, 168–169, 170
Shopping centers:
  anchored, 36
  mini-malls, 35–36
Speculation, 9, 10, 14–16
Street patterns, 99–100
Subsidized housing programs, 69–70

Taxation:
  of commercial properties, 229
  of income properties, 18, 228
  as neighborhood analysis factor, 114
  property taxes, 114
  regional growth affected by, 80–81
  of residential properties, 228, 229
  tax-deferred exchange, 18–19, 46,
    228–231
  tax shelter, 18–19, 45–46, 228–231
Tax-deferred exchange, 18–19, 46,
    228–231
  financial investments and, 19
  Individual Retirement Accounts, 18–19
Tax shelter:
  depreciation, 18, 228–229
  real estate investment as, 45–46
  tax-deferred exchange, 18–19, 46,
    228–231
Tenancy in common, 49
Tenants, 198–199, 200–207, 210–211
  credit checks, 206–207
  evictions, 221–222
  rental agreements, 207–210
  selecting, 203–206
Title, 48–49, 162–163
  "clouds" in the title, 162–163
Tract homes, 127
Trust deed, 160, 167–168

Zoning ordinances, 105, 116–117, 277,
    278